# THE PURPLE BOOK

# THE PURPLE BOOK

## A Progressive Future for Labour

*Edited by Robert Philpot*

Biteback Publishing

First published in Great Britain in 2011 by
Biteback Publishing Ltd
Westminster Tower
3 Albert Embankment
London
SE1 7SP
Copyright © Robert Philpot and the individual contributors 2011

ISBN 978-1-84954-117-6

10 9 8 7 6 5 4 3 2 1

A CIP catalogue record for this book is available from the British Library.

Printed and bound in Great Britain by
CPI Group (UK) Ltd, Croydon, CR0 4YY

# CONTENTS

Acknowledgements                                                        vii

Foreword: the new centre-ground                                          ix
*Ed Miliband*

Introduction: today's choice before Labour                               1
*Robert Philpot*

Renewing our offer, not retracing our steps:                            19
building a sense of national purpose
*Douglas Alexander*

An effective state, not a big state: forging a national strategy        32
*Peter Mandelson*

Back to the future: the decentralised tradition                         45
and Labour's way forward
*Paul Richards*

Reviving our sense of mission:                                          61
designing a new political economy
*Tristram Hunt*

Making markets genuinely free:                                          80
redistributing power to all
*John Woodcock*

Empowerment and transparency:                                           97
a new settlement for public services
*Patrick Diamond*

Breaking the link between demography and destiny:                      116
how to restart the engine of social mobility
*Alan Milburn*

Eliminating 'power failures': a new                              129
agenda for tackling inequality
*Liam Byrne*

Securing social justice:                                        144
savings and pensions for all
*Rachel Reeves*

Restoring Labour's moral economy:                               158
the role of National Insurance
*Frank Field*

Putting families first: universal care from cradle to grave     166
*Liz Kendall*

The authors of their own lives:                                 183
stronger communities and the relational state
*Tessa Jowell*

A state in society for all:                                     200
better homes in stronger neighbourhoods
*Caroline Flint*

Cutting crime and building confidence:                          215
empowering victims and communities
*Jenny Chapman and Jacqui Smith*

One Nation Labour:                                              231
tackling the politics of culture and identity
*Ivan Lewis*

Good government and thriving economies:                         245
rejuvenating England's cities
*Andrew Adonis*

From centralism to localism:                                    255
building cooperative communities
*Steve Reed and Paul Brant*

Letting the people decide:                                      270
redistributing power and renewing democracy
*Stephen Twigg*

Conclusion: a progressive future for Labour                     282
*Robert Philpot*

Author biographies                                              304

# Acknowledgements

'Writing that chapter was like giving birth,' one of our contributors remarked after theirs had gone through its final iteration. It is a credit to all of our authors that, faced with extremely tight deadlines and multiple requests for revisions, additions and further information, each responded with admirable levels of patience. Our thanks to them all. My thanks also to Progress's chair, Stephen Twigg MP, and vice chairs (especially Tristram Hunt MP, Liz Kendall MP, Rachel Reeves MP and John Woodcock MP) who have contributed chapters to the book, and who provide much wider service to the organisation. Throughout this project another contributor in particular, Andrew Adonis, has offered a great deal of support, encouragement and advice, for which I am very grateful.

*The Purple Book* was conceived early in 2011 and we have been very lucky in Biteback Publishing for all their help in bringing it to fruition in such a short space of time. Many thanks to our editor, Hollie Teague, and to James Stephens, who helped shape the book in its initial stages.

This year marked Progress's fifteenth anniversary. Without exception those who I have been fortunate to work with at the organisation over the years are, in my unbiased opinion, the best in the business. Their passion, enthusiasm and loyalty are the key to all that Progress has achieved. Many former colleagues have become firm friends, both personally and of the organisation.

I'd like to thank especially the current Progress team – Richard Angell, Adam Harrison, Matthew Faulding and Simon Jeffrey – who have made our fifteenth year Progress's most successful and productive ever. It is a small team with big achievements to its name thanks to the hard work each and every one of them puts in. In terms of this book, Richard and Adam deserve special thanks – they have applied their customary intelligence, diplomacy and humour to this project. It wouldn't have happened without them. I should also mention our intern Felicity Slater, who performed a number of extremely tedious – but absolutely vital – checking and proofing duties in the book's final stages.

Finally, to my parents and to Paul, for all they have given me over the years, but especially for last year.

*Robert Philpot*
*August 2011*

# Foreword: the new centre-ground

*Ed Miliband*

I am delighted to welcome this collection of *Purple Book* essays as contributions to the discussion about the kind of Labour Party we need to build for the future.

You may not agree with all the views expressed in this book. Nor do I. But I believe strongly that a vibrant debate across the party, in all its colours, is a necessary condition of renewal and of returning to power.

Last year we suffered one of our heaviest electoral defeats, bringing the curtain down on the longest period of government in our party's history.

The speed with which Labour has got back on its feet is testament to the energy, dedication and unity of those in our party. We have recruited 65,000 new members, won by-elections, and gained hundreds of council seats.

I am proud to be leader of our great party. And I am proud of our record in government.

But as well as celebrating our resilience and recovery, we have a duty to face up to the realities of our situation. In the 2010 election the electorate sent us a clear message, and we have a responsibility to confront the hard truths behind this result if we are to learn from what we got wrong and earn back the voters' trust.

That's why Labour has spent a lot of time this year listening to what people have to say – about us, about their lives, about the current government and about the kind of Britain they want – so that we can be in a position to offer our country hope for the future.

Above all, in my first year as Labour leader, I have learned two things about Britain in 2011. First, the scale of the challenge that faces our country and our party. But second, a source of confidence: that there is a new centre-ground emerging in British politics, one which Labour can and must occupy.

In Britain today, millions are anxious and insecure. Although they work hard and do the right thing, the 'squeezed middle' feel they don't get the rewards that they should. And they see and experience the contrast between their own experiences and those at the very top whose income and wealth has been consistently rising.

Parents worry that their kids will do worse than them – whether measured in terms of jobs, housing or income. What I call the 'promise of Britain', the idea of continuing progress across generations, is more under threat than at any time in living memory. It is a notion of progress that is not just about what people earn, but about their quality of life and the hours they work.

And people also see the weakening of the communities and values that matter to them – responsibility, our obligations to each other, a sense of solidarity, and people's ability to have a say in shaping the places where they live.

These concerns – a new inequality between the rich and the rest, the fate of young people, renewing the values of community – all mark out a new centre-ground in Britain.

Showing that we understand this new terrain marks a crucial staging post for us as an opposition. But addressing these challenges will require courage for us to change and shed old orthodoxies – wherever they come from.

To encourage responsibility in our society, we must be willing to speak out about the responsibilities of the powerful – from politicians to bankers to those who run the press.

To create good jobs at good wages, we must champion the role of small businesses against established interests in both the public and private sectors that can hold them back.

To tackle the issue of falling living standards, we must be willing to acknowledge and address the inequalities that scar our society and have damaged our economy.

And to make government a fit and proper servant of the public, we must face up to the need to reform the state, and give people more control over the public services on which they depend.

A common theme across these challenges is that we will need to take on some of the powerful vested interests in our country. That is, in fact, where we have always been strongest as a political party.

Learning from our history in government and daring to change the way we do politics is not easy. I know many will find this path uncomfortable and unfamiliar.

But that is why I welcome, and take encouragement from, the debates being opened up in this book.

# Introduction: today's choice
# before Labour

*Robert Philpot*

The author's verdict was unforgiving. The Labour government, he declared, 'did not fall with a crash, in a tornado
from the blue. It crawled slowly to its doom.' And the blame
for this catastrophe was its alone: 'It will not soothe the
pain of defeat with the flattering illusion that it is the inno-
cent victim of faults not its own. It is nothing of the kind.
It is the author, the unintending and pitiable author, of its
own misfortunes.'

R. H. Tawney's damning assessment of the fall of the
1931 Labour government, presented the following year in
his essay *The Choice Before the Labour Party*, is one that few
today would dispute.[1] The more self-critical in Labour's ranks
will, however, recognise the parallels with the death, if not
the overall record, of the Labour government, which was
defeated in last year's general election.

Indeed, the scale of Labour's defeat in 2010 – in which
the party polled its second lowest share of the vote since 1918
– was akin to that of 1931. The 6 per cent drop in Labour's
vote mirrors almost exactly the decline in the party's vote
between 1929 and 1931. Then, too, of course, Labour had
been at the helm when the country faced a seismic economic
shock not of the government's making – although, unlike
Ramsay MacDonald and Philip Snowden, Gordon Brown

and Alistair Darling took bold and decisive action to prevent a recession turning into a depression.

Eighty years on, the lesson from 1931 rests, in part, with the aftermath of defeat. Then, too, Labour's defeat was followed by a coalition government – one which came close to destroying the Liberal Party. Perhaps more importantly, however, 1931 was the only occasion on which Labour's ejection from office was not followed by an even worse defeat at the subsequent general election. In 1935, the party fell far short of returning to power, but under Clement Attlee's leadership it recovered substantial ground. After Labour's defeats in 1951 and 1979, the party fared far less well: on both occasions its share of the vote and seats in the subsequent general election both fell. And the one apparent post-war exception to this rule – Harold Wilson's surprise defeat in 1970 – is itself not clear-cut: in February 1974, Labour returned to office without a majority, on a share of the vote which was lower than that which it had polled four years previously, and lower than that polled by the Conservatives.

But, mixed though its fortunes were in 1974, Wilson's victory stands out for another reason: it is the only occasion upon which Labour has managed to return to government within five years of losing power.

## A little cold realism
This history is not repeated to depress Labour's supporters or to detract from the solid progress the party has made under Ed Miliband's leadership during the past year. Rather, it is rehearsed to remind all those who believe that the coalition must be defeated at the next general election of the scale of the challenge ahead. As Tawney's essay declared, Labour needed a 'little cold realism' now it had had an 'interval in which to meditate its errors'.

The causes of Labour's defeat in 2010 were endlessly rehashed during last summer's leadership election, although only a superficial consensus has been achieved. It is agreed that winning a fourth term was always going to be a great challenge. Add to that the deepest and longest recession since the 1930s; the scandal over MPs' expenses which, justifiably or not, hit Labour hardest; and a perception that, on immigration and welfare, the party had lost touch with the voters, including many of its erstwhile supporters, and some marvel at Labour's achievement in denying the Conservatives an outright victory. And all this before account is taken of Labour's failure to renew itself after Tony Blair's departure from No. 10 in June 2007 and Brown's widely acknowledged difficulties in communicating with the electorate.

But, if it is to truly understand the lessons of its defeat, and how to address them, Labour needs a deeper analysis. Polling commissioned by Demos's Open Left project in the immediate aftermath of the general election provides a detailed snapshot of public opinion. It found that 'voters who left Labour at the last election are more likely to have views in common with the mainstream of public opinion than with voters that stayed with Labour'.[2]

This divergence in attitudes was particularly apparent on issues surrounding the role of government. Demos's research revealed that 'people who voted Labour in 2010 are much more comfortable with a bigger, active state [and] they are less likely to see public sector cuts as a priority'. The authors went on: 'The polling data shows that more than one in four of the voters that Labour lost said they saw government as "part of the problem not the solution", compared with just over one in ten voters that Labour retained. More than half of voters who stuck by Labour at the last election consider government to be "a force for good" but among voters that left Labour this view fell to just one in three.'

Indeed, the depth of Labour's difficulties is demonstrated by the views shown towards the NHS – the public service for which voters have the highest regard and satisfaction and for which the party received the most credit for its performance in government. Here, 33 per cent of the voters Labour retained agreed that the priority should be to 'avoid cuts'. But among the voters that Labour lost, that proportion fell to 13 per cent, while 55 per cent believed that the priority should be to 'seek greater efficiency and end top-down control'.

Other findings suggested the limited appeal of statism. Over one-fifth of voters agreed that 'central government interferes too much in local services like schools, hospitals and the police. They should leave it to the professionals,' while 33 per cent of voters opted for an alternative, but equally sceptical, view of the state that, 'people should have more choices and control over local services – otherwise professionals or government bureaucrats end up deciding what happens'.

There is, as Patrick Diamond argues in his chapter, what many on the left view as an apparent paradox here: 'The financial crisis of 2008–9 was initially understood as a failure of liberal market capitalism, but quickly transformed into a crisis of public debt and government deficits. Unfortunately for the left, popular fury against the financial system has not been accompanied by a restoration of faith in the power of government. While the crisis was fuelled by irresponsible banking and financial deregulation, it is the role and size of the state which has returned to the centre of political debate.'

Labour's problems are not unique in this regard: since the onset of the financial crisis, social democratic parties across Europe have suffered a string of defeats – in Germany, Sweden, Finland, Holland and Portugal – while prospects for the Spanish socialists look bleak next year.

But, as international polling for Policy Network demonstrated this spring, this negative view of the state, and the parties most closely associated with it, has not as yet – as it did when the stagflation of the 1970s stretched the consensus in favour of Keynesian economic management to breaking point – translated into an upsurge in support for neoliberalism.[3] Instead, suggests Policy Network's analysis of the data, 'at the heart of it lies the question of trust: in state action [and] in the market economy... Faced with frighteningly low levels of trust in the state and the market, with widespread concerns about government redistribution and the role of corporations, as well as high degrees of cynicism towards the ruling elite (of which social democratic parties are now seen to be part), social democrats seem to be on the back foot like no other political contender.'

Three of Policy Network's findings, which go to the heart of the argument of this book, are worth more detailed consideration.

First, people are palpably frightened by the concentration of power in the market economy. Some 85 per cent of Britons (a higher figure than in Germany, the United States or Sweden, which were also surveyed) agree that large corporations care only about profits and not about the wider community or the environment. Voters expressed concern about the harsh impact the market has on vulnerable individuals, while barely one-fifth of Britons cited the positive effects it has on jobs and opportunities as an advantage of the market economy.

Second, voters still see, however, the advantages of the liberal, competitive functions of the market economy. Competition is cited as the primary advantage of the market economy by half of British voters, while 44 per cent value the wide choice of goods and services it provides.

Third, concern about concentrations of power in the market economy, its impact on the vulnerable and scepticism about its ability to create jobs is mirrored by a lack of faith in the role of the state as a counterweight. Only 16 per cent of Britons believe that government could stand up to 'vested interests'; nearly four in ten are concerned about the extent to which the state has been captured by those interests; and only 17 per cent think that politicians will represent their interests. Indeed, scepticism about the efficacy of state action leads 29 per cent of British voters to question whether there are, in fact, any

advantages at all to government-led action to improve societies. Unsurprisingly, a plurality of voters in all four countries
surveyed – and 39 per cent of Britons – believe that centre-left
governments tax too much with too little public benefit.

It barely needs stating that such levels of distrust about
the efficacy of government present a particular problem for
Labour. Indeed, if we look at some of the challenges facing
Britain over the next decade – reforming capitalism to restore
growth in the light of the lessons of the financial crisis,
tackling the plight of the 'squeezed middle' by ensuring the
proceeds of that growth are fairly shared, addressing the lack
of affordable childcare and the massive increase in social care
costs that the nation will have to bear as a result of the ageing
society, and reversing the decline in home ownership – none
of these can be tackled without government playing a role.

However, as then governor Bill Clinton argued in the
early 1990s when, following a series of election defeats, the
centre-left was last forced to fundamentally examine its
approach towards the state, 'those who believe in government
have an obligation to reinvent government, to make it work'.[4]
Thus, as Policy Network's polling demonstrates, the necessity
of reinventing government cannot be separated from the task
of tackling concerns – also very apparent – about concentrations of market power. This, then, is the outline of the emerging new political centre – which demands concentrations of
power be bust open to restore the voters' trust in the efficacy
of the state and the ability of the market to create wealth
sustainably and shared fairly.

Is Labour up for this challenge? Tawney's 1932 essay warned
of the 'void in the mind of the Labour Party' which leads us
into 'intellectual timidity, conservatism and conventionality,
which keeps policy trailing tardily in the rear of realities'. The
challenge of ensuring that policy does not 'trail tardily in the
rear of realities' has been met by Labour before through the
process of revisionism. But the party has also responded in the

past to defeat by engaging in 'intellectual timidity, conservatism and conventionality'. This is the choice before the Labour
Party today and it is to the latter option that we turn first.

## The politics of evasion

There is, of course, a school of thought that Labour should
adopt a 'safety-first' strategy for opposition. This way of thinking was, indeed, the reaction of some to the party's fourth
consecutive defeat in 1992, and it has made an occasional
appearance since May last year. In their excellent study of the
failure of the US Democrats and other centre-left parties to
come to accept the real causes of their defeats in the 1980s,
and what it would take to recover from them, Elaine Kamarck
and Bill Galston labelled this mindset 'the politics of evasion'.
'Democrats have ignored their fundamental problems,' they
argued at the time. 'Instead of facing reality they have embraced
the politics of evasion. They have focused on fundraising and
technology, media and momentum, personality and tactics.
Worse, they have manufactured excuses for their presidential
disasters, excuses built on faulty data and false assumptions,
excuses designed to avoid tough questions. In place of reality
they have offered wishful thinking; in place of analysis, myth.'[5]
    Miliband has made clear his determination to resist the
politics of evasion, arguing that 'one more heave just won't
do'.[6] As he recognises, this way of thinking confuses short-
term tactics for a long-term strategy. And it shies away from
forcing the party to confront difficult choices, mistaking a
conversation within the Labour Party for a conversation with
the country. It overplays the significance – welcome though
they are – of mid-term by-election or local election victories.
It overemphasises the importance – vital though that is – of
better organisation on the ground, believing that progress can
be measured simply by better targeting of resources or higher
voter identification statistics. And it overestimates the consequences – important though they may turn out to be – of the

inevitable difficulties and unpopularity that most mid-term governments run into.

But perhaps most pernicious of all for the party's chances of recovery, it can, as Douglas Alexander suggests in his chapter, 'risk blaming the voters and not ourselves for our defeat'. In its present incarnation, the 'safety-first' strategy assumes that the coalition's deficit-reduction plan, the consequent public spending cuts, and the risk that George Osborne drives the economy back into recession, will provoke a wave of public anger that Labour can exploit at the next general election. That may all be true – although opinion polls continue to suggest that more voters still blame Labour for the spending cuts than they do the coalition.

But morally, such a strategy has little to commend it: those who are suffering most from the cuts – and would suffer most in a recession – are the poor and the powerless, those who it is the Labour Party's first duty to defend. Politically, it has even less: it is a gamble that takes Labour's fortunes out of its own hands and, at root, assumes the party is little more than a bystander in its own story. It suggests that a relentless attack on its opponents and a return to the old politics of 'dividing lines' will provide the voters with an opportunity to correct the 'mistake' they made of failing to re-elect Labour last May. Such a strategy will fail for the very simple reason that it forgets that elections are not simply a referendum on the performance of a government: they are a choice between government and opposition; their accounts of the present and their visions of the future.

None of this is to deny the element of truth contained in the old adage that oppositions do not win elections, governments lose them. But it is also true that faced with a choice between a government they do not like and an opposition they do not trust, most voters will opt for the former. Governments may lose elections, but oppositions have to win them, too. The story of Labour's defeat in 1992 and its victory in 1997 demonstrates this perfectly. Faced with a choice in 1992 between a disliked government, presiding over a recession, and a distrusted opposition, voters chose the former. By contrast, when faced in 1997 with a choice between a disliked government – now presiding over a recovery – and an opposition which had worked hard and relentlessly to earn the trust of the voters, the electorate gave the latter a landslide victory.

Some of the 'safety-first' adherents will, no doubt, disapprove of this book because of the final characteristic that defines their politics: a dismissal of any discussion of ideas and policy as the self-indulgent antics of 'wonk world', far removed from the concerns of the 'ordinary voters' for whom they claim to speak. This view is bolstered by the notion that any debate or discussion is not only a distraction from the 'real task' of winning elections, but is detrimental to it: suggesting that to offer any view that has not first been expressed by the leadership risks giving the impression to the voters that the party is divided, and divided parties do not win elections.

What *The Economist* has termed 'Westminster's anti-intellectualism' is, in fact, one important obstacle to Labour's renewal. Indeed, it betrays a lack of understanding about the link between a party's intellectual vibrancy – its ability to think about its purpose and beliefs, and how these fit with the country's future needs and challenges – and its electoral health.

That link is not hard to prove. Look at the fate of the premierships of Brown, Jim Callaghan or John Major: each appeared bereft of new ideas, not only politically but intellectually exhausted. Callaghan's government, of course, was not entirely without new ideas, but it lacked the political will to bring them to fruition with disastrous effects. Most famously, it rejected proposals drawn up by the No. 10 Policy Unit to allow council tenants to purchase their homes. Bernard Donoughue, the head of the unit and the man responsible for drawing up the plans, later remarked: 'It gave Mrs Thatcher a winning election card. The left-wing reactionaries in the party had won... The heart of the problem, much wider than the issue of selling council houses, was that our Labour government was trapped in the outdated prejudices and undemocratic structures of its party organisation. Because of this, we failed to appreciate and respond to the changing realities and aspirations of many of our own supporters.'[7]

Similarly, the Royal Commission on Industrial Democracy, chaired by Alan Bullock, led nowhere. Even concessions to the unions that workers on company boards would be there as their representatives and not the entire workforce failed to buy off what David Marquand has termed the 'unholy alliance between industrial conservatives' in the TUC, CBI and Cabinet who combined to smother the proposals.[8]

Indeed, as Blair noted in a speech marking the fiftieth anniversary of its election, even the Attlee government ran out of intellectual steam in the space of barely five years. Its three main weaknesses, argued Blair, were, 'First, a failure to recognise fully the realities of the new world order, manifested in the attitude of the government towards Europe; second, a reluctance to modernise the institutions of government itself – what Kenneth Morgan calls the Labour government's "stern centralism"; and third, a tendency to look back to the problems of the 1930s, not forward to the challenges of the 1950s.'[9]

And it is not only governments but oppositions, too, whose fate is determined by the perception that they are unwilling to face the future. Throughout the 1950s, Labour appeared more concerned with defending its past achievements, worthy though they were, than with thinking about the challenges of the future. As Denis MacShane has argued, 'In the 1950s, Labour opposed the creation of commercial television, premium bonds and betting shops. No to *Corrie* and no to a flutter pleased bishops and the fellows of All Souls. But was that where the great British public was?'[10] Writing in 1954, Hugh Dalton, Chancellor of the Exchequer in Attlee's government, provided his answer. 'People were very content with the Tories. They had stolen the Socialists' clothes (full employment, welfare state, etc.),' he suggested. Indeed, in some moods he could 'see no reason, except crass conservatism, for voting Labour now'.[11] Labour's opposition in the 1980s and the Tories under William Hague, Iain Duncan Smith and Michael Howard were similarly intellectually moribund. Each were repeatedly rejected by the electorate.

By contrast, consider the story of oppositions: Wilson and the 'white heat of technology' in the 1960s; Margaret Thatcher and Keith Joseph's development in the 1970s of what would eventually emerge as Thatcherism; and, of course, the welter of ideas which accompanied Blair and New Labour in the mid-1990s – which appeared to be at the cutting edge of new ideas and thought. Opposition has few pleasures. The time and space to think is not only one of them, it is also the surest way out of it.

### Back to revisionism

There is, of course, an alternative to the 'politics of evasion'. Writing a couple of months before Labour's general election defeat last May, James Purnell and Graeme Cooke's *We Mean Power: Ideas for the Future of the Left* offered a passionate justification for, and explanation of, Labour's revisionist tradition. 'True revisionism,' they argued, 'is the opposite of abandoning our principles. It is an attempt to return to them. An ideology is a combination of three things: values, an idea of society and the methods by which to implement them. Labour has spent much more of its history arguing about the third, about means: which industries to nationalise, whether to abandon unilateralism, what the trade union block vote should be. The revisionists have always tried to push the debate back to the first two – to values, and to society, with the means following from a clear understanding of both.'[12]

This is the challenge for Labour today, and it is to meet that challenge that *The Purple Book* offers a first, necessarily incomplete, contribution. Our title has provoked some comment, with some seeing it as an attempt to mix Labour red and Tory blue and others drawing comparison with *The Orange Book*. Today's Liberal Democrats do not, of course, have a monopoly on the use of colours in book titles: *The Orange Book* derived its title from the 1928 *Yellow Book*, while Labour has had the likes of the *Red Paper on Scotland*. The *Orange* and *Purple* books are alike in one sole but important respect: both attempt to revive a tradition from our respective parties' history that we believe has relevance for the future. But while *The Orange Book* attempted to revive economic liberalism, *The Purple Book* attempts no such thing – this has, after all, never been part of Labour's story. We, instead, attempt to revive Labour's decentralising tradition of participation, self-government and 'moral reform'.

So, why purple? Because we feel it represents the centre-ground of British politics. Unlike the Americans, we do not normally describe constituencies as safe 'red' or 'blue' ones or swing 'purple' ones, but if we did, the purple constituencies would be those marginal ones – in the vast majority of which the main fight is between Labour and the Conservatives – upon which the outcome of elections is ultimately decided.

Labour's revisionist tradition is a rich and strong one. Its origins lay in the publication of the *New Fabian Essays* in 1952 and, most famously, Tony Crosland's *The Future of Socialism* in 1956. Labour's first revisionist leader, Hugh Gaitskell, captured well the essence of its philosophy in the speech with which he launched his – unsuccessful – attempt to change the old Clause IV. Labour, he argued, must adapt 'to be in touch always with ordinary people to avoid becoming small cliques of isolated, doctrine-ridden fanatics, out of touch, with the main stream of social life in our time'. The party should not, he urged, 'wave the banners of a bygone age'.[13]

It was precisely this argument that Labour's revisionists of the 1980s and 1990s – Blair, Brown, Neil Kinnock and Peter Mandelson – made to the party and which set it back on the

road to electability. Revisionism's importance – and its relationship to New Labour – is underlined by Paul Richards in his
chapter in this book. It is, he argues 'the only reason we still
have a Labour Party. Without revisionism – which New Labour
dubbed modernisation – the Labour Party would have clung to
outdated policies and be weighed down by dusty ideology. It
would be a political sect, not a governing party.'

The case for the continuing relevance of New Labour –
with its insistence on the necessity of separating means from
ends – hinges on its proponents' acceptance of this place
within the revisionist tradition. This point is made by two
of our authors. As Alexander suggests in his chapter, New
Labour was 'composed of positions, personnel and policies.
The personnel have changed and the policies for the 1990s
are not going to be the solutions to the problems in the 2010s.
But the positions – a determination to prioritise credibility
on the economy and a willingness to take bold steps on crime
and antisocial behaviour – are ones we would reject at great
cost to our prospects of winning back power.'

Similarly, Mandelson makes the case that New Labour
'cannot simply rely on the policy solutions we deployed when
last in office. But we can retain the central revisionist insight
embodied by New Labour: that as a party we are at our best
when we are neither sectional nor regional, but national, challenging ourselves to make reforms to achieve greater social
equality in ways that will attract support from those living in
very different social circumstances.'

### Electoral strategy and the challenge of blue Labour

New Labour's great electoral insight, therefore, was its understanding that the party could no longer win by relying on
its traditional base of support but needed instead to build
a cross-class alliance. At times, however, the debate within
Labour's ranks appears to suggest that the party must rebuild
either its 'core' working-class vote or its support among

southern middle-class voters. This was always a false choice – one which New Labour successfully overcame in its three election victories – and it is even more so now.

As a new analysis of the British Values Survey by Graeme Cooke of ippr suggests, understanding the new electorate means 'engaging with "Voter-3D": class, geography and values'. He suggests three broad values dispositions within the electorate: the 41 per cent of voters who might be classed 'pioneers' and who are global, networked, innovators, ethical and seek self-actualisation; 'prospectors' who, at 28 per cent of the electorate, value success and status, are ambitious and seek the esteem of others; and the one-third of Britons who are 'settlers' and have a strong sense of the need for rules, value the local, are wary of change, and seek security and belonging. But these value dispositions cut across different classes and 'it is certainly not the case that the formerly industrial north is full of "settlers", metropolitan areas only have "pioneers" and "middle England" is a sea of "prospectors",' Cooke argues. While avoiding micro-targeting and 'pick and mix politics', he concludes, Labour must assemble a 'broad majoritarian pitch that has something to appeal to all values [and] sentiments'. This, in turn, requires the party to break out of the 'straitjacket' of the 'working-class northern core versus middle-class southern swing'.[14]

In the period since the general election, blue Labour has offered its own analysis of Labour's time in office and made a valuable contribution to the debate about where the party goes next. Its principal 'guru', Maurice Glasman, has pitched it as 'an attempt to improve and strengthen the early days of New Labour' and argued that it is the 'place where New Labour needs to go next'.[15] There are certainly some shared insights and concerns with *The Purple Book*. Blue Labour has recognised the importance of issues like welfare reform and immigration, understood the complexity of the debates around the meaning of fairness (whether our conception is based around the notions of need or desert can produce radically different policy outcomes), and, most particularly, shares an antipathy to 'top-down' statism.

Nonetheless, the limitations of blue Labour are also clear. To return to Cooke's analysis of the values dispositions of the electorate, it is clear what blue Labour's appeal might be to those with 'settler' sentiments, but less apparent when it comes to the 'prospectors' and, especially, the 'pioneers'. Blue Labour appears also to have moved beyond an understanding of the need to acknowledge and respond to voters' concerns about immigration to an anti-immigration position with suggestions of a halt to the free movement of labour within the European Union. Perhaps most importantly, though, while revisionism seeks to ensure that Labour remains connected to the world as it is, and the future challenges changes in society and new aspirations will bring, blue Labour all too often appears fundamentally backward-looking. Rather than reassuring the public that Labour understands, and will help people to manage, the process of change, all too often blue Labour seems to suggest that the party should attempt to persuade the electorate that it can resist it. This is a false promise and Labour should not make it.

## Revising New Labour
But New Labour, too, must itself guard against becoming a conservative force, stuck in the world of 1994 rather than 2011. Indeed, Labour's revisionists have made this error before. Writing in the aftermath of Labour's fourth general election defeat in 1992, Marquand noted that, 'the values embodied in the ... social democratic middle way – a combination of personal freedom and social justice; of individual fulfilment and public purpose – are as compelling as they always were. But ... the instruments through which the revisionist social democrats of the 1960s and 1970s tried to realise their values broke in the hands of the governments which relied upon them.'[16]

For many, this would be an apt description of New Labour's final years in government. And the solution that

Marquand proposed nearly twenty years ago is as relevant today as it was then: 'If revisionist social democracy is to recover intellectually as well as politically, if it is to serve as a governing philosophy after an election as well as providing a platform from which to fight one, it must itself be revised.'[17]

A 'revising of New Labour' requires four things. First, a willingness, in the words of Miliband, to escape the 'false choices' around Labour's electoral strategy.[18] Second, an honest account of New Labour's period in office and its lessons. Third, a willingness to confront the division within the left on the role of the state. And, finally, the development of new policies – guided by the principle of redistributing power – to confront the new challenges facing Britain over the next decade. Crucially, these must be explicitly based on a recognition of the need to restore the public's shattered faith in the ability of the state and the market to widen opportunity, demand responsibility, and strengthen communities.

**Reclaiming the decentralist tradition**
Attitudes towards the role of the state have long divided what, in the broadest sense, we might term the left. Marquand has famously highlighted this with his distinction between 'democratic collectivists' and 'democratic republicans'. The former 'were content with the existing state, but for them it was the agent of social transformation, guided by science, reason and their own grasp of the dynamics of historical change – legitimate because it was the emanation of an overarching society that transcended the individuals who composed it'.[19] By contrast, 'democratic republicans' advocated 'civic activity versus slothful apathy; and, most of all, government by vigorous discussion and mutual learning versus passive deference to monarch, capitalist and state'.[20] G. D. H. Cole drew a distinction in British socialism between reformists and revolutionaries and, more saliently for this discussion, 'federalists' and 'centralisers'. And Peter Clarke's *Liberals and Social Democrats*

has pinpointed the division between 'mechanical reformers', who 'believe that recalcitrant human nature can be prodded into the right path only by coercion, and that the primary aim of those who seek social change must be to get their hands on the instruments of coercion', and 'moral reformers', who believe that 'social change is above all the product of persuasion and leadership, and state-imposed progress is inherently suspect'.[21]

Thus, as *The Purple Book* seeks to demonstrate, abandoning statism does not require Labour to shed its identity or adopt the political traditions of its Liberal or Tory opponents. Instead, it requires us to rediscover an old tradition rooted deep in Labour's history which is right for new times. Indeed, if we look at the manner in which the Conservatives have attempted over recent years to appropriate the agenda around mutuals and co-ops, to take just one example, we see that rediscovering our decentralist tradition allows us to reclaim what is rightfully ours, rather than attempting to claim for ourselves what belongs to another.

Democratic republican, mechanical reform or federalist, what we term the 'decentralist tradition' is a rich one. It is the tradition of those such as the Levellers and Thomas Paine who fought and argued for a widening of political rights; of the ethical socialism of Tawney and the guild socialism of Cole; of the cooperative movement, Robert Owen, the Rochdale Pioneers and William Morris; of the self-organisation ethos by which the working class built the early trade union movement, the friendly societies and other institutions that reflected their belief in self-help; and the municipal 'gas-and-water socialism' of the inter-war years.

However diverse this tradition, there is a common thread running through it. Resting on the principles of participation and self-government, it challenges the statist approach that Labour's role should be to win elections, seize the commanding heights of the state – at a local or national level – and use the power it has acquired to redistribute resources from the few to the many. Instead, the decentralist tradition, as Richards describes, requires the left to 'create new centres of governance, power and wealth creation, as an alternative to both the central-ised state and the private sector'. This should be the guiding objective of a future Labour government, and the narrative with which the party describes its mission as it seeks to attain office once again. *The Purple Book* begins to set out how.

1   Richard H. Tawney, 'The Choice Before the Labour Party', *Political Quarterly* (1932) vol. 3, no. 3, pp. 323–45

2   Richard Darlington (ed.), *Open Left: Why Voters Left Labour* (London: Open Left/Demos, 2010).

3   *The Quest for a New Governing Purpose* (London: Policy Network, 2011).

4   Bill Clinton, keynote address to the Democratic Leadership Council's Cleveland Convention, 6 May 1991.

5   Elaine Karmack and William Galston, *The Politics of Evasion* (London: Progressive Policy Institute, 1989).

6.  Ed Miliband, speech to the Fabian Society Annual Conference, 15 January 2011.

7   Bernard Donoughue, *The Heat of the Kitchen* (London: Politico's, 2003).

8.  David Marquand, *Britain Since 1918: The Strange Career of British Democracy* (London: Weidenfeld & Nicolson, 2009).

9.  Cited in Philip Gould, *The Unfinished Revolution: How the Modernisers Saved the Labour Party* (London: Little Brown, 1998).

10  'Labour's lost decades', *Progress*, March 2011.

11. Cited in Peter Clarke, 'The Making of the Post-War Consensus', in *A Question of Leadership: From Gladstone to Thatcher* (London: Hamish Hamilton, 1991).

12. James Purnell and Graeme Cooke (eds), *We Mean Power: Ideas for the Future of the Left* (London: Demos, 2010).

13. Cited in Philip Gould, op. cit.

14. Graeme Cooke, 'Still Partying Like It's 1995: Class, Culture and Capitalism and the New Political Sociology of Britain', presentation at ippr, June 2011.

15. 'Labour isn't working', *Progress*, May 2011.

16. David Marquand, *The Progressive Dilemma: From Lloyd George to Kinnock* (London: Heinemann, 1991).

17. Ibid.

18. Ed Miliband, speech to Progress Annual Conference, 21 May 2011.

19. David Marquand, *Britain Since 1918: The Strange Career of British Democracy* (London: Weidenfeld & Nicolson, 2009).

20. Ibid.

21. Cited in David Marquand (1991), op. cit.

# Renewing our offer, not retracing our steps: building a sense of national purpose

*Douglas Alexander*

Fresh from experiencing Labour's 1987 general election defeat, I headed to the United States in the autumn of 1988, to study at the University of Pennsylvania.

At the time Michael Dukakis, the governor of Massachusetts, was running for President. He roared out of the Democratic convention with a seventeen-point lead over George H. W. Bush. And then, unbeknown to the candidate, I started volunteering for his campaign.

On polling day I spent many cold hours handing out fliers at a subway station in north Philadelphia. Literally everyone I met was voting Democrat. And so it seemed that maybe, just maybe, America was heading for a Dukakis–Bentsen presidency.

Early the next morning, it became clear what was actually happening outside the Democratic heartlands. Dukakis had not won Pennsylvania. He had been defeated across the country and lost the electoral college 111 to 426.

The risk then, and the risk now, is experiencing a crushing defeat without fully understanding it. Four years later the man who introduced Dukakis at that Democratic convention – Bill Clinton – proved that he both understood the defeat, and understood what it took to win.

Labour achieved a great deal in office. Leaving government

we looked back with pride at much of what had been done – Sure Start centres across the country, civil partnerships, dozens of new hospital buildings, and hundreds and thousands of pensioners taken out of poverty, to name but a few.

But that pride – and the defensiveness that generally goes with it – can at times risk blaming the voters and not ourselves for our defeat. And understanding Labour's defeat – with honesty and humility – is the first step back to power.

## A wider view

The scale of the defeat bears a brief recap. Just over a year ago, Labour suffered its second lowest share of the vote since 1918. The 6 percentage point drop in Labour's vote share was almost the same as after the collapse of the National government in 1931. Labour won only 10 out of around 200 seats in the south of England outside London.

Various accounts of why Labour lost have circulated since the defeat. Some focus on street-level support, arguing that Labour's approach to immigration or the welfare state contributed decisively to defeat. Others focus on how we lost permission to be heard when we lost the support of media or business elites. Yet these analyses, important though they are, reflect the common tendency to find explanations that simply validate previously held beliefs. A deeper account demands a wider view.

And that wider view confirms that Labour is not the only centre-left party with cause for concern: the French and Danish centre-left have not won in a decade while, following the crash, the German and the Swedish centre-left all polled their lowest-ever votes for at least twenty years and, in the case of the Swedish Social Democrats, their lowest since 1923. When Clinton and Tony Blair were winning power, the centre-left was regularly winning against the right. Now it is the centre-right that is regularly coming off better in electoral contests with the left.

Of course each of these setbacks has had distinctive features reflecting distinctive national circumstances. Yet it seems undeniable that here in Britain, and internationally, the market failure of the global financial crash has ended up damaging the electoral position of the centre-left much more than the centre-right.

In part that can be explained by the specific steps that have been taken by our centre-right opponents. There are clear and common threads in the 'magpie politics' appeal for votes made by the centre-right in countries as diverse as Canada, New Zealand and Sweden. Each offers a traditional economic appeal with an assertion of compassion and concern for issues such as poverty not associated in recent years with the right.

But our defeat in Britain cannot only be explained by our opponents' recognition of the electoral appeal of a politics – albeit insufficiently – combining credibility and compassion.

We have to examine what is still relevant in the New Labour prospectus that saw us through three general election victories. New Labour was composed of positions, personnel and policies. The personnel have changed and the policies for the 1990s are not going to be the solutions to problems in the 2010s. But the positions – a determination to prioritise credibility on the economy and a willingness to take bold steps on crime and antisocial behaviour – are ones we would reject at great cost to our prospects of winning back power.

Our challenge is not to retrace our steps to a pre-1990s settlement on the centre-left but to forge an authentically new settlement for the 2010s and 2020s. And honestly examining our positions on the central issues of the role of the state and on the market is, I believe, vital to understanding the problems that face our party today.

That examination and that debate is needed, and it is needed now. Of necessity, many key areas cannot be covered here. Issues such as crime – not least with the latest riots – or the future development of devolution form essential parts of the analysis of other contributions to this book.

But my take on 'purple politics' is the almost paradoxical claim that New Labour was both powerful and partial and that our future success depends on drawing the correct conclusions about what to retain and what to reject as we renew our political project.

So while this analysis does not seek to write a manifesto, it does seek to analyse the defeat, see how the Conservatives and Liberal Democrats are changing, and look at some of the tools we will need to come back.

In my view, this work starts with a new analysis of the role of both the market and the state.

### Markets, aspiration and fairness

The role of the market in our lives has always been central to Labour politics. For much of the twentieth century, the debate in the Labour Party was about to what extent the state should control what the country produced and to what extent it should be left up to the market. The original Clause IV represented Labour's early belief that the more the state controlled, the better for everyone.

In moving away from that, starting with Tony Crosland through to the mid-1990s modernisers Blair and Brown, Labour moved from being market-phobic to being market-sceptics to finally being seen as market-enthusiasts.

But for those who take pride in having been part of the party's modernisation in the mid-1990s, the problems we have seen in recent years should be genuinely troubling. Internally, and externally, we had argued hard that Labour had to accept and harness the creative power of markets – only to then govern during one of the great market failures of modern times.

In fact, some of the language endorsing the market in all its forms and impacts – talk of being relaxed about the super-rich or a golden age of the City – reflected an apparently uncritical embrace that was a product of the anxieties of the past. Yet the politicians who made these statements were not bad people. They were progressive people who – in the face of repeated electoral defeats and continuing media hostility – forged a progressive settlement for their time.

In retrospect it is hard to overestimate the scale of intellectual defeat felt by the centre-left in the wake of the 1992 general election defeat. The response was to offer an apparently uncritical account of globalisation, in part motivated by the desire to prove that Labour understood the productive power of modern market economies.

The deal that was offered to the public was this: that the taxes generated by growth – in particular facilitated by globalisation in the decade after 1997 – would be redistributed into building schools, hospitals, and lifting children and pensioners out of poverty.

But the global financial crisis left Labour looking as if we had confused good times with a good system. In truth, the weaknesses of that 1990s progressive settlement were already being felt years before the collapse of Northern Rock. It is not simply that, with this approach, Britain was too heavily reliant on the continued growth of financial services.

Take, for instance, the issue of living standards. In 1997, we won on the idea that we could continue to promote rising living standards, but that we could combine it with a more decent society. But by 2010, living standards were being squeezed and, just as economic boom turned into economic bust, record investment in public services was set to be replaced by significant cuts to public expenditure.

Ed Miliband has highlighted how, 'since 2003, those at the top have seen their living standards continue to rise at extraordinary rates, while those of the rest have stagnated. For most, flat wages, rising prices, longer working hours, and the burden of debt and insecurity are increasingly being placed on them and their kids.'

If we needed to sometimes overcompensate in our language during the 1990s to prove that we really did want a better capitalism, rather than to abolish capitalism, then thirteen years in office acting as pro-market progressives should remove that worry.

Now, instead, our focus should be on how we achieve that better capitalism in a very different environment. The coalition government has adopted a politics of austerity that risks delivering an economics of decline. We need positive and specific answers when we are asked how we can build an economy where ordinary people, not just the elite, have the power to make a success of their own lives. We can show just how unlikely it is that an unreconstructed anti-government strategy is going to deliver the sustainable, stable growth people want to see.

But to match that intellectual renewal we also need to make the emotional link to why market economies, however flawed they are, in the end, are better than the alternatives.

Here the invention of my friend the late David Cairns comes in useful. He thought up the 'conservatory principle': that no one should be allowed to lead the Labour Party unless they understood the desire to own a conservatory. And certainly the charge has been levelled that Labour politicians do not instinctively understand why people want small improvements to their standard of living. Being the party of holidays, home ownership, and an HD TV is something that the party's ethical socialist tradition has always struggled with.

Now, of course, only talking about material concerns, whether it is tax cuts and council house sales or extra spending and public provision, can create a diminished politics. There is more to life than earning and owning. Moreover, the word 'aspiration' appears more often in the political lexicon than in the public one.

But, in fact, aspiration – the holiday, the house, the television – can be about far more than the material. The holiday might be the one time we get to spend the hours with our kids that our parents, home by 6pm, never questioned. The house is a project, an inheritance and a guarantee against disaster. The television is a chance to relax and be distracted from the intensity of modern work.

So aspiration does not have to mean one thing, or consumption for its own sake. But understanding aspiration means understanding how the loss of savings, the loss of a home, seeing too much of your paycheque disappear before it reaches your bank account put people's dreams at risk.

The route to economic credibility has to start from a real understanding of aspiration. If you do not understand what is at stake, you will never understand why people need such reassurance on economic issues: reassurance that you will do everything possible to avoid economic crashes, that you will not suddenly introduce unforeseen taxes or store up problems by constantly borrowing money to fund day-to-day spending.

It is hard to prove your commitment to these guarantees but it is the only way you earn the stewardship of the country's economy. Whether it is through a focus on productivity of public spending, on taxation or on the audit and scrutiny of your policy offer, to be credible means finding means by which you can make people believe that you believe it.

And in this way, strangely, our ability to take tough decisions that will be painful for some people today is inseparably linked with our ability to offer rising living standards in the future. That is why when I was shadow work and pensions secretary we made the decision to work with the government on a number of its proposed welfare measures, rather than oppose every cut. Accepting some cuts as necessary is a prerequisite for being able to say that some things will be protected.

It is that bedrock of mainstream economic credibility and the hope of a return to rising living standards that could allow us to reject the false choice between aspiration and fairness.

In 1994, the economic test was to prove Labour really was comfortable with a private sector-led economy. In 2015, the tests the public set us will be very different. Voters will trust us not to try and implement a wages policy but they will need to trust us to protect their living standards too. They will trust us not to bring back pre-Thatcher union laws but they will care as much about how we bring the public sector finances into balance over time. They will trust us not to start nationalising industries but we will need to earn their trust that we will ensure public spending is efficient and effective.

## Understanding state failure

The extent to which the public judge that a political party 'gets it' reflects its approach not only to the market but also to the state. During our time in office we killed for a generation the argument that a publicly funded NHS could not meet the rising aspirations of the British people. The effectiveness of state action – by both the Bank of England and the Treasury – in preventing recession turning into depression made the case anew for a government response to macroeconomic emergencies. Policies like the national minimum wage showed that regulation did not always have to be an enemy of jobs and growth. And the fact that child and pensioner poverty were reduced by deliberate government policy showed that we had it within our power to address the fundamental problems of our society.

But Labour's increased spending also exposed two fundamental weaknesses in our approach to the state that we had not much worried about in 1997. An efficiency argument on waste hurt our credibility while a fairness argument on welfare challenged our moral authority.

By focusing on how the state could do good, at times we

lacked a language for state failure. And that left us fighting a referendum on the virtues of the public sector – the big state versus small state argument – rather than on a choice between action and inaction.

To continue to build the case for the state taking some action, we allowed ourselves to confuse processes with results in our arguments. We talked about spending on particular areas reaching a certain proportion of GDP and used the word 'billions' as if it was the conclusive point in an argument.

With such a monochrome palette, at times we looked as if we thought there was no problem that government could not or should not solve. But when people angrily raised something like GP pay or the salaries of local government chief executives, we did not have much to say.

Now, in opposition, we should be able to address these changes. We have won the argument that the state can be effective – responding to financial crisis and providing public services – and the Conservatives have accepted it. So we can be more willing to take a serious look at how the public sector can swell, how wage bills can spiral and how managers can lose sight of the needs of the people they are supposed to be serving.

It will not be easy changing the public's view of us on these issues. Scepticism towards politicians blends with a scepticism towards government and that makes the advocacy of the capacity of government to help improve lives a tough task. The answer has to be to balance the necessary resources with the necessary reform. It is the right thing to do in terms of efficiency, and the wise thing to do in terms of electability. People need to believe we are as serious about productivity as we are about investment.

But the record of Labour's time in office is under assault not simply in terms of efficiency but also in terms of fairness. Its fairness was challenged for too little action at the top of the income scale and, simultaneously, for too much action at the bottom of the income scale.

In the minds of some voters, some of the very policy tools designed to make society fairer – like housing benefit – became a source of resentment, rather than a source of pride. Too often they reinforced a sense that when we talked of fairness we were talking about someone else. In fact – by often seeming to reward those who were not working hard or in having rules that were flouted by significant numbers – they too often came to be associated with unfairness.

So if we are going to sustain the case for taking action to keep inequality in check – and part of that strategy involves cash transfers – then we are going to have to remake the political case for action at the bottom of the income scale as surely as we need to remake the case for action at the top of the income scale.

Here again, the idea of aspiration could be a guide to navigating the difficult questions about fairness at the top and at the bottom.

It is completely legitimate to want to work hard, build a good business and earn significant sums in the process. It is not legitimate to want to earn mega-bonuses for undertaking behaviour that actually puts the business you are employed in more at risk.

No one starts off aspiring to a life on benefits. No one really hopes for a job where they can only afford to get by because of a top-up to their income from the state. But people do know that awful things can happen, and they want the state to be ready to help if they do.

We need to redesign our welfare state with that in mind. A foundation of our original welfare state was the idea that those who worked would be rewarded: for many it feels like the welfare state pulls in the opposite direction, not because they have to pay taxes, but because of the manner in which they receive benefits.

There is more that can be done to enhance the legitimacy of welfare through conditionality – taking greater action to enforce the duty to work, while if necessary providing support to make sure the jobs are there. And we need to say that hoping that others will pick up after us if we are able but don't want to work, is utterly unacceptable. No one starts off with that aspiration but too many end up there.

But we also need to be aware that for many people on average salaries who worried for their jobs during the recession, the prospect of getting or losing £65 a week was just not relevant to them despite years of paying into the system. Rethinking welfare means looking less to compensation and more to contribution as a guiding principle in our welfare state.

## A sense of national purpose

As a party, we are only just now grappling with a number of these issues. To re-evaluate how we won three elections, to retain the good lessons of government while changing the things that the electorate told us they were sick of, is an immense challenge.

After losing the argument in 1979, it took us eighteen years to get back into office. When the Tories lost the argument after Black Wednesday, it took them eighteen years to come back.

To come back in one term is not Labour's normal experience, but it can be done. In setting up a review of our policies and our party structures, Ed Miliband has given us the processes by which this task can be undertaken.

By the time of the next election, the processes that have been set up on the reform of our party and the review of our policy will be complete and the outcomes will be there for the public to judge.

I believe that there will be fundamental questions by which they will form that judgement: Do we meet the threshold of credibility in all of our policy proposals but most importantly on the economy? Have we genuinely learned from the message that voters sent us in 2010 – and have a new account of fairness at both the top and the bottom? Does the way we manage the party give confidence to people that we could effectively manage the country? And do we offer a positive change and a sense of national purpose that people in Britain genuinely want and believe in?

That last point is crucial. Even if people think you are credible on the economy, that you get what is going on with their lives and that you have some valuable policy proposals, that will not be enough to deliver victory. People might have done all the calculations and worked out that they would be better off with a particular party – and then vote a different way or not at all. Many might only judge on an impression they have built up from the tone of our language and half-remembered bits of newspaper coverage.

The type of renewed policy agenda we need will not itself be sufficient unless we renew the way we emotionally engage the electorate.

As class distinctions have weakened, what inspiration that could be found in being 'the working-class party' is declining. In a mobile, fast-changing society simply 'standing up for my area' does not cut it either. And, for all the dreams of some pro-Europeans, a transnational story has not emerged in Britain.

The national level – an enduring community of association – is still looked to for inspiration. At that level, there is a complex debate about identity which is as much about the past as the present. What Labour needs is a way of looking towards the future, because Labour wins when it invites people to be part of a better future. A conversation about national purpose is our best route.

That means taking this debate beyond the market and the state and asking the question: 'What is Britain for?' I could be wrong, but my guess is that people will answer that Britain is for fundamentally progressive measures at home – like the

NHS – and internationalist measures abroad. Synchronising our pride and our patriotism with our best instincts could allow us not merely to criticise but to compete with everything this government can offer.

Few parties ever manage to come away from a bad defeat, look hard at their record, salvage what was good and learn from what was bad, and come up with something new and inspiring in a matter of four or five years. That is the scale of the task before the Labour Party today.

We could shy away from that task, stay in a defensive crouch and hope our luck turns. I do not think it would work. But I believe the Labour Party is more than that: Britain needs us to learn from both our victories and our defeats, and so renew our offer to serve the country.

# An effective state, not a big state: forging a national strategy

*Peter Mandelson*

Almost a year to the day after the 2010 general election I returned to Hartlepool in the north-east of England. I was reflecting on what the town had been like when I was first elected in 1992 and the changes it had undergone during the Labour government after 1997.

Hartlepool had become a depressed, rather sullen, down-at-heel place by the early 1990s. As I knocked on doors I discovered people who did not think things could get better, whoever was in charge. They were not inspired by Labour, however much they wanted to see the back of the Conservatives.

In 1997, there was greater enthusiasm for us. Perhaps it helped that Tony Blair, too, represented a north-east constituency, and people thought he would not let down the people of England's poorest region.

Overwhelmingly, Hartlepool, like many constituencies elsewhere, emerged with a hugely positive legacy from the years of Labour government. New school buildings, a freshly built primary health and diagnostic centre as well as the revamped general hospital, a lot of renewed public housing and the town's parks, community areas and seafront greatly changed for the better. The changes were epitomised by the construction of a new home for the town's college of further education. Without doubt, Hartlepool had come on in the world in a nation that benefitted from tremendous regeneration.

Britain's once-crumbling, Thatcherite infrastructure of public services inherited by the Blair government could now boast 3,700 schools either rebuilt or refurbished, as well as hundreds of wholly new schools with 42,000 more teachers; over 100 new hospitals with over 44,000 more doctors and 89,000 more nurses who help perform 3 million more operations per year since 1997; the biggest programme of council house building for twenty years; and over 3,500 Sure Start centres.

For all the Guardianistas' complaints of New Labour authoritarianism, Labour's social reforms have made Britain more liberal than ever before. Civil partnerships, better rights for gay people, ethnic minorities, pensioners and parents (including record maternity pay and, for the first time, the right to paternity leave) have clearly left their mark on British society. Free museum entry, free swimming for children and some of the cleanest public spaces for a century have played their part, too. And, with more police than ever on Britain's streets, crime came down by one-third, domestic violence down by two-thirds and rape convictions went up by a half.

Yet my constituency lay in a region that was most susceptible (or least resilient) to economic shocks. As economic change took its toll in the 1980s and 1990s, alternative sources of employment did not come naturally or quickly. What saved the region from sinking were the large foreign-owned enterprises whose investment the region had successfully attracted in earlier periods.

From 1997 to 2007, jobs picked up as annual growth averaged at 2.9 per cent, allowing living standards to rise and inflation to be tamed. Yes, incomes did race away at the very top (much faster than I had ever imagined was likely fifteen years ago, and in many cases with boards and shareholders too careless in ensuring a proper justification of executive pay based on increased performance). But if it had not been for Labour's redistribution of income through tax and benefit changes, inequality would have been far higher. By 2007 UK average wages were 59 per cent ahead of where they were in 1997 – only two other countries in the Organisation for Economic Cooperation and Development could match this – and real disposable income grew by one-fifth from 1996 to 2008. On Labour's watch, half a million children were lifted out of poverty, the new educational maintenance allowance kept children in school, pensioner credits greatly reduced poverty in old age while the winter fuel allowance, free TV licences and bus passes were introduced for all the elderly, some more in need than others.

Labour invested in the workforce, too. We created a record number of students in higher education, a majority of who were women. The New Deal and a new system of skills training helped over a million people into work, while the number of apprenticeships was doubled. As a result of signing up to Europe's Social Chapter, full-time workers were given statutory rights to twenty-eight days' paid holiday for the first time, and part-time workers are now afforded many of the same protections.

This is what a 'progressive state' means in practice. Real, practical changes that make a difference to the lives of millions of our fellow citizens. So let's not fall for the canard that voting does not change anything.

I do not know whether to laugh or cry when I hear Conservative ministers saying now that the problem with the north east is that it became too reliant on public spending and public sector employment. As if that was what people chose. Of course towns like Hartlepool were glad to have public investment but, given the choice, its people would have preferred the continued presence of the steelworks, the General Electric Company and other large industrial plants, the engineering firms, the busy port and the many small businesses supplying the bigger companies. Like elsewhere, progressive policies, implemented over many years of active Labour government, central and local, kept the town afloat. Far from public sector investment squeezing out private sector growth, as the Conservative world view imagines, increased public expenditure was the only platform on which a revived private sector would be capable of flourishing. But it still needs that strong private sector in order to flourish.

Now, the 'progressive state' will become smaller and less generous as a result of the hole blown in the nation's finances by the banking crisis and we know who will pay the price. In vulnerable parts of our country there will be less fairness; fewer opportunities will exist for individual advancement than in those places where the private sector is more vibrant and there is more money splashing around.

The world may not have been transformed during our time in government but the individual lives of millions of our fellow citizens were improved, saved or made better by the actions of the progressive state advanced and nurtured by us. Britain had become a better place because of thirteen years of New Labour in government.

**Reassessing New Labour**
At the 2010 election we lost not because of our record, but because voters were not convinced we were the right choice for the future. The excitement that propelled New Labour to victory in 1997 and sustained two further victories had almost faded away by the time we reached last year's election. A mixture of drift and uncertainty about what New Labour meant had set in. Perhaps it was asking too much to sustain that original excitement and flair, that sense of bold New Labour purpose, over such a long period of time as well as through such a profound global financial and economic crisis. Difficult, but not impossible.

As we regroup and rethink our way forward, we should

take pride in our achievements. New Labour was, and remains, a highly successful governing philosophy. Our new generation of leaders are perfectly at liberty to call it something else if they prefer. But the governing principles that New Labour embraced – above all the commitment to a successful market combined with the determined pursuit of social justice – remain attuned to the issues that will shape the politics of the second decade of the twenty-first century. They will remain the basis of the successful renewal of social democratic politics in Britain.

We fought and won on the centre-ground where the swing voters are to be found. Now some suggest we should look elsewhere for electoral support by proposing reconnection with (what is left of) the traditional working class on the basis of a nostalgic longing for a lost communitarian past. I doubt if my former supporters on the Hartlepool estates would understand what they are on about and, if they did, they would reject such patronising assumptions about their aspirations and ambitions.

The problem with killing off New Labour and putting nothing in its place is that it leads us to clutch at straws and grab at any passing sentiment. This is what has happened with blue Labour, which seeks to reconnect the party with its old, post-war, apparently white and male, industrial working-class base. These people have moved on, to other jobs, to other aspirations and, in the main, to an entirely different identity. I do think blue Labour's espousing of 'community' is attractive and reminds me of Blair's pre-1997 belief in local renewal (before our top-down actions in government fell short of our pre-election commitments). I also think that motivating people to bring about improvements in their lives and neighbourhoods is where Labour should be rather than ceding the 'big society' to the Tories. But blue Labour's platform of 'faith, family and the flag' lacks economic content – by far the biggest challenge facing the country – and its romantic ideas about working-class people turning back the clock is misplaced. Labour's people live in the real world and, above all, want secure, well-paid employment and a safe future for their children, which is why more activist growth and industrial policies are needed. This future is not going to come from the sort of populist, anti-immigrant, Europhobic, anti-globalisation language used by blue Labour. And however important it is to address the economic concerns of young people attracted to the English Defence League, the idea that we should reconnect by entering a dialogue with this organisation beggars belief.

We should avoid a binary and simplistic debate about New Labour, for or against. There were plenty of tensions, compromises and trade-offs over our thirteen years in power that we should acknowledge and reconsider.

Perhaps our pro-aspiration and pro-business politics came to define New Labour in a rather narrow economistic and individualist view of the world. Arguably our enthusiasm for public sector reform gave too little recognition of the values of the public realm and the commitment of its workforce.

Labour's approach to public service delivery meant change was rapid in some areas but also too top-down and driven too much from the centre in other cases. With the collapse of our ideas for regional government we did little, outside Scotland and Wales, to reverse Britain's historic trends towards centralisation. A big challenge for Labour's current rethinking will concern the distribution of political power, particularly in England, and its model of change in public services and social policy.

**Progressive growth and wealth creation**
But in our thinking about the future, our starting point should be to acknowledge what we did well in advancing the progressive state – one that combines as much belief in the power of wealth creation as it does in the need for wealth

distribution – and then identify what we need to do differently and better next time.

Labour has to be the party not only of the progressive state but of progressive growth. We do not believe – and never did – in the free-market trickle-down theory of economics. But economic growth, driven by a combination of competitive markets, sustained innovation and responsible business, provides a rising tide that can lift all boats – and it is the foundation of everything else we want to achieve for society.

Simplistic attacks on 'finance capitalism' will not win us back many votes. We must not allow the sensible arguments for a more long-termist business culture and for Britain to learn the valuable lessons of German and Swedish success to become naive anti-capitalist posturing. Equally, we need to go further in our thinking about growth than we did by the end of our period in government.

Ed Miliband has recognised that we cannot win or govern on the basis of being against the injustice of the cuts, however passionately we feel, if we are not economically credible ourselves. Our political opponents have got some way in trashing our economic record in order to harm our credibility. The right says it all went wrong because Labour spent too much. I do not think that can possibly explain the crisis. After catching up for years of underinvestment in public services, ahead of the financial crisis, the growth in public spending was being brought down into line with the medium-term growth rate for the economy as a whole. This would have put debt on a declining path if the banking crisis had not struck.

Yes, as a government we made mistakes. All governments do. We were too oblivious to the risks of financial deregulation. We assumed that the tax revenues that came through in a boom were permanent and sustainable and would not collapse in a bust, as they did. But it is a grotesque distortion of the truth that the crisis was the making of Gordon Brown, or Blair for that matter. It was the breakdown of the global financial system that struck so hard at a Britain that had become dangerously over-dependent on financial services. We left our industrial activism far too late, relying for too long on thirty years of Whitehall's belief that ministers and markets do not mix.

When the crisis broke, we made the right calls to save the banks and blunt the impact and duration of the ensuing recession. In the run-up to the general election, we also made the right economic judgements to deal with the deficit in a carefully managed way: tax rises, spending cuts and growth measures.

Our mistake was not to spell out in more detail the implications of the spending cuts so that people could see we were serious. By refusing to be clear that our deficit plans were sufficient, we were unable to persuade the public that the Tories' plans were excessive.

But this does not diminish the fact that the Darling Plan represented a better judgement than the Osborne Plan, which has frontloaded the necessary cuts on to an economy too weak to withstand them and has not offset them by building on our government's growth strategy designed to rebalance the economy.

The main driver of growth is innovation based on competitive markets. But this does not obviate the need for smart, strategic action by the government to pump-prime certain investment and contribute selectively to the heavy lifting of early stage technology or product development and market entry where market forces alone cannot or do not do the job themselves.

There is not a country I know in the world where there is more naivety than in Britain about the difference governments can make in supporting business. We suffer from the mistakes of our past, from the 1960s and 1970s, when instead of government picking winners, losers picked the government. This led us into the belief that markets alone must deliver sustainable and balanced growth, with too narrow a role for government in delivering the consistent policies and long-term private and public investment needed for all sectors of the economy to flourish.

This requires the kind of activism I envisaged when I was first at the Department for Trade and Industry in 1998 and which I returned to when I rejoined the government at the Business Department ten years later. The knowledge of continental Europe and the rest of the world I gained as trade commissioner encouraged me to see the sense of government helping to facilitate investment in innovation, skills and technology, as well as taking steps to ensure that its own capital investment receives a higher priority and that shareholders are motivated to take a more long-term view of investing in the corporate sector.

We need to recognise that the financial system has a key role to play in the real economy. The City and financial services are a huge global asset for the UK, not least as the financial capital of the EU's single market. However, as the financial crisis showed,  that asset can become a liability unless we get regulation and incentives right. New Basel III capital and liquidity rules – if internationally implemented – are essential. New mechanisms for quickly and effectively resolving failing banks are also vital, both to handle market sentiment and protect the credit system. And banks and their boards need to improve their ability to understand, manage and avoid excessive risk.

We have to recognise that tighter capital adequacy rules will mean less easy mortgages and more difficult access to finance for small businesses. Public policy has to address these issues with a new housing policy based on more building for rent and shared equity. There has to be additional finance available for industry based on public–private venture capital and business growth funds. We also need to align our financial system with the need for national infrastructure development to be better privately financed.

These issues are central because at the heart of our electoral dilemma is how we can offer a good future of better quality jobs for Britain's 'squeezed middle'. This has to be based on new sectors and growing businesses, with greater specialisation, that successfully combine our manufacturing and engineering prowess with the expanding demand for services, supported by a population capable of taking on higher skills and higher productivity. If those New Labour aspirant supporters who came to feel overlooked by us towards the end of our time in government are to be won back successfully, our core offer will have to be an economic and industrial strategy that delivers this promise of more and better jobs in the coming decade.

**The battleground ahead**
Let me conclude this chapter by making some political observations – born of a lifetime, literally, in the service of the Labour Party – about the possible battleground we will face at the next election and whether this is likely to be framed, again, by a 'post-crisis' agenda as 2010 was.

Fundamentally, Britain will still be coming to terms with austerity and the massive hole in the economy and public finances created by the global financial crisis. We know the economy will not be growing quickly and real incomes will not be rising.

In my view, this means three things. First, we must show how our policies will ensure value for money and higher productivity from our public services and continuing reform to strengthen their delivery. Second, we must keep the tax burden as low as possible – living standards will be squeezed enough as it is. And, finally, we must develop policies to keep our economy competitive and innovative and to create more higher-value jobs.

Our 1997 manifesto described the New Labour approach as being 'wise spenders, not big spenders'. This is, and should remain, a core principle of our party. We need to be 'effective state' social democrats, not 'big state' social democrats.

In this light, and in contrast to the Tories, one of the most difficult questions for social democrats in the future is how do we continue to deliver quality public services in a period of public spending constraint?

We reject the argument of those on the right who argue that the state is an obstacle to human freedom and who espouse a vision of the good society based on a smaller state, shrinking public services and essential support delivered somehow through the voluntary sector with top-ups and opt-outs for the wealthy few.

Equally, we unashamedly reject those who espouse the centralising or controlling state, arguing that the solution to every problem in our economy and society is to have more state. What matters is not big or small government, but whether it values opportunity for all, responsibility from all and fairness across society.

Our conception of the role of government must evolve yet further. It is clear to me that we must continue to transfer power to parents, pupils and patients. We must recognise that the solution to many of the challenges facing our country will have to be found in the communities in which people live, working in partnership with public services, rather than an expanded central state.

Debate will also be shifting to broader questions about a post-recovery Britain. How will higher levels of home owner-ship and house-building be sustained? In what other ways will governments be able to give people greater control over their lives? What are the next stages of the agenda on child poverty? How will we provide, and finance, social care for our ageing population? And how will all of these questions be refracted through increasing global interdependence; indeed, how will Britain craft its relationship with Europe following the travails of the eurozone?

In other words, what kind of national strategy does Labour want to offer Britain and how should this be rooted in the challenges of the future? In developing this strategy, we should recall what we learned a long time ago: that there is no future for us as a party of class, merely representing sectional trade union interests. My grandfather, Herbert Morrison, spoke and wrote of little else as he organised Labour's efforts to prepare for the 1945 general election. We knew that, to be successful, we had to be a cross-class alliance of 'conscience and reform', as a later leader, Hugh Gaitskell, put it. We went on to accept Tony Crosland's explanation that there were no good reasons of principle for us to believe that public owner-ship is the ark of the social democratic covenant.

The Croslandite conception of equality remains a leitmo-tif for revisionists within the party. The essential goal for the progressive state should always be to strive for better social equality – not equality of outcome but a genuine equality of opportunity in a society where those who do not succeed as they wish are guaranteed a fair deal.

The goal of greater social equality guided New Labour's public service reform agenda as did our unprecedented investment in schools, hospitals, housing and the creation of Sure Start.

Yet, in today's post-crisis Britain, the challenge of social equality is perhaps more pronounced than in Crosland's epoch, or indeed when New Labour first entered govern-ment. The re-emergence of an, at times, brutal 'fairness gap' as a result of public sector retrenchment is reversing many of New Labour's most important social reforms. There is a real danger, once again, that today's school and university leavers will become part of a 'lost generation'.

Clearly, we cannot simply rely on the policy solutions that we deployed when last in office. But we can retain the central revisionist insight embodied by New Labour: that as a party we are at our best when we are neither sectional, nor regional, but national, challenging ourselves to make reforms to achieve greater social equality in ways that will attract support from those living in very different social circumstances.

It is time to move on, to think through and set out what the progressive state needs to accomplish over the next decade, and how our policies will achieve this. The public will be ready in the coming year or so to focus on what comes next after the coalition. We should be in a position to offer some good answers.

# Back to the future: the decentralised tradition and Labour's way forward

*Paul Richards*

There are some socialists who do not think that the problem of the organisation of life and necessary labour can be dealt with by a huge national centralisation, working by a kind of magic for which no one feels himself responsible; that on the contrary it will be necessary for the unit of administration to be small enough for every citizen to feel himself responsible for its details, and be interested in them, that individual men cannot shuffle off the business of life on to the shoulders of some abstraction called the state, but must deal with it in conscious association with each other; that the variety of life is as much an aim of true Communism as equality of condition, and that nothing but a union of these two will bring about real freedom.

*William Morris, 1889*

Within the British socialist tradition, two broad strands of thought warily coexist. One is the familiar social democratic model, whereby socialists win elections, take over the organs of the state at a national or local level, and use the system to redistribute resources from the few to the many. The second, expressed by William Morris at the start of this chapter, is the cooperative or self-government model, where socialists create new centres of governance, power and wealth creation, as an alternative to both the centralised state and the private sector.

One side will describe the other as control freaks, wanting to meddle in every area of public life, from the frequency of fish fingers served in the nation's school canteens to the numbers of times a hospital floor must be mopped. The other side will complain about the utopian dreamers who believe everyone is straining at the leash to become members of their local swimming pool management committee, if only given the chance. It is the difference between those who believe Labour politicians are elected to wield power on behalf of those without it and those who believe Labour politicians are elected to give power away.

This chapter reviews the decentralist, or federalist, tradition within Labour's political thought, and the implications for the modernisation of the Labour Party.

**Labour's local roots**
Let us start at the beginning, with Labour's patron saint and first leader, Keir Hardie. Hardie learned the organisational skills that served him well as the architect of the Labour Party not in politics, but in the temperance movement, in his union, and in the non-conformist church.

Aside from a scattering of hotels and pubs bearing the name 'temperance', but now serving alcohol, the movement has left little obvious legacy. When Hardie was a teenager, working long hours in the coal mines, he threw himself into the temperance movement. Temperance attracted the political left: radical Liberals and the early socialists. The movement was built on local lodges with their banners and insignia, public meetings, parades, dances, outings and recruitment drives to encourage people to sign 'the pledge'.

Caroline Benn makes the point in her biography of Hardie that:

strongly allied to the working-class self-help ethic, the pledge brought many advantages. A great deal of the social organisation and widespread appeal of later move-ments – including the Cooperative Society, trade unions and Clarion Clubs, even the ILP and Labour Party – were based on early temperance organisations. For temperance societies were not merely campaigning bodies organising parades and marches (which later political parties and trade unions adopted as well) but ... friendly societies organising sick clubs and funeral funds.[1]

Hardie's teenage zeal for temperance was matched in his early twenties by his conversion to Christianity. He joined the Evangelical Union, a non-conformist sect of the United Succession Church, rooted, not in the 'respectable' liberal middle classes, but in its working-class membership. At the age of twenty-one, Hardie was chosen as secretary of the Lanarkshire Miners' Union, with a brief to recruit and build the union among the Lanarkshire coalfields. Church, union, temperance. These were the three pillars of Hardie's early life, and where he learned how to build a political movement.

Hardie's background was not unusual among the Labour pioneers. They were 'community organisers', building their churches, unions, temperance branches, and then the Labour movement, from the grassroots upwards. It is oft-repeated, but worth saying again, that the Labour Party, unlike the Tories or Liberals, began life outside of Parliament as an affiliation of trade unions, socialist groups and local branches, striving to break into the citadels and take power through the ballot box. Unlike Labour, the other parties began life inside the political system, and were forced to look outwards as the franchise was extended.

It is not surprising that the organisational background of Labour's founders influenced their political beliefs. The history of the Labour Party is the history of the swirling eddies of its ideology and policies, with competing programmes and platforms, each with their passionate advocates, vying for primacy. By rejecting orthodox European Marxism, and adopting instead the studied vagueness of Clause IV in 1918, the Labour Party allowed itself maximum flexibility of action. The restatement in 1994 strengthened the ethical basis for policy, and disentangled policy from the values that should underpin it.

Into the mighty river of British socialism flow the tributaries of radical liberalism, trade unionism, anarchosyndicalism, Christian Socialism, humanism, cooperativism, Fabianism, and the belief in the equal rights of all men and women. In more recent times, the political movements of the late Victorian and Edwardian period have been joined inside Labour's walls by environmentalism, anti-racism, feminism, campaigns in support for equality for gays, people with disabilities and other marginalised and oppressed groups, and internationalism.

**Centralisers versus federalists**
The absence of a single doctrine is a source of great strength, allowing Labour to be a broad church with only occasional fractures from the left or right. The socialist writer and theoretician G. D. H. Cole made the argument that socialism in Britain could be divided along two axes. The first was between reformists and revolutionaries. Thanks to its founding in 1900 as a parliamentary party seeking to win seats in Parliament for working men, Labour has no revolutionary tradition. The tilt within British socialism has always been firmly towards reforms to the system, not its violent overthrow. The Marxist academic Ralph Miliband decried this 'parliamentarianism' in his book *Parliamentary Socialism* in 1961, calling Labour's 'devotion' to Parliament the 'fixed point of reference and the conditioning factor of their behaviour'.[2]

But the second of Cole's axes has more relevance today. This one is between federalists and centralisers. Cole himself

belonged to the federalist camp. As one of the leading proponents of guild socialism in the 1920s and 1930s, he invented
a complex alternative system of industrial organisation and
democratic participation which would replace both private
industry and parliamentary democracy. Workers would be
members of guilds, based on their trade or industry, and each
guild would send delegates to a commune. Each commune
would comprise industrial guilds, a cooperative council (representing consumers), a collective utilities council (running water,
gas and electricity), a cultural council and a health council
(providing healthcare free at the point of need).

Guild socialism was thus an expression of the widespread
view in the first decades of Labour's life that socialism was
not the same as the state. The early pioneers, with their roots
in liberalism and local self-organisation, did not look to the
state for help; they looked within themselves and their own
communities. Indeed, they had a healthy distrust of the state,
which was often associated with repression and anti-trade
unionism. Early Labour manifestos complained about high
taxes and burdens on the individual.

The Victorian belief in 'self-help' ran deep in working-class
culture. It emphasised thrift, education, advancement through
hard work and, seen through the prism of working-class life,
contributed to the early trade unions, the friendly societies
(which provided social insurance), working men's clubs, lending libraries and a range of other institutions and organisations
run by volunteers, funded by their members and dedicated to
collective security, wellbeing and progress. Thus the British
working class constructed, brick by brick, a 'big society' as a
deliberate bulwark against the misery of capitalism, the terrible
uncertainties of unemployment and the inadequacies of the
existing systems of welfare and healthcare.

## The cooperative ideal

The most important of these organisations was the cooperative

movement, founded in the mid-nineteenth century to provide
local food and services to communities without exploitation
or profit-motive. The ideas of Robert Owen, Dr William
King of Brighton and the Rochdale Pioneers have shaped a
worldwide movement which predated and outlived communism, and which today has the seeds of an alternative socialist
society. The key insight of the co-op is that each member is
equal, and power should be shared democratically within the
organisation. The cooperative ideal does not rely on the state,
but on self-organisation.

Despite the close ties between the Labour Party and the
cooperative movement, including Labour and Co-op Party
sponsorship of MPs, the cooperative movement is not a
formal part of the Labour Party structure. In 1900, the founding conference of the Labour Representation Committee
heard Mr J. T. Chandler, chair of the parliamentary committee of the TUC, report that although the Cooperative Union
had been sent a written invitation to attend the conference,
alongside the Independent Labour Party, Fabians, Social
Democratic Federation and trade unions, they had not come.
Hardie sought to include them in the constitution that was
being drawn up. But on the second day, the cooperators were
excluded from the Labour constitution. By not pitching up at
the Memorial Hall in February 1900, the mighty cooperative
movement missed the chance to become enmeshed into the
structure and constitution of the Labour Party.

If the co-op, representing millions of consumers (especially women) had secured an equal share of the votes and
influence as the trade unions inside the Labour Party, British
socialism in the twentieth century might have run an entirely
different course. Instead of being dominated by industrial,
and then public sector workers, the Labour Party might have
represented a broader coalition of workers, professionals and
consumers, like the Swedish socialist party, perhaps with the
same degree of electoral success.

## Gas-and-water socialism

Thirteen of the original delegates to the Labour Party conference were councillors. Within the Labour tradition is the strong influence of 'municipalism': the belief that local government can be an instrument of local reform and improvement. Joseph Chamberlain, as the radical Liberal mayor of Birmingham, proved that strong local government could transform the lives of working people by establishing municipal gas and water companies, clearing the slums, building parks, libraries and public baths, and regenerating the city centre. The centrepiece is Corporation Street, named to celebrate the transformatory power of local government. In 1882, Chamberlain had a love affair with Beatrice Potter who, as Beatrice Webb, went on to lead the Fabian Society and develop 'municipal socialism' (dismissed by its critics on the left as 'gas-and-water socialism').

Where it held power in local government in the years before the Second World War, Labour developed what we would call 'localism': running municipal utilities, hospitals, tramways, housing, baths, libraries, schools, parks and employing armies of direct labour. The London County Council in particular provided citywide strategic governance, under left-wing 'progressive' leadership between 1889 and 1904. Leading members of the Labour Party to serve in local government in the pre-war period include Clement Attlee (mayor of Stepney); Herbert Morrison (mayor of Hackney), George Lansbury (mayor of Poplar) and Sidney Webb (representing Deptford on the LCC for eighteen years).

At the 1918 party conference, which adopted Clause IV of the constitution, another resolution was passed in favour of decentralised, municipal socialism. It stated:

> That in order to avoid the evils of centralisation and the drawbacks of bureaucracy, the conference suggests that the fullest possible scope should be given, in all branches

of social reconstruction, to the democratically elected local governing bodies; that whilst the central government department should assist with information and grants in aid, the local authorities should be given a free hand to develop their own services ... in whatever way they choose.[3]

The resolution went on to say that councils should not only continue to provide education, sanitation, police, water, gas, electricity and tramways, but also extend into housing, parks, town planning, libraries, the provision of music and popular recreation, and the retailing of coal. This was the Labour federalists' 'Clause IV moment'. Alas, it remains unfulfilled.

**Federalism defeated**
In 1945, Labour inherited a system of wartime institutions and regulations, comprising mostly nationalised, state-run bodies for the direction of industry, manpower and welfare, for example the Emergency Medical Service (EMS) – the forerunner of the National Health Service. The 'evils of centralisation and the drawbacks of bureaucracy' were ignored. Faced with the choice of dismantling these monoliths, or co-opting them to peacetime purposes in pursuit of Labour's manifesto pledges, ministers chose the latter. This was the moment when the cooperative, decentralist, localist and municipalist traditions within British socialism were trampled under the boots of central planning, state control and nationalised corporations.

As David Blunkett and Keith Jackson wrote in *Democracy in Crisis*: 'The party turned largely to nationalisation, not local control, and to national rather than local administration as it set out to build some advance positions for democracy in a capitalist state.'[4]

Most contentious was the formation of the NHS between the passage of the NHS Act in 1946 (opposed, never forget, by the Tories) and the start of the service in 1948. Aneurin

Bevan opted to create a national structure, pulling together the mixture of pre-war voluntary and municipal hospitals and clinics and the wartime EMS. He was opposed in Cabinet by Morrison, who wanted a role for municipal hospitals in the new NHS. If Morrison had won the day, local government in Britain would have retained a strong role in the delivery of healthcare and disease prevention, and councils would have been more powerful actors within the state.

Politics in the UK might have been less focused on Westminster and more devolved to powerful local town halls, if councils were responsible for public health, as they soon will be under NHS reforms. With local authority hospitals and clinics as part of the tapestry of socialised healthcare, the NHS would have been less of a monolith. Bevan's concession was a plan for a network of local 'health centres', on the model of the Finsbury Health Centre which pioneered local services in the 1930s, but this radical public health plan never fulfilled its potential. The NHS was, and remains, a service to mend the injured and ill, not to improve public health through preven- tion of disease and unhealthy habits. It remains, too, a service run from the political centre, despite waves of reforms from both Labour and Tory governments.

The 1945 Labour government, in creating British Railways, the NHS, the National Coal Board and the rest, forged the impression that socialism equals nationalisation and state control. It was this false impression, against the backdrop of the Cold War with the Soviet Union and the eastern bloc, and the manifest failure of aspects of the centrally run welfare state, that the Tories mercilessly exploited to attack Labour in the 1970s and 1980s.

It need not have been so. Little in Labour's ideology or ethos suggested that nationalisation, rather than different democratic or cooperative forms of ownership and control, should take precedence. The favoured phrases before the war, 'socialisation' or 'public ownership', do not necessarily equal nationalisation. Indeed, the 1918 version of Clause IV itself refers only to the 'common ownership of the means of production, distribution and exchange, and the best obtainable system of popular administration', which Sidney Webb deliberately left open to interpretation, and to the inclusion of municipal and cooperative models of ownership.

The sociologist A. H. Halsey pointed out that: 'The movement that had invented the social forms of modern participatory democracy and practised them in union branch and co-op meeting, thereby laying a Tocquevillian foundation for democracy, was ironically fated to develop through its political party the threats of a bureaucratic state.'[5]

The decentralist tradition refused to die in the post-war period, despite this being the age of the nationalised institution. A robust critique of nationalised industries and social services grew up on the left of politics.[6] There was a revived interest in the role of cooperatives and workers' control of industry. In 1971–2, shipyard workers on the Upper Clyde refused to see their yards close, and organised a 'work-in' to keep them open. There was a revival of interest in cooperatives. In the 1980s, a new municipalism was developed by Labour councils such as Sheffield, as a 'dented shield' against the Thatcher government's policies. There were fleeting vogues for 'participation' and 'industrial democracy' in the 1970s and 1980s. Harold Wilson asked Alan Bullock, the Labour-supporting historian and academic, to chair a commission on workers' representation on company boards. The result in 1977 – the Bullock Report – was rejected by the trade unions and was never implemented. The unions' objection rested on the report's recommendation that the workers' representatives be directly chosen, not selected by the union bosses.

### New Labour's missed opportunities

Labour's 1997 manifesto aimed for 'democratic renewal of our country through decentralisation'. The first term was characterised by referenda to establish a Parliament for Scotland, an Assembly for Wales and an elected mayor for London. These reforms have changed the democratic landscape for the better, and it seems unlikely that even the most centralising Conservative government would reverse them (although the Tories did abolish London-wide government in 1986).

However, the early successes in devolution were not built on. The next stage – regional government – fell at the first hurdle when the referendum to establish a north-east assembly was rejected, 78 per cent to 22 per cent. Further referenda were postponed, then dropped altogether. Like electoral reform for the Commons, a decisive defeat in a referendum pushed regional government off the agenda for a generation. The move to elected mayors similarly faltered after an initial wave of success. The reform of the House of Lords, while successfully removing the hereditary principle, ground to a halt when no alternative democratic system could be agreed upon. Lords reform has now become a key bargaining chip in the coalition government's internal machinations. Given the Liberal Democrats' ineffectual role within the coalition, and their toxicity with the public, it is entirely possible a democratic second chamber, resisted by most Tories, will remain unfinished business.

New Labour's enthusiasm for democratic reform waned after the first term. Despite Donald Dewar's description of devolution as a 'process, not an event', in reality it was a series of events, not a process. The second term was dominated by the war against Islamist terrorism and public service reform. On the latter, the greatest missed opportunity was the failure to introduce local ownership and democratic control over public services. The Blair government recognised that monolithic state institutions, the legacy of previous Labour governments, were incapable of meeting modern demands and, crucially, keeping the middle classes onside. This point – that public services must be good enough to maintain the support and use of those affluent enough to be able to pay for private alternatives – is a vital insight for Labour. Once a service ceases to be universal because the middle classes desert it, it risks becoming a poor service for poor people.

Labour's reform programmes were based on creating internal markets, competition between suppliers and freedom to innovate. In a telling passage in his memoirs, Tony Blair describes the evolution of New Labour's approach to reforming the public services:

> At first, we govern with a clear radical instinct but without the knowledge and experience of where that instinct should take us in specific policy terms. In particular, we think it plausible to separate structures from standards, i.e. we believe that you can keep the given parameters of the existing public service system but still make fundamental change to the outcomes the system produces. In time, we realise this is wrong; unless you change structures, you can't raise standards more than incrementally. By the beginning of the second term, we have fashioned a template of the reform: changing the monolithic nature of the service; introducing competition; blurring the distinctions between public and private; taking on traditional professional and union demarcations of work and vested interests; and in general trying to free the system up, letting it innovate, differentiate, breathe and stretch its limbs.[7]

This approach undoubtedly led to improvements in the public services, most obviously in the NHS and in primary schools. The missing ingredient in New Labour's reform programme was any shift in ownership or control over local services. They remained services done to people, not co-authored or co-owned. A notable, and laudable, exception was the creation of foundation trust hospitals within the NHS, fashioned by one of New Labour's

leading decentralists Alan Milburn. By April 2011, there were
137 foundation trusts. They are free from central control and have
an element of local democratic control through local memberships, governors and boards. Some foundation trusts wrote the
Rochdale principles of cooperation into their constitutions.
There are 1.76 million members of foundations trusts, more than
all the UK political parties in the UK combined.

However, despite sporadic experiments with local ownership and control, the Labour Party left office in 2010 with the
fundamental pattern of ownership of state assets and control
over services mostly unchanged since 1997.

**Next time: the lessons**
Not only was this a missed opportunity to create a vibrant
not-for-profit sector, to shift the economy towards mutual
ownership models and to create local platforms for democratic renewal, where citizens could learn the basic repertoire
of democratic activity; it was also a strategic error in political terms. If the levers of the state remain in the hands of
ministers in Whitehall, when they fall into the hands of the
Conservatives Labour's achievements can be reversed.

Take the example of Sure Start centres. These were
conceived, uncharacteristically for the Treasury, as locally
owned and managed centres for child development. Although
sited in deprived neighbourhoods they were open to all and,
following their launch in 1998, poor and affluent parents mixed
on equal terms. They were modelled on successful schemes in
the USA and Scandinavia, and soon established themselves as
a New Labour success story. The visionary civil servant who
developed Sure Starts, Norman Glass, wrote in 2005:

> Anarcho-syndicalism came rather late for me – between
> the arrival of New Labour and the Spice Girls' first
> album. What I learned from visits to successful early
> years programmes and local communities was that it was

necessary, in the case of early years at any rate, to involve
local people fully in the development and management
of the programme if it was to take root and not simply be
seen as another quick fix by middle-class social engineers.[8]

Yet in 2005, the centralising tendency within the government swooped and placed them under state control, diluted
their original cooperative, self-governing ethos and turned
them into yet another government programme. The tragedy now being played out is that if a service such as Sure
Start remains the creature of Whitehall it can be diluted,
diverted, or abolished when one set of ministers is replaced
by another. Coalition ministers are strangling Sure Start
centres to death, an act of injustice that would have been
far more different to conduct if the ownership of assets
and democratic control of Sure Starts rested with their
local boards, not the Department for Education. Surely the
great lesson for the next Labour government is that the risk
in 'letting go' of state-run services such as health clinics,
swimming pools, parks and woodland, children's centres
and other assets is far less than the risks of their abolition or
privatisation by a future Tory government.

### The necessity of revisionism
Labour is a revisionist party. Revisionism, defined as the
application of timeless values to changing challenges and the
rejection of policies set in stone and worshipped as idols, is the
only reason we still have a Labour Party. Without revisionism
– which New Labour dubbed modernisation – the Labour
Party would have clung to outdated policies and be weighed
down by dusty ideology. It would be a political sect, not a
governing party. Each wave of modernisation is denounced
by its opponents as a betrayal and a shift away from the true
path. Yet at every stage the results have enhanced Labour's
electoral prospects and performance in government.

A look at any Labour manifesto proves the point: policies swiftly sound old-fashioned, quirky, quaint or locked in
time and place. Labour's 1900 manifesto called for an 'end to
compulsory vaccination' and 'abolition of the standing army'.
In 1906 'Chinese labour' was a big issue for the manifesto. In
1923, Labour pledged to place 'the drink traffic under popular control'. Even Labour's 1997 manifesto, with its modest
pledges and promises to give schools 'access to computer
technology', belongs firmly to the mid-1990s, an age before
the internet and the ubiquity of mobile phones.

Policies are outdated almost as soon as they are produced.
Values endure. This is the essence of revisionism. The latest
phase of revisionism, of which *The Purple Book* is a part,
must be guided by the decentralist tradition. It can give us a
template for policies across a range of areas – from the public
services to the democratic system itself. It provides us with a
convincing antidote to the 'big society', increasingly understood as a fig-leaf for traditional Tory demands for a smaller
state and lower public spending. It also provides us with an
internal challenge to the default setting that Labour's answer
to everything is some arm, institution or agency of the state.
This was the tangent that Labour pursued in 1945 and has
wrestled with ever since.

The next phase for Labour should be a return to the
socialism of its founders, based on the 'little platoons' of
locally owned and run bodies, under the benign guidance of a
smaller, strategic state. More Hardie, less Stalin; more co-op,
less National Coal Board. Back to the roots of socialism, not
its byways and meanders.

As T. S. Eliot advises us in the *Four Quartets:*

> We shall not cease from exploration,
> and the end of all our exploring
> will be to arrive where we started
> and know the place for the first time.

1   Caroline Benn, *Keir Hardie: A Biography* (London: Hutchinson, 1992).

2   Ralph Miliband, *Parliamentary Socialism: A Study in the Politics of Labour* (London: Allen and Unwin, 1961).

3   Cited in David Blunkett and Keith Jackson, *Democracy in Crisis: The Town Halls Respond* (London: Hogarth Press, 1987).

4   Ibid.

5   A. H. Halsey, *Change in British Society* (Oxford: Oxford University Press, 1978).

6   For a review of this critique see Paul Richards, *Labour's Revival: The Modernisers' Manifesto* (London: Biteback, 2010).

7   Tony Blair, *A Journey* (London: Random House, 2010).

8   'Surely some mistake?' *The Guardian,* 5 January 2005.

# Reviving our sense of mission: designing a new political economy

*Tristram Hunt*

The big questions of contemporary western politics – how to respond to the continuing globalisation of labour markets, climate change, increasing immigration, rapid technological advancement and chronically ageing populations – are all economic ones. Yet despite the obvious repudiation that one would have expected the financial crisis to have dealt to neoliberal economics, in Europe and across the developed world, it is to a resurgent right that voters have turned for answer.

Nowhere is this phenomenon more pronounced than here in Britain where, with breathtaking ruthlessness, the government has successfully reframed the crisis in the minds of the electorate. The political agenda is not dominated by talk of how to correct the problems associated with unregulated market power, but about how to correct the problems associated with unrestricted government spending.

In our journey back to government, it is essential to get our economic agenda right. Our starting point must be the acceptance of this uncomfortable political reality: that the public has accepted the government's explanation of the financial crisis. Of course we must be robust in explaining that the deficit was only 2.1 per cent in 2007–8, compared with 11.1 per cent in 2009, after the seismic shock to the economy delivered by the financial crisis. We should also continue to point out that in 2008 the extent of Conservative anger at our levels of spending led them to match our commitment to public investment to the last penny.

But politics is not an empirical social science; it is about people's perceptions and emotions, their hopes and insecurities. Directing an incredulous public to the relevant graphs is not a winning strategy.

Rather, the first component of our economic approach must be to accept the need to develop a clear strategy for deficit reduction. We are right to say that the Conservatives have turned the 'means' of deficit reduction into an end in itself, and that this reflects the paucity of their aspirations for Britain. Yet a vital means it remains: there is nothing progressive about running a large budget deficit or wasting money on interest repayments that could be invested in schools, hospitals or Sure Start centres. This is the crucial insight the electorate has already realised and until we move beyond the 'why' and 'who' arguments about deficit reduction, and articulate with more clarity the 'how', we will not regain our voice.

## Choosing positive freedom

The second component must be nothing less than the full-scale development of a new political economy, one built around the task, intrinsic to the purpose of the Labour movement, of distributing power to those who lack it. The exercise of power is the most basic, fundamental political act for any member of a free and fair society; in its absence, citizens lack the capabilities to lead a full life of their choosing. The type of freedom brought about by the distribution of power is positive freedom, the freedom to carry out a given action, physically. This contrasts with negative freedom, freedom from interference, which is the only freedom that animates the right.

In choosing positive freedom, we reject the false dichotomy of choosing between freedom and equality, as greater equality is instrumental in creating the kind of society required by the pursuit of positive freedom. Furthermore, the pursuit of distributing power is, crucially, an economic goal that is sufficiently pluralistic to accommodate the importance that different individuals will place upon different aspects of the good life. Yet it also recognises that a fundamental part of the good life is provided by human relationships and a sense of community. Without the sense of solidarity and shared fate that resilient communities foster, we lack the power to resist the dual forces of market and state.

It is this sense of resistance that is a uniquely Labour contribution to social democracy; the distribution of power and the pursuit of real, positive freedom has always been a leitmotif for the Labour movement. In the depths of the 'terrible thirties', the last time that Britain faced a financial implosion of such magnitude, the Christian socialist R. H. Tawney placed it at the heart of his 1944 essay *We Mean Freedom*:

> A society in which some groups do much of what they please, while others can do little of what they ought, may have virtues of its own: but freedom is not one of them. It is free in so far, and only in so far, as all the elements composing it are able in fact, not merely in theory, to make the most of their powers, to grow to their full stature, to do what they conceive to be their duty and – since liberty should not be too austere – to have their fling when they feel like it.

It was Tawney's model of social citizenship that inspired the architects of the post-war welfare state, providing a vital contribution to arguably the greatest intellectual transformation of the twentieth century: the Labour movement's embrace of the democratic state as a means to alleviating market injustice. Faced once more with a Conservative–Liberal coalition, complete with its own version of the Geddes Axe, it is to this tradition within the Labour movement that we must turn for inspiration. Because, before our post-1945 embrace of statism, the movement was acutely aware that the state, too, could be an agent of injustice. Marx and Engels' assertion that the state was simply a committee for managing the affairs of the bourgeoisie did not seem fanciful to a movement suffering from a series of anti-labour judgments, from the Tolpuddle Martyrs to Taff Vale.

For in becoming too reliant on the state as the only means of resisting market outcomes, we have forgotten our associationalist heritage as a movement of democratic grassroots activists: our history of cooperatives, mutual societies and trade unions. It is by turning to this heritage that we can help revive our sense of mission, to distribute economic power to those who lack it and build a new political economy around this goal.

## A new political economy

But if distributing power is to become the raison d'être of our new political economy then we currently lack the apparatus to achieve it. Indeed, the Labour movement currently faces an intellectual crisis every bit as big as its political one. This is because the dominant Croslandite model of political economy – the best way of advancing social justice is through accepting free market capitalism as it is and redistributing the proceeds of its 'perpetual' growth, which was stretched to its limits by New Labour – has run its course.

That is not to undermine the significant feats of New Labour in redistributing economic power. Lifting 500,000 children out of relative poverty, halving the number of people in absolute poverty and the creation of a national minimum wage are achievements that we should be proud of and defend. Most significantly of all, New Labour used the proceeds of the ten years of growth over which it presided to rebuild the public realm. The current debate's fixation upon the impact of globalisation in creating polarised patterns of 'winners and losers' is understandable – it is right that Labour should be primarily concerned with improving our ability to create a better society for the 'losers'. Yet this should not detract from the fact that New Labour did create vast swathes of 'winners', empowering people from all backgrounds with the skills to succeed in a knowledge-based economy. Nobody could possibly deny that the Britain New Labour bequeathed to the coalition was more likely to be seen as an innovative, open-facing hub of technological and creative excellence than it was in 1997. Yet, for a variety of reasons, more of the same is no longer a suitable response to the economic challenges of today.

First, the central assertion of *The Future of Socialism*, that growth could continue ad infinitum, recycled in Gordon Brown's claim to have ended 'boom and bust', and that it was possible to eradicate the cyclical fluctuations in demand inherent to all varieties of capitalism, has been shown, with emphatic violence, to be flawed. Resilience to these fluctuations, in the form of tighter fiscal policy and a less cavalier attitude towards borrowing, must be one important component of our new political economy.

Second, the overreliance on resource-based redistribution as the only successful strategy for creating a better society does not truly capture the importance of power: that resources are nothing without the power to use them. To characterise, crudely, there is no point giving somebody a tax credit if they lack the capability to access basic services or feel completely disengaged from society. Or, more saliently, in relation to economic power it is no good providing someone with financial support through unemployment benefits if that person is not supported by being placed on an active welfare-to-work scheme.

Rather than redistribution, we should be shifting our focus to what the political economist Jacob S. Hacker has called 'pre-distribution' or 'the way in which the market distributes its rewards in the first place'. The contemporary policy trend, whether through financial market deregulation or the weakening of union rights and employment legislation, has shifted the 'pre-distribution' of economic power in favour of those at the top. In shifting our focus towards 'pre-distribution' not only will we focus on market reforms that encourage a fairer distribution of power in the economy before redistribution, but we will also avoid the perennial political pitfall that excessive reliance on redistribution generates: the ease with which the Tories deploy their populist, well-rehearsed 'tax-and-spend' arguments. Of course, resources remain important; their ability to enable people to expand their choices, horizons and opportunities should not be understated. However, the left has always argued, rightly, that everything of value cannot be reduced to money or measured by price.

As that irrepressible proto-socialist John Ruskin wrote in *Unto This Last* in 1860:

> It is impossible to conclude, of any given mass of acquired wealth, merely by the fact of its existence, whether it signifies good or evil to the nation in the midst of which it exists. Its real value depends on the moral sign attached to it, just as strictly as that of a mathematical quantity depends on the algebraic sign attached to it. Any given accumulation of commercial wealth may be indicative, on the one hand, of faithful industries, progressive energies and productive ingenuities: or, on the other, it may be indicative of mortal luxury, merciless tyranny, ruinous chicanery.

Even now, Ruskin's critique has lost none of its force. Indeed, it is the Croslandite model's inability to stand in a critical relationship with the way the market concentrates existing distributions of power and inequality that is the third reason we turn to. One of the shortcomings of the New Labour project was our failure to regulate the banks and our reluctance to intervene in market outcomes. However, as our economy becomes ever more exposed to the rapid change that globalisation and increasing technological development will bring, it is no longer enough just to equip the labour market with the skills necessary to succeed. All-out resistance to globalisation is not an option. Neither is closing our markets: openness and competition remain unparallelled in their ability to stimulate innovation and drive efficiency. Instead, what is required is a strategic, interventionist response to managing the economy. This should include the encouragement of regional specialisation and selecting 'winners' based upon their ability to contribute jobs, develop labour market capacity and compete internationally. Put simply, globalisation means that governments can no longer be ambivalent about the means by which wealth is created.

This lack of a critical analysis of market outcomes also had one other profound impact, implicit in Ruskin's critique. It prevented us from distinguishing between different types of capitalism and growth. We must reject the argument that the 'avenue to economic dynamism is to let capitalism be true to its atavistic, red-in-tooth-and-claw instincts; that to make a distinction between good and bad capitalism is fundamentally to misrepresent its character.'[1] The idea that there is nothing but neoliberal capitalism and traditional socialism is absurd. There are, of course, many variants of capitalism, capable of distributing varying degrees of economic power to its citizens. The goal of our new political economy should be simple: to pre-distribute as much economic power as possible, to the lowest levels possible, while remaining sensitive to personal freedom and individual aspiration. This task will prove impossible without generating growth. But just as we can critically choose the type of capitalism we want, we must also be explicit about the type of growth we mean, too: growth that is socially fairer, reduces inequality, delivers securer work, is more environmentally sustainable and, above all, benefits all regions and not just the City of London.

But if this sets out the aspirations for a new political economy, it does not outline a process for getting there. The final failing of the Croslandite-New Labour model was its reliance on statist intervention, whether through resource-based redistribution or public service investment as the means for bringing about political change. Sober assessment of the long-term economic trends would suggest that, even were such statism still desirable (and it is not), we are unlikely to enjoy the conditions favourable to its enacting that we enjoyed pre-2008, if and when we return to power.

The Resolution Foundation's first report for the Commission on Living Standards reveals the shocking statistic that, given the impact of the recession, living standards will not even reach their 2001 levels until 2015. Even before the recession, median wages for people on low to middle incomes were flat from 2003 to 2008, with disposable income falling in every region except London during this period. The 'squeezed middle' is a political reality and, furthermore, is one that is here to stay.

And all of this is before we even begin to consider the potential damage the government might inflict on the economy during the intervening period.

All of which intensifies the need to develop new, non-statist means of political change. Trade unions, mutuals and cooperative societies, and free voluntary associations of all different hues – all share a common belief that through democratic association their members are protected from excessive concentrations of power, whether that be from global markets or an intruding state. In particular, the role of cooperative and mutual models of ownership has been explored to see whether they can provide the launch pad for a new policy platform.

However, the majority of interpretations have focused on their ability to reinvigorate our approach to public services and so to recast our understanding of the relationship between citizen and state.

Others have highlighted their use as a tool to highlight

the authenticity of our vision of society when contrasted to
the deficiency of that most audacious of Cameroonian land
grabs, the 'big society'. Both of these tasks require swift and
urgent attention, particularly that of developing a construc-
tive, positive response to the 'big society'. However, a road less
well-travelled is the role that cooperative and mutual models
of ownership can play in reforming the private sector and
developing a different approach to the economic task we have
set ourselves: the 'pre-distribution' of economic power. The
first step is to examine the history of the British cooperative
movement.

**Rediscovering our cooperative past**
Our cooperative roots can be traced back, most obviously
to the Utopian socialism of Robert Owen, and the attempt
to craft an alternative, 'cooperative' philosophy during the
early nineteenth century. Owen's starting point was that
conditioning, not character, was the key to man, who 'is a
compound being, whose character is formed of his constitution, or organisation at birth, and of the effects of external
circumstances upon it, from birth to death'. Original sin was
a fallacy and what was instead required was an educational
and social ethos designed to draw out the cooperative best
in mankind. At his factory at New Lanark, he operated a
beneficent commercial dictatorship cutting working hours,
eliminating underage employment, restricting alcohol sales,
improving conditions and introducing free primary education. In *A New View of Society, or Essays on the Principle of the
Formation of the Human Character*, Owen detailed how his
experiment could be magnified for society at large and, in so
doing, helped to drive through the 1819 Factory Act limiting
working hours in the textile industry.

Owen's solution was to establish a series of communes,
which entailed a retreat from 'the old immoral world'.
More productive was his following of Owenite socialists,

with their criticism of modern competition, who grouped together under the aegis of the British Association for the Promotion of Cooperative Knowledge. 'The selfish feeling in man may fairly be called the competitive principle,' announced the leading Owenite William Lovett, 'since it causes him to compete with others, for the gratification of his wants and propensities. Whereas the cooperative may be said to be the social feeling that prompts him to acts of benevolence and brotherly affection.' An economy based on the competitive system was condemned as inherently inequitable and unstable: wealth was concentrated, trade cycles became more extreme and poverty deepened. While Owen himself increasingly focused his efforts on reforming religion and ending 'the unnatural and artificial union of the sexes' in marriage, the Owenites during the 1830s built a political programme around cooperation and a moral sense of value based on labour-time and just transfer rather than 'the doctrine of wages'. This led to the establishment of a series of cooperative shops in London and Brighton, 'labour exchanges' for the direct marketing of goods and trade unions to advance the cause of labour.

From this tradition emerged the better-known Rochdale Society of Equitable Pioneers, with a clear focus on retailing unadulterated foodstuffs at competitive prices. At their peak, cooperatives played an indisputable central role in working-class life. The historian Peter Gurney described the cooperative store as the 'defining feature of working-class community and neighbourhood life'. They were a way of providing services for the benefit of one another, based on values of reciprocity and mutual assistance rather than a desire to maximise profits. These ideas were crystallised in the idea of the 'divvy', the dividend paid out to the cooperative member. The divvy became part of the rhythm of people's lives, the little bit of money that kept the wolf from the door, or the means for working-class families to build a small reserve of savings.

But the cooperative societies provided more than just financial assistance. They also acted as a repository for social capital, organising events that fostered community cohesion. In 1950 the Buckingham Co-op Societies' dairy department was able to attract more than 3,000 people to their annual sports day. As one co-op member wrote in 1958, 'All our wants, or at least all our needs, could be supplied... Yes, all of us – men, women and children alike – were well looked after by the Old Co-op. It could feed, clothe, shelter and in the end, bury us.' Even in his last journey, the true cooperative member brought a 'divvy' as a final payment to those left behind. This vision, of a self-sustaining community bound by relational ties of common endeavour is authentically Labour. Written on our membership cards is a proud proclamation of this vision. The history of the cooperative movement is intertwined and inseparable from the history of our own Labour movement.

## A new model of the firm

But buried within this nostalgic portrayal are some important insights for developing a modern approach to the pre-distribution of economic power in a globalised world. First, it demonstrates the undeniable potential for democratic association as a means to increase social capital. Clearly there is a world of difference between the Buckingham Cooperative Society of the 1950s and a modern, employee-owned, retail giant such as John Lewis. But that does not mean that the Labour Party should not loudly advocate for communities to come together to form the 'little platoons' that can contribute in the fight against the 'Bowling Alone' phenomenon and turn deep-seated trends towards a more atomised, individualistic society, on their head. We are right to place this type of activity, influenced by the community organising tradition, at the heart of the vision for party reform.

However, this history also illustrates a profound contrast in values, between the ethos of cooperatives on one hand and the competition-driven ethos of the dominant model of corporate governance in modern capitalist economies, the shareholder-return model, on the other. The cooperative model emphasises the importance of solidarity, accountability, responsibility for your fellow member and at its very heart gives you an increased democratic stake in the direction of the firm. In comparison, the ultimate goal of the shareholder-return model is the bottom line, with little value placed upon the quality of the relationship between firm and employee. Will Davies has described it as 'a particularly acute attempt to assert the power of financial capital over industry, making return on investment the single benchmark against which all of a firm's managerial, technological and employee actions could be measured'.[2]

Yet, if we are serious about tackling the inequalities of economic power, pre-distributed by existing market forces, then this is a challenge we can no longer ignore. The sociologist Richard Sennett has written about the way that 'modern firms destroy the capacity for human beings to tell a coherent story about their lives or to develop the capacity for craft'.[3] Tony Blair's former strategy adviser and the new director of NESTA (National Endowment for Science, Technology and the Arts), Geoff Mulgan, has also observed that 'there has been a long-term trend towards more people wanting work to be an end as well as a means, a source of fulfilment as well as earnings'.[4] We should never be relaxed about situations where employees are disempowered as a result of their existing employee-employer relationships.

But what, other than advocacy, can we really hope to offer? The idea of *Mitbestimmung* or 'co-determination', intrinsic to the German social democratic model, where employees have direct managerial responsibility, should certainly be an aspiration. But interventionist legislation to create this would seem to be a wrong option. Although we did enjoy some notable legislative successes in this area during our period in government, developing new legal forms such as the asset-locked

Community Interest Company, the best innovations from the social enterprise sector did not occur because of legislation. Besides, those innovations can largely be characterised as bringing private sector insight into the ethos-driven third sector. Reversing the direction of this flow is long overdue. Labour should actively encourage the formation of mutuals and cooperatives, and other inherently democratic models of the firm, as a means to organically encouraging the *Mitbestimmung* end.

There is a wide body of research to suggest that these models of shared ownership help to empower staff and increase their overall wellbeing.[5] There is also evidence to suggest that they make more responsive and efficient businesses. Increased power begets increased engagement and, so the argument goes, this leads to greater efficiency. The recent success of the cooperative economy would seem to reinforce this argument: between 2007 and 2009, a period when the overall turnover growth of the whole British economy contracted by 1.8 per cent, the cooperative economy's turnover grew a staggering 24.6 per cent.[6]

The easiest policy response available is to provide tax breaks, incentives and reducing the regulatory burden for new mutual start-ups or spin-outs. In Italy, the success of the mission-driven 'social' cooperative movement, which grew as a response to the challenges of social and labour market integration in the late 1980s and early 1990s, was built upon preferential rates of VAT, corporation tax, tax exemption for charitable donations and privileged public procurement rules. Labour could commit to waiving the VAT charge on public service contracts for cooperatives, charities and social enterprises that deliver on specific social outcomes. This will allow such organisations to tender for such contracts on an equitable playing field with the VAT-exempt public sector.

On cooperative spin-outs from public services, we could ease the regulatory burden by committing to funding the discrepancy between existing employee conditions and the new

mutual ones for a period of two years. One of the biggest challenges faced by small mutual spin-outs is matching the terms
and conditions of public sector contracts which, under TUPE
(Transfer of Undertakings, Protection of Employment) legislation they are legally obliged to offer. Providing a small amount
of funding for a two-year 'TUPE holiday' would not ultimately
solve the problem of renegotiating contracts, but it would
alleviate this challenge at the crucial moment of spinning-out,
reducing staff and union anxiety, and allowing the new cooperative breathing space to develop a sustainable business plan.

We should also fully commit to transferring assets to
community groups, where appropriate. The work of Elinor
Ostrom, the political economist who won the 2009 Nobel
prize for economics, has sharply illustrated the idea that
resources, or 'shared commons', can be effectively managed
by the people who use them as opposed to governments. The
cooperative model is the perfect embodiment of this spirit;
pubs, schools or even the British Waterways network of
canals could easily be transferred to new community cooperatives. Indeed, buried in the darkest reaches of our 2010
election manifesto are tentative propositions for precisely
these initiatives, initiatives that for all of its 'big society' blus-
ter, the government is reluctant to match.

As far as employee share-ownership is concerned, Labour
should consider, despite the potential for a tax loophole to be
created, reversing our 2003 decision to remove the tax break
on creating employee benefit trusts. To ensure that share-
ownership becomes a reform that empowers the lowest-paid
members of a firm and those who generally have less power to
take advantage of such schemes, we could hardwire progressive
considerations into the policy: tax breaks the firm receives as
part of the scheme might only apply if a significant threshold
of shares have been distributed to all members of staff.[7]

However, perhaps the most important thing to do will be
to provide new mutual forms with adequate access to capital.

Whatever the size of the investment fund that is eventually awarded to the Big Society Bank, Labour should consider improving on it. We should also resist the disingenuous appropriation of this idea by the Conservatives: it was a Labour government that set up the initial Social Investment Taskforce. And, as part of the strategy for regional, inclusive growth, we should look at developing strong, well-funded regional investment funds.

## Remutualising the financial ecosystem

There can be no doubt that the banking crisis gave the mutualism movement fresh impetus. In the wake of such an unprecedented crisis it was perhaps inevitable that something which can allow people to exert democratic control over previously unaccountable financial institutions would be bumped up the policy agenda. Labour knows that it did not do enough to rein in the actions of the banks during our time in office. But our previous caution should encourage boldness now. We should not be too timid to move our mutualism agenda into the financial sector. Not only can this help to shake up the existing pre-distributions of power with the sector, and the economy more broadly, but it should also create a more stable and secure financial sector. A variety of commentators from across the centre-left have long argued that the financial system should be as diverse as possible and last year, borrowing an old Will Hutton metaphor, *The Economist* wrote that 'just as an ecosystem benefits from diversity, so the world is better off with a multitude of corporate forms'.[8]

These commentators are right. Labour must seriously consider proposals that promote the growth of a financial sector more grounded in our values. Britain's financial services industry is among the least diverse in the world, a situation exacerbated by the Thatcherite policy of aggressively encouraging building societies and credit unions to demutualise. A new generation of financial cooperatives and mutuals can play a vital role in redressing this balance; a diversity of institutions will help to maintain the stability of the whole financial system.

However, this task is not easy. Financial mutuals can have more difficulty in securing capital and the impact of sharing the proceeds of growth can also sometimes lead to slower capital accumulation. These disadvantages make it unlikely that, left to its own devices, the market will provide this new generation of financial mutuals. Merely vacating the space, as the government is doing, will not work. Providing incentives for other banks to capitalise fledgling mutuals, providing community investment tax relief for people who use them, and the Employee Ownership Association's proposal for expanding the existing Share Incentive Plan so that it benefits all members of a firm and is not merely a way of enhancing executive salaries, are all ways that Labour could provide the right structural framework to allow mutuals to flourish.

One proposal that Labour should definitely commit to is my colleague Chuka Umunna's campaign to remutualise Northern Rock. Similarly, Labour should actively consider ensuring that the 600 branches that Lloyds TSB was ordered to sell off as part of the interim report of Sir John Vickers' Independent Commission on Banking be sold to new or existing mutual organisations. This would prove far more effective at leveraging the kind of responsible and engaged shareholders required to regulate financial excess than the Deputy Prime Minister's proposal to distribute shares to every taxpayer in Britain. Notwithstanding the expense and the administrative burden, the main problem with this idea is its financial illiteracy. Even if a decent entry price could be guaranteed, the bank's share price is likely to collapse as millions of new owners, as is likely, immediately cash in their shares. Similar voucher schemes, such as in the Czech Republic, merely resulted in unscrupulous private investors buying up the shares at discounted rates. In this scenario it is difficult to see how the public finances would be best served by these proposals.

However, we must be careful when developing a mutualism agenda for the financial sector not to present mutualism as a panacea for the sector's problems. A thorough critical interpretation of the financial crisis is required in order to learn the appropriate lessons; to blithely suggest that mutuals are inherently unrisky or that their employees were immune to indulging in the practices that caused the crash, would be wrong. Indeed, while the Co-operative and Nationwide emerged from the recession in positions of relative strength, it was only the buy-outs of the latter that saved the Cheshire and Derbyshire building societies in 2008, and the Dunfermline in 2009, from going to the wall. Rather than prohibit risky investment for these smaller firms, their mutuality may actually have encouraged it. Denied the easier access to capital enjoyed by non-mutuals, they were forced higher up the 'risk curve' and thus proved more exposed to the riskier tranches of subprime mortgages and credit default derivatives.

The fate of the Cheshire, the Derbyshire and the Dunfermline highlights two key insights that must inform the type of new mutual we seek to encourage. First, that financial mutuals are businesses: they must compete. Any new mutual that attempts to detach itself from the rest of the financial sector is unlikely to acquire enough business to survive. And, second, that governance structure alone guarantees neither success nor sensible sustainable investments. It is people, not structure, that really determines the behaviour of any organisation; unless the new mutuals' members, employees and shareholders desire the right type of investment then the benefits of mutualising the financial ecosystem will be unrealised. The new mutuals we encourage must embrace the ethos and values that underpinned the nineteenth- and early twentieth-century cooperatives. They need to once more play an active, democratic role in their members' lives. At the very least this should include optional education and training programmes to improve their members' financial literacy.

Intrusion into the private sector will be politically difficult. We should not delude ourselves into thinking that public anger at bankers' bonuses will automatically neutralise those 'overreaching state' arguments. The interim Vickers report has largely focused on the internal structure of Britain's biggest, diversified banks. But part of its scope is to explore ways of 'reducing systemic risk in the banking sector'. We await its final conclusions in September, but it remains amazing that the only serious reforms to emerge from the financial crisis are of public services. By carefully promoting financial mutuals, Labour can tread this political tightrope and help to create a more equitable, stable and democratically account-able financial sector.

## Redistributing economic power

This article only offers an embryonic contribution to a policy platform that might return Labour to power. But even the most inventive policy agenda in the world will not deliver us victory unless we fully appreciate the size of the challenge we face: it is no exaggeration to say that our crisis is every bit as big as that faced by Tawney and his colleagues in the midst of the Great Depression.

Electoral success is based on two factors: economic competence and the ability to communicate a compelling vision of a future society. Without a clear strategy for deficit reduction, Labour will fall at the first of these two hurdles. Embracing more democratic models of ownership can help to communicate the vision of society and our values of solidar-ity, cooperation, reciprocity and community empowerment in ways that the public can understand. That society works best when people work together and share in each other's fate. That when people are trusted to help deliver a better soci-ety, they will respond responsibly and effectively. And that the route to a better society, to real empowerment, is to give people a truly democratic stake in that society.

These models of ownership should also form part of our new political economy, the development of which is the only way we can truly satisfy these two preconditions for success. The goal of distributing economic power through institutions of democratic association is a uniquely Labour story, deeply embedded within the intellectual traditions of our movement. This and the pursuit of positive freedom that it engenders must become the raison d'être of our political economy. We must reject the false choices that many will suggest to its achievement; between equality and individual freedom, prioritising the middle-class progressive vote or the working-class communitarian vote, or between the politics of aspiration and the politics of preventing insecurity.

It is to the task of developing this political economy that we must all, with urgency, now apply ourselves.

1    Will Hutton, 'Liberal Social Democracy, Fairness and Good Capitalism', in Michael McTernan (ed.), *Priorities for a New Political Economy: Memos to the Left* (London: Policy Network, 2011), pp. 25-26.

2    William Davies, *Reinventing the Firm* (London: Demos, 2009).

3    Richard Semnett, *The Corrosion of Character: The Personal Consequences of Work in the New Capitalism* (New York: Norton, 1998).

4    'After Capitalism', *Prospect*, 26 April 2009.

5    For a good example, see John Craig, Matthew Home and Dennis Morgan, *The Engagement Ethic* (London: Innovation Unit, 2009).

6    *The UK Cooperative Economy 2010: A Review of Cooperative Enterprise.* (Manchester: Cooperatives UK, 2010).

7    For a full exposition of this policy, see Will Davies, *Reinventing the Firm* (London: Demos, 2009).

8    'Schumpeter', *The Economist*, 19 August 2010.

# Making markets genuinely free: redistributing power to all

*John Woodcock*

If Labour is serious about handing power to individuals and if it is serious about winning the battle of ideas again, it must recast its uneasy relationship with the concept of markets.

To successfully and enduringly challenge the ascendency of the right and to map a way forward for the country in this new era, we need to reclaim from conservatives the right to define what makes markets free and fair. That requires us to rethink our fundamental arguments about the relationship between government, the individual and the economy. As we seek to devolve the power of the state to communities and individuals we must similarly devolve power in the market to employees, businesses and regions.

Labour has rarely, at heart, been a protectionist party. In splitting from the Liberals in the early twentieth century, the labour movement never wholly split from the free trade argument. The internationalist foundation of the Labour Party informed a belief that protectionism inevitably proved deeply damaging to working people both at home and abroad, whatever its short-term attractions. When Labour first entered government in 1924, it was on the basis of a free-trade bloc with the Liberals following the defeat of the Conservatives' protectionism at the ballot box.

Indeed, markets have provided the majority of working people in Britain with standards of living that previous generations could not have dreamed of through ensuring lower costs and greater availability of food, consumer goods and travel. In recent decades, the market was the essential basis of the information technology revolution, which has served not only to support wealth creation, but has facilitated a shift of power towards individual consumers and has been both a trigger and tool for movements demanding greater democracy.

Throughout Labour's history the underlying credo has been that economic growth is the basis on which social reform, rising living standards and equality of opportunity can most effectively be built. Whether explicitly stated or not, the reliance was always on market forces, tempered or corrected as necessary, to deliver that growth. In *The Future of Socialism*, in many ways the founding text for the story that eventually became New Labour, Tony Crosland was clear that greater levels of equality not only can be, but are most likely to be, achieved alongside a free market. While Crosland's vision was that 'the subjection of all life to market influences' was a thing of the laissez-faire past, his prescription relied on an export-led market economy to provide economic growth. Similarly, he saw a free – and in many cases less regulated – market as the means by which the availability and affordability of consumer goods and services could be increased for working people. These concepts inspired the social market thinkers of Labour's mainstream throughout the late 1970s and early 1980s. While its prominent proponents, such as David Owen and Roy Jenkins, split from Labour, in many ways the influence of their thinking remains stronger within Labour today than it does in the contemporary Liberal Democrats.

New Labour, under Tony Blair and Gordon Brown, also explicitly recognised the ability of liberal markets to provide opportunities and standards of living where more restrictive economic policies had consistently failed, and sought to

harness the wealth they generate for social democratic ends.
As Ed Miliband said in his speech to the British Chambers
of Commerce:

> In the 1990s, New Labour's core insight was that a
> successful and dynamic market economy is the founda-
> tion on which a strong and just society must be built.[1]

But the left, including New Labour, has never sought to
contest the basic definition of what has been termed a free
market, broadly: the minimisation of government regulation
to achieve the most efficient distribution of goods. We need
to question that now, at a time when progressive politics is
at a low ebb across the world. The failure of government to
regulate financial markets effectively has perversely weakened
the progressive left's political creed, which states that it is the
principle role of government to protect the individual from
the inherent inequities of market forces. Instead, the crisis of
financial capitalism has drawn people towards parties who
state the answer is less government, not more.

With the public's refusal to embrace a 'progressive
moment' in the wake of the government-led bailout of the
banks, the left's historic ambivalence towards markets has
unexpectedly left us flat-footed.

To get back on track we should restate a basic principle that
has endured in the 111 years since Labour was founded in large
part by private sector trade unionists at the Memorial Hall: it
is part of Labour's DNA to accept that markets should be as
genuinely free as possible for all participants – be they producers, consumers or employees – because of the innovation and
wealth that freedom generates. But we go beyond this, too. Just
as elsewhere in *The Purple Book* we seek to reform the state in
part by looking back to earlier inspirations for decentralised
socialism, so too we must look to how the market can not only
be free itself, but how it can empower people to be free. In the

times we live too many now feel that neither the state nor the market can empower them. It is Labour's job to make sure that both do. That is why Labour under Ed Miliband's leadership accepts that markets are here to stay but are not immutable; instead, we are seeking to win the argument over what it is that we want the market economy to do for its participants.

## After the crash: three prescriptions for a better market economy

To look to the future we must first look at our recent past to decide what should be the enduring lessons we take from the financial collapse, particularly in the context of Labour's failure to sustain itself in office after it.

As Prime Minister, Brown probably did more than anyone else to lead the global response to avoid economic disaster. He was, of course, right to identify the need for a tighter international regulatory framework to increase transparency and prevent a repeat of the situation where markets were devoid of scrutiny and excessive power was wielded destructively and irresponsibly. And he correctly identified that a political lesson of the crash was the importance of government action 'where markets fail'. As he told the TUC in September 2009: 'The lesson of the 1930s is that whenever banks collapse and markets fail, governments cannot stand aside; they must ensure that the savings of people, their mortgages, their credit, are all protected and that they must intervene to save jobs.'[2]

But the success progressive parties have had in defining the role of government in the event of such a monumental collapse has proved insufficient to convince electorates that they should be trusted to govern in the post-crisis age. Instead, national debates have been more focused on the question of how we get our economies back on track. And there, argument between parties on the left and right has rightly centred on what is the optimal role for government to shape and stimulate the market economy – not whether we should retreat from market capitalism itself. Labour has not, therefore, retreated into an anti-market comfort zone. As shadow business secretary John Denham has said: 'The next Labour government will have to be relentless, a single minded focus, in creating the conditions for private sector growth. That means, without any ambiguity, creating the conditions in which companies compete within fair markets.'[3]

Yet to do so successfully and convincingly, we must over-come an inherent disadvantage that has held us back for decades in the battle with the conservative right to shape the kind of market economy we want. We must explicitly recognise, and be comfortable with, what in fact we implicitly accepted decades ago: that markets are the only effective way to deliver the kind of economy and the kind of society we want.

Instead of outright opposition, the danger for the progressive left is surely this: if we attack the free market dogma of the Tories without a coherent and boldly set out counter-proposition of what kind of markets we think are best, our position can too easily be misconstrued as unerr-ingly taking the side of government in a battle of state versus market. Indeed we can sometimes deceive ourselves into thinking that we are against markets, when in fact we are engaging in an argument over the kind of market we want and the optimal role for government in achieving it. This is in contrast to the Tory version of the free market, which seeks to hack back the state. We, though, understand that the state and the market have a strong inter-relation-ship and that to weaken one weakens the other. Our true position is arguing for a more equitable and, crucially, a more economically efficient kind of market economy to a Conservative Party that remains instinctively hostile to the concept of state intervention.

But misalignment between the rhetoric we adopt and our actual position on markets not only impedes the thinking we need to do to renew, it also risks leaving us seeming out of step in a world where belief in enterprise economies as the best foundation for advancing our goals is remarkably entrenched in the UK and across the world.

A poll of 20,791 individuals across twenty countries conducted by the Program on International Policy Attitudes of the University of Maryland in 2005 found a clear majority in all but France believing that 'the free enterprise system and free market economy is the best system on which to base the future of the world'. Around 66 per cent of people in the UK agreed compared to 27 per cent who disagreed – above the global average of 61 per cent versus 28 per cent.

An attempt to redefine what we mean by free markets can take inspiration from Isaiah Berlin's seminal 1958 essay *Two Concepts of Liberty* that drew a distinction between negative and positive concepts of liberty.

Negative liberty, wrote Berlin, equates to 'freedom from' – the absence of external interference. Positive liberty, on the other hand, is 'freedom to' – the freedom to reach one's true potential. In many areas of social policy, as progressives we have been successful in building a narrative of positive freedom, defining ourselves as the would-be conquerors of William Beveridge's five giant evils. Yet in the economic sphere, the conservative right has achieved rhetorical primacy. The 'free' in 'free markets' has come to be universally accepted as defining a negative liberty, the near-total withdrawal by government from the functioning of the market. The closer you can get to that theoretical paradise of total freedom through absence of government involvement, the better.

So, besides adopting more measured cuts to public spending to prevent market slowdown, if Labour is to become the progressive champion for markets that work for people? What steps can we take to ensure they deliver genuinely progressive ends? Three broad areas to consider are: new models of the firm and ownership; regularly reviewing regulation; and defining fairness and intervention in the economy.

## New models of the firm and ownership

In the private sector, we should support models that concentrate power in the hands of a more diverse set of constituents.

The global cooperative economy, a prime example, is responsible for an aggregate turnover of more than $1tn, with over a billion people being members of a cooperative around the world. Owned by stakeholders from within the business – whether that is the staff, customers, the local community or a mixture of these – it is this element that allows these businesses to challenge the stereotype and redistribute power and dividend in ways difficult for a more conventional business model. Mutuals are clearly on the rise in the UK, partly thanks to the efforts of a decade of Labour in government to support the sector and the determination of organisations like the Co-operative Group of stores, which has been able to buy itself into the 'Big Five' supermarkets in the UK.

But we should seek to understand how other countries, like Spain where the large and multifarious Mondragon Cooperative Corporation is based, have for so many decades been more successful in fostering mutual ownership than the country whose Rochdale Pioneers produced the first modern consumer co-op.

We should be prepared to place greater faith in the 'enterprise' element of cooperatives, questioning whether mutuals are held back in the UK by the fact that our law on cooperative societies only covers organisational governance and not employment issues. In Spain, members of cooperatives are treated solely as co-owners and therefore self-employed in law. In the UK, overlapping legal structures that can treat workers in co-ops as both co-owners and employees often risk confusion that may impede the dynamism that co-ops need to compete.

So Labour in opposition should work with its sister organisation the Co-operative Party to re-examine comprehensively whether further legal or cultural steps are needed genuinely to level the playing field and produce a significant change in their viability and existence. At their best, progressives can work within the framework of dynamic, enterprising markets to pioneer models that spread power and wealth widely across communities.

We should also engage seriously with the emerging concept of shared value capitalism, the idea of business moving beyond the basic concepts of social responsibility into a world view where operating in socially and economically beneficial ways is economically advantageous; that business should not simply do good, but do well by doing good. This is an idea gaining favour with some of the world's leading companies, including Google, General Electric and Johnson & Johnson, and represents a rebuff to the conservative orthodoxy that the best thing government can do for business is simply to get out of the way.

But most importantly, rather than either railing against their inherent inequities or using acceptance of them as a tool to show that we can be trusted with economic orthodoxy, we should embrace and shape for ourselves what we mean by a genuinely free market – empowering workers and challenging the long-held orthodoxy that says a market can only be free when the state withdraws fully from it.

**Regulation and fairness**
Those on the left should never fall into the trap of assuming regulation comes at no cost. There should clearly be limits to intervention: challenging the notion that the optimal level of intervention in any market is zero does not mean that it can be perpetually increased without impact.

How to do that is a difficult question for any government. In its final term the previous Labour administration examined, but ultimately rejected, the idea of regulatory budgets that would have imposed strict limits on the level of increased cost that departments could place on businesses through new regulations.

Regulatory budgets could have provided a check on those regulations whose utility was outweighed by the cost of implementing them. Yet they were perhaps too crude a mechanism and could themselves have been burdensome to implement in Whitehall. Most importantly, budgets would struggle to adequately capture the areas where regulation improves the economic efficiency of markets as well as providing a social good.

In opposition, Labour will need to scrutinise the application of sunset clauses, which would time-limit certain new regulations. While we should have confidence that we can continue to win our case on particular issues and take opportunities to improve legislation to make markets work better, Labour is right to be wary that sunset clauses could increase uncertainty for businesses who complain that unexpected changes greatly increase the expense of complying with regulation. Above all, any Labour government worth its salt should guard against attempts to use parliamentary chicanery to sweep away important protections that are currently embedded in the statute book.

But we do need a new approach which recognises that Whitehall, local government and agencies have often seen increased regulation as a first rather than last resort; that governments of all stripes have at times allowed stated ambitions on controlling the growth of regulation to be trumped by competing priorities. The last Labour government's groundbreaking work measuring, and seeking to minimise, the unnecessary cost to businesses from new regulations should not be forgotten in this new era. Instead, the new programme for government that Labour presents will be founded on a radical overhaul of our approach to regulation. We will seek to end the culture that too often places unnecessary burdens on well-run businesses but is ineffective in changing the behaviour of their badly-run competitors.

That approach should be ingrained in the thinking of western progressives seeking to ensure their economies remain competitive against emerging countries who are often prepared to accept far lower standards of environmental, safety and social security protection.

Yet whatever mechanisms we agree on to control the unnecessary growth of regulation, we must keep in mind that in an overwhelming number of cases, total withdrawal of government action restricts opportunities rather than expands them, and so perverts a genuinely free and open market.

Of course, even traditional free marketeers did not advocate the law of the jungle. They stipulated that a basic level of regulation was necessary to enforce two conditions that they deemed essential to the functioning of a free market: property rights and no barriers to entry. But we have never properly challenged the minimalist interpretation that defined absence of barriers to entry as being purely the absence of legal barriers.

To reclaim this debate and genuinely become the party that champions and rewards individual aspiration, the question we should ask of any market is what the appropriate minimum level of intervention should be to make it genuinely free: that is, free to allow all potential participants – producers and consumers – to have a fair chance of participating successfully within it.

### Fairness and intervention

Besides constantly keeping under review how free a market is against the social impact it has, we must consider how we decide to define fairness. In areas like health and schools we decide that fairness means that access to services should never be impeded by personal income or location. So in health, the rules for access to the NHS have been drawn very tightly and specifically since its creation.

Compare that to the market for broadband, where, rather than stipulating everyone must have free access at the point of use, we implicitly define fairness as consumers having the opportunity to enter the market by purchasing a service at a reasonable price. Therefore, government intervention in the market has taken the form of investment to eradicate the minority of 'not spots' in pockets of the country where no service was available to customers, coupled with a strong regulator designed to ensure lower prices for consumers through competition between providers.

Such targeted intervention can be the means to injecting fairness into a market that otherwise does not meet social need. How do we make this a reality while continuing to champion the liberal private sector or cooperative enterprise as ways that ensure Britain remains competitive in an ever-advancing global economy? And how does our ethos differ from that of the Conservative right in these areas?

It differs because right across the economy, and at every level, we are seeing the damage perpetrated by a government that has regressed to the traditional view that government is the principle barrier to strong individuals enjoying economic success, rather than a potential facilitator of that success and disperser of power across the market economy.

Nowhere is this more apparent than in the role the new administration is prepared to countenance for government in driving growth in sectors of the economy.

In the last years of the Labour government, Lord Mandelson, then business secretary, gave increased energy and focus to a policy he described as 'industrial activism': identifying where greater government intervention in sectoral markets could help build the capacity of businesses and their employees. This was more than a short-term response to the global economic crisis, though of course job creation and economy diversification were vitally important at such a time. The strategy also sought to equip British industry for the challenges of the coming decades, but this has been systematically scaled back in scope and ambition by the new government.

Thanks to the short-sighted withdrawal of a government

loan, the support given to Sheffield Forgemasters has become the best-known example of this. Forgemasters was chosen for a loan, not to prop up a struggling firm, but because it demonstrated that it had the skills base and the ability to break into an emerging marketplace – pressure valves for a new generation of nuclear power stations.

By carefully targeting support within certain sectors, government sought to intervene to open up and increase freedom for British firms to reach their true potential in emerging markets, creating jobs and raising skills. There were examples where we missed a trick during our last period in office. Renewable energy technology is an area where Labour began the work to facilitate market entry by UK firms, but should have acted faster in a global market that is predicted to grow in value from £33bn in 2006 to £139bn in 2016. In future, targeted loans or other forms of support from government could help British industry break into markets of this size – and in doing so can help to redistribute power in the economy, supporting small businesses, cooperatives and firms in economically deprived areas.

Far from calling a halt to this approach as ministers have now done, government should be learning from what was most effective through the global recession to develop a targeted activism for the leaner decade ahead. We need to get better at pre-empting global trends in industry, considering the demographic, environmental and sociological changes that will shape future markets.

How do we avoid simply replicating the shortcoming of the 'picking winners' policy of past decades – only this time with sectors rather than individual companies? We should recognise that there should always be a role for political leadership in crucial decisions on our future – ministers need to make decisions and be held accountable for them by the electorate. But we should not entrust the future competitiveness of the UK economy, even to ministers as good as Mandelson, without being prepared to consider re-engineering the way government itself promotes entrepreneurial risk-taking in its public servants.

The banking system boiled over partly because a system developed that gave huge financial rewards to short-term fluctuations in value at the expense of longer-term stable returns. But Whitehall, which can make decisions every bit as critical as an investment bank, still represents the other extreme. The government's shareholder executive is full of bright people with private sector experience. But it still lacks the prospect of basic risk and reward that – for all the faults that were laid bare in the financial crash and must now be corrected – has driven growth and innovation in the private sector for many decades. So we should consider a bold recasting of incentives in the public sector which more effectively rewards genuine sustained success that facilitates economic growth in emerging sectors, seeking to attract the very best talent that currently is captured by high salaries in the private sector.

There has been a similar retrenchment in the government's will to help drive regional and local economic success under the Conservatives. Businesses and working people seeking to succeed across the country are being held back by shrinking support to help every region of the country reach its full potential.

With total central government funding of around £2.26bn, the regional development agencies sought to promote economic development, business efficiency, employment, skills and sustainable development. The new local enterprise partnerships are being asked to do more (including local business regulation and national infrastructure implementation) and better with no guaranteed central government funding, just ad hoc awards from a £1.4bn regional growth fund and a £400m LEP capacity fund, both spread over four years.

The regional development agencies were not perfect. There were variations in how effective they were at targeting investment where there was a genuine need for it to drive private sector growth. And Labour never cracked the accountability question once its early big idea of regional assemblies had been resoundingly rejected. But on the whole they worked. Now there are concerns about a new system which has centralised investment decisions over a much smaller pot in Whitehall. The reduction in support for local economies is so great that it calls into question the government's role in stimulating economic success in areas cut off from the established engines of growth in the UK.

A party that believes in positive action to make markets free in a way that empowers individuals should make the case for regional and local intervention in the economy where playing fields are not level. If there are barriers to firms growing and creating jobs in parts of the country, like my constituency of Barrow and Furness, we should redouble our efforts to remove those barriers, rather than accepting the idea floated by the current government that people should just move to where the jobs are.

It is not simply social justice and a desire to sustain communities that insists we should act in this way. We should also be prepared to act on the grounds of economic efficiency: as the previous administration's industrial strategy explicitly recognised in its final years in office, participants in a labour market and industrial capital are 'sticky' – they cannot just uproot at the drop of a hat. Taking a minimalist view of what makes markets free rejects government intervention to boost regional economies. But this will not drive greater efficiency: it will actually necessitate diverting more money to the cost of economic failure in higher benefit bills and lower tax receipts.

Seeking greater accountability for interventions to boost regional and local economies is difficult. Previous attempts to give greater decision-making capacity to regions or sub-regional areas have had mixed success in capturing the public's imagination. On the other hand, centralised decision-making in Whitehall is too remote. Many infrastructure improvements, such as significant transport schemes, require a coordinated action on a scale greater than the boundaries on which local government currently operates. We should do what we can to make the new local enterprise partnerships a success but consider how the successful model of directly elected mayors could operate more widely and with greater economic powers without leaving at a disadvantage areas that do not fall within a definable city-region.

Most radically, a commitment to new forms of intervention in markets should lead us to consider whether we can empower business to have a more effective say over what happens to the wealth they create. One issue we could explore is whether there is a way to give enterprise partnerships a greater say over the distribution of revenue from business rate taxation without recreating the inequity and inefficiency of the government's current reform of the rates. As shadow communities secretary Caroline Flint has rightly pointed out, the Tories' plans for localisation of business rates risk severely impoverishing areas with low business density at which increased business support could most effectively be targeted.

That problem would need to be addressed and the accountability of enterprise partnerships would need to be strengthened beyond the current loose groupings. But if a workable proposition could be found, it could inject genuine vitality into local investment and decision-making that has too often been absent in recent decades. That would address a basic gap in political systems around the world, where the principle of no taxation without representation does not directly apply to businesses, who pay their taxes yet have no formal say in how it is spent.

Consumers must be strong in any market economy that genuinely empowers individuals and enables them to prosper. Yet the coalition government is determined to dismantle the framework Labour created to empower consumers and uphold fair competition and fair treatment in domestic markets. Consumer Focus is being scrapped, and the Office of Fair Trading and the Competition Commission are being merged.

We should pledge now that Labour will restore government's role as champion of the consumer in the UK economy through creating effective levers of redress for individual consumers without recreating the downsides of the United States' class action culture. And we must explore new ways to champion diversity in markets against the concentration of power in any one body, be it the state or an overly dominant market leader.

For individuals seeking to succeed at work, the new administration has retreated from the last Labour government's commitment to offer continued support to enable people to better their chances of getting back into the labour market or progressing within it. Far from accepting a more limited role for intervention to empower people to succeed in the labour market, it is time to examine what role a lean but active state could play in facilitating access to support for job seekers, which goes beyond the minimum level currently available to all who have met basic contributory requirements or whose family income is below a certain level.

### Guaranteeing genuine freedom
These ideas are among many that we should consider as the progressive left seeks to shape a world that will remain dominated by markets at all levels. The new programme for government that we construct must be tested by a Labour Party that has the courage to take on the right and redefine what makes a market genuinely free.

New Labour's success in the 1990s came in convincing people we were serious about ending the false choice between economic efficiency and social justice.

But that must not be a once-in-a-generation repositioning of policies to capture the centre-ground. To give progressive ideas the best chance of dominating the post-crisis global economy, we should move on from the false debate that sets free markets against government. Instead we should define a new role for government as guarantor of genuine freedom for all within markets. From national intervention down to individual support for working people, the test for government action should be whether it spreads genuine power and freedom better than the status quo, which still too often hoards power and wealth in the hands of the already privileged.

Labour must never lose its burning passion to tackle the injustice we see around us. But if we are to succeed, we need to show the public that we understand the world we seek to shape. Above all, we need to demonstrate we are prepared to tackle the failures of both market and state that hold people back. So let's embrace a new radicalism that shapes the market economy in the name of true freedom and fairness for all.

1  Ed Miliband, speech to the British Chamber of Commerce, 7 April 2011.
2  Gordon Brown, speech to the Trade Union Congress, 15 September 2009.
3  John Denham, speech to ippr North, 26 May 2011.

# Empowerment and transparency: a new settlement for public services

*Patrick Diamond*

T he financial crisis of 2008–9 was initially understood as a failure of liberal market capitalism, but quickly transformed into a crisis of public debt and government deficits. Unfortunately for the left, popular fury against the financial system has not been accompanied by a restoration of faith in the power of government. While the crisis was fuelled by irresponsible banking and financial deregulation, it is the role and size of the state which has returned to the centre of political debate. Voters rightly fear the unrestrained power and inequality of markets, but remain doubtful as to what government can do. According to the latest evidence, many believe that centre-left parties are too prone to increasing taxation while failing to manage public expenditure wisely.[1] The demise of neoliberalism has not rejuvenated support for the interventionist state.

Indeed, the error so often made by social democrats has been to confuse anger at the excesses of the market with public backing for the traditional state. This does not mean that anxieties about the ferocious squeeze on lower and middle incomes together with soaring inequality at the top are unfounded: they remain deeply resonant with British voters. Nonetheless, antipathy to New Labour's heavy-handed and centralist approach sowed the seeds of public disillusionment well before the financial crisis. The centre-left will not be trusted to govern until it recasts the state's role as an agent of economic and social progress.

That insight has profound implications for the future of Britain's public services.[2] This chapter does not provide a detailed audit of Labour's performance in government over the last thirteen years.[3] It is clear that public services face a series of challenges today that pose fundamental questions about how they should be organised and run. They have to cope with rising expectations among those who use public services. They have to accommodate rising costs. They have to deal with the new right critique of bureaucratic failure. And public services have to respond to the social and economic challenges of globalisation after the crisis.

This chapter contends that such challenges will be met only if Labour seeks to rebuild confidence in an empowering state. Incompetence and bureaucratic centralisation erode trust not only in political parties, but in institutions and the role of government as a force for good. That requires the next Labour government to prioritise the decentralisation and redistribution of power in the name of a fairer and more equal society. The most fundamental assumption that should guide the party's programme is that power must be located at the lowest possible level consistent with the public good. This animating vision must drive the next phase of institutional adaptation and reform.

The chapter begins by addressing the case for empowerment in public services, located within the communitarian and pluralist strands of the British Labour tradition. Decentralising power in order to emancipate citizens and local communities has deep roots in Labour's history, as exemplified by Thomas Paine, Robert Owen, William Morris, R. H. Tawney, G. D. H. Cole and latterly Paul Hirst. The participatory socialist tradition has always valued self-government and bottom-up action, instead of relying on monolithic national institutions to uphold and sustain the common good. The empowering state transcends both free markets and centralising government, ensuring a decisive shift in the balance of power towards individual citizens and communities. Nonetheless, an agenda of empowerment is insufficient given the range of challenges facing public services as they seek to square the circle of rising expectations and rising costs in conditions of austerity. Too often the debate about public services has detached the structure of provision from how they should be financed. This chapter argues that Labour has to reframe the debate about financing in the context of the fiscal squeeze and the long-term structural challenges confronting the British state.

The centre-right has succeeded in casting the size of the state as the central issue in British politics, but it is imperative to redefine the terms of debate concerning the quality of public goods and public infrastructure. The connection between taxation, public services, and economic and social cohesion needs to be restated as an essential component of a dynamic and socially cohesive society. Proper debate about the nature and scope of taxation, including how to fund public services, will be critical to the legitimacy of British democracy and the vitality of the public domain. Empowerment and public investment must go hand in hand.

### The tradition of self-government

Before reviewing the evidence for different models of public services and exploring how they might respond to new challenges, it is essential to draw out the implications of different conceptions of markets, state and civil society. Social democratic governments over the last century have been characterised by a deep paradox of purpose, torn between competing statecrafts, each of which is a legacy of the past.

On the one hand, there is the tradition of 'mechanical reform', which is essentially top-down and dirigiste. It is assumed that not only economic life, but social and personal behaviour will be managed through regulation and intervention by the centralising state. Labour's approach in the NHS and schools has often been portrayed as 'mechanical', despite the onus on devolution, liberalisation and quasi-markets. On the other hand, there is the tradition of 'moral reform', sustaining an implacable faith in the empowerment of individuals through an enabling and 'steering' state.[4] Earlier conceptions of the Third Way emphasised partnership, democratic renewal and citizen participation, though these were rarely translated into new models of provision.

The tensions and contradictions between such approaches are self-evident. Over the last decade, the traditional model of the top-down, centralising state has been broken as the result of constitutional reform. However, a new model has not yet emerged that genuinely empowers individual citizens and localities. There is a marked tendency to conduct debate in terms of simplistic caricatures such as centralism versus localism, big state versus small state, and 'public good' versus 'private bad'. The centre-left should have the confidence to cultivate a more sophisticated and nuanced approach. At the same time, progressives need to determine how they can guarantee a fairer distribution of power.

Labour should opt emphatically for a conception of moral reform, embracing the tradition of 'self-government' elaborated by Harold Laski, Richard Crossman and J. P. Mackintosh. This demands active engagement in the public sphere in return for the devolution of power and control. Moral reform is preferable because if communities feel a stronger sense of ownership, new coalitions of support will be forged that help to sustain public investment. The pace of improvement might be slower, but change is more likely to embed and endure. In any case, mechanical reform erodes public and professional confidence in the efficacy of the state.

The tradition of self-government is not about rolling back the state, nor asserting that greater localism is a panacea. Trusting people is risky because people can be wrong: localities may be small-minded, insular, even corrupt. They may lack the capacity to exercise control, and it becomes harder to safeguard access and equity. Indeed, any attempt to shift power and control from the centre leads to dilemmas. To ensure accountability, for example, governments have imposed centralised targets in return for investment. Incentives might conflict with bottom-up, peer-driven pressures to improve, however, and national targets and regulatory oversight can reduce the scope for local experiment and innovation.

Any credible programme for devolving power has to explicitly acknowledge such trade-offs. Nonetheless, the relationship between the state, public institutions, communities and citizens will continue to change regardless of whether 'empowerment' is an explicit objective of government policy. The great failing of past social democratic governments has been the misguided belief that they will achieve radical domestic reforms through the existing machinery of the state. The aspiration of forging an active industrial strategy, for example, has been constantly derailed by the dominance of the Treasury in economic policy-making. The Treasury's essentially liberal, free market instincts have sought to prevent the emergence of an active and developmental state. It is precisely the top-down and elitist nature of the British state that has most frustrated progressive ambitions.

### The case for empowerment

There has long been a fundamental divide between the neoclassical right and the social democratic left on the role of the state and public services in British society, reflecting contested conceptions of personal liberty and social justice. The right continues to believe that 'empowerment' is about freedom from restraint, a conception of negative freedom. Its claim is that people attain control over their lives only when the state gets out of the way, leaving the ethic of 'social responsibility' to fill the void.

In contrast, progressives elaborate a conception of empowerment as the expression of positive liberty: not merely freedom from interference, but the capacity to do and to be, which is enabled by public goods and public services. This is what the Nobel Prize-winning economist Amartya Sen envisages in the concept of 'capabilities'.[5] Capabilities are a variety of freedom: the substantive freedom to achieve 'functioning combinations'. Less formally put, this is the freedom to develop and sustain various conceptions of the good life and the common good.

There is an affinity between the capabilities approach and Tawney and Tony Crosland's conception of democratic equality.[6] The implications for public services are quite profound:

- The capabilities model does not mean treating individuals as if they are the same, but treating people according to their circumstances;
- Those circumstances are defined by the individual receiving support, hence the importance of personalised provision and an awareness of the barriers that prevent choice;
- This approach emphasises the importance of local and tacit knowledge, hence the value of devolution and the decentralisation of power;
- The notion of capabilities does not demand equality of outcome, but rather that people should be enabled to make choices concerning the outcomes of their own lives: it is not authoritarian, but enabling.

In essence, this amounts to a strategy of equalisation through empowerment: enabling individuals and communities to take greater responsibility for their own lives. The claim that uniformity of provision ensures equality of outcome ought to be contested. Social democrats need to acknowledge that state intervention has left a multitude of social and economic ills untouched. Class divisions have been entrenched while social mobility appears to have slowed down dramatically since the 1950s.

The claim of this chapter is that decentralisation and devolution are critical agents of change in public services, but there are other reasons why devolving and decentralising power remain critical to the progressive cause. First, a top-down, centralising state is wholly inconsistent with the forces that are reshaping politics and today's economy. The future challenge of global economic competition requires a state that is agile and responsive with the strategic capacity to regulate and shape markets.

Britain is an increasingly diverse society where needs and aspirations differ greatly between localities. Social and economic change has fragmented identities, breaking down traditional occupational and geographical hierarchies, and creating a more complex distribution of spatial disadvantage. The most salient fact is 'hyper-diversity': many neighbourhoods that were relatively homogenous in terms of ethnicity and social class are now more mixed.[7]

The rapidly changing make-up of communities underlines the case for localised strategies that promote equity and well-being in accordance with Sen's vision of enriching capabilities.[8] The cultivation of the civic is inescapably concerned with the politics of place in contemporary Britain. The hollowing-out of civic life is felt in the erosion of local democracy and local public institutions, but there is also incredible civic energy that can be released by a subtle combination of community leadership and bottom-up reform.

The empowering state should also be based on a balance of rights and duties for the individual as well as the state. Much of what governments have sought to achieve requires the active engagement of citizens. Public health, safer neighbourhoods, a better start for disadvantaged families depend not only on the delivery of services, but how citizens choose to help themselves. This is best achieved where services are located closer to people with discretion to vary provision according to local circumstances and needs. Finally, individuals lead complex lives where they may be materially richer, even with the downturn and squeeze on median incomes, but are also increasingly anxious and insecure. They need personally tailored services that give confidence as well as care, empowerment as well as higher standards. These are more likely to be delivered where power and control are properly devolved from the centre.

## The public services Britain needs

Britain has entered a period of radical change: indeed, the structural environment for public services will be markedly different by 2015. The government is applying the tightest squeeze on public spending since the Second World War, while demand is rising sharply in health and social care: cuts and reprioritisation are the key drivers of change. Structural reform is overturning existing arrangements. Whether the purpose is greater localism or enhanced competition, a phase of major change is underway. One of the key challenges for any opposition party is to determine which reforms to consolidate and which to reverse. At the same time, Labour should have the confidence to elaborate its own model of active and participative provision which takes account of the varying nature of public services:

| Type of service | Examples |
|---|---|
| Some public services are universal and are 'purchased' and organised on our behalf: we use them as citizens. This applies particularly to regulatory services and public infrastructure. | Street cleaning, refuse collection, emergency healthcare, road maintenance, policing and environmental protection. |
| Some public services are organised universally but structured to provide a degree of choice. The state cannot afford unlimited supply, but theoretically organises sufficient or surplus capacity to provide for consumer preferences. | Schools and GP registration are the most familiar examples. |

| Some public services enable citizens to choose from a wide but approved list of state-funded providers. | Free nursery entitlements, direct payments for the recipients of social care, university places and, increasingly, hospital elective care. |
|---|---|
| Some services combine all or most of the features outlined above. | Hospital care is the best example since choice can be applied to elective care, but is less applicable in emergency cases requiring a more universalist approach. |

Any initiative that seeks to devolve power and diversify provision has to acknowledge that no model will be suitable across all contexts: it is necessary to maintain a range of levers and drivers of change. Six principal approaches can thus be identified.

First, the empowerment of local government. There must be a new settlement for local government giving real control over policy and performance rather than just the limited conception of 'earned autonomy'. This has to include greater fiscal freedoms and a reining in of the target culture.

Second, the use of both 'voice' and 'choice'. Placing power and control in the hands of citizens requires a variety of governance strategies: individual and collective choice should be extended through greater use of 'purchaser-provider' models. The separation of purchaser and provider enables public bodies to purchase services on behalf of citizens, allowing for the removal of failing providers, improving responsiveness and incentivising innovation. This model is not a panacea and may be inappropriate, for example, in relation to primary care in the NHS. But it has been the direction of travel in key public services, notably state education, since the early 1990s. A future Labour government ought to give local education authorities explicit regulatory powers to oversee the development of education services in each local community, monitoring access and equity while ensuring a flourishing local ecology of schools. Another aspect is widening personalised budgets, crucial to any strategy of empowerment, including

for adult skills and helping long-term unemployed people
back into the labour market.

Third, the creation of more self-governing institutions. The
progressive agenda means nurturing genuinely self-governing
institutions built on the model of foundation hospitals in
the NHS. In his seminal essay *The End of Laissez-Faire*,
John Maynard Keynes referred to the importance of semi-
autonomous public bodies that lie between the individual and
the state, whose criterion for action is the public interest. This,
he argued, helped to sustain an appropriate 'balance of powers'
between market, government and civil society.[9] Academy
schools, for example, ought to be reconstituted as public
interest bodies incorporating a wide array of community and
stakeholder interests. Similarly, early years and Sure Start
centres should be granted much greater self-autonomy.

Fourth, the acceleration of the notion of citizen redress.
Devolving power to the citizen means recognising the importance of 'coproduction', as well as a clearly defined contract
between users and providers focused on mutual rights and
duties, including proper rights of redress where services fail
to deliver basic standards. For example, if schools fail to
meet minimum attainment standards for more than three
successive years, a competition should be triggered to bring
in alternative providers. Parents should also have the right to
trigger competitions for new schools where standards fail to
improve. Separately, the onus on coproduction in public services includes developing mechanisms of 'affiliative welfare',
such as timebanks that encourage reciprocity and mutuality
between citizens.

Fifth, the granting of more rights to community ownership.
Citizens should have additional freedom to own and manage
public assets including equity stakes in social housing, as well
as leisure facilities and public amenities owned by the community, capturing the spirit of the early cooperative movement.
One important example is Community Land Trusts (CLTs),

which develop housing and other assets at affordable levels for long-term community benefit. The value of land and equity is permanently 'locked in' by separating the value of the building from the land it stands on, while CLTs are often run according to cooperative and mutual principles. There are currently around eighty CLTs across the UK, but Labour should stimulate their expansion by widening access to capital financing. This drive for community ownership is not inconsistent with a greater role for democratically elected local government.

Finally, the building of a decentralised 'steering' state. This echoes the principles of 'reinventing government' pioneered by Bill Clinton and Al Gore to reform the US federal government in the 1990s. The danger is that localities will be compromised by the constant flow of centralised edicts going against the tide of bottom-up reform. Therefore, the structure of government departments needs to be reviewed, accompanied by radical reform of the civil service. As a first step, the Department for Communities and Local Government ought to be abolished altogether, while the Wales Office, the Scotland Office and the Northern Ireland Office could be merged into a single Department of the Nations. This is not about arbitrary cuts in central capacity, which governments so often fail to deliver. Instead, all programmes and agencies at the centre should be subject to a public value test: decentralising and removing functions altogether, focusing resources on the frontline, and enabling neighbourhoods and communities to devise their own solutions. Labour has to show that it is willing to apply high-octane reforms to an excessively centralised and bureaucratic state.

## Future funding pressures

It would be quite wrong, however, to detach the debate about the structure of public services from the future financing of the public realm. The coalition is determined to reduce the size of the state, having announced cuts of at least 25 per cent in departmental budgets, and a planned reduction of the public sector deficit through a combination of 73 per cent spending cuts (£74bn) and 27 per cent tax rises (£24bn) over the next four years.[10] The financial crisis is estimated to have permanently weakened the UK public finances by about 6.5 per cent of national income, or £90bn a year. Fiscal retrenchment to shrink the UK budget deficit is accepted across the ideological divide, but the centre-left needs to recast the terms of debate.

The Conservatives have sought to reduce the deficit without considering what future level and quality of public services Britain will need. They have not faced up to any of the fundamental challenges, from changing demography to new technology. Ministers insist that improved services will simply be delivered through efficiency savings, but this is illusory. The table below illustrates that spending is likely to keep rising as the result of long-term fiscal pressures:

| | 2008 | 2018 | 2028 | 2038 | 2048 | 2058 |
|---|---|---|---|---|---|---|
| Education | 5 | 5.6 | 5.8 | 5.6 | 5.5 | 5.6 |
| Pensions | 7.6 | 8.1 | 9 | 9.9 | 9.9 | 11 |
| Health | 7.4 | 7.9 | 8.6 | 9.2 | 9.6 | 9.9 |
| Total (age-related) spending | 20 | 21.7 | 23.4 | 24.7 | 25 | 26.6 |
| Other spending | 20.4 | 19.1 | 18.9 | 18.6 | 18.1 | 18 |
| Total spending | 40.5 | 40.8 | 42.3 | 43.3 | 43.1 | 44.5 |

Source: HM Treasury (2008) Long-Term Public Finance Report: an analysis of fiscal sustainability

Nonetheless, these estimates may still be relatively conservative: recent research has shown that an additional 6 per cent of GDP will be needed to meet the social costs of ageing by 2030 alone.[11] In the coming decades, the proportion of elderly people is likely to increase substantially.

This trend results from a combination of factors, including increasing life expectancy, and the ageing of two large cohorts born in the 1940s and 1960s. They have a direct impact on age-related expenditure such as state pensions and healthcare. Alongside HM Treasury forecasts, this will increase to 47 or 48 per cent of GDP the share of national income allocated by governments within the next twenty years. The challenge will only be met by refocusing and restructuring public services, while facing up to hard choices about the composition of the UK tax base.

The centre-left has to cultivate a more open and honest debate about the future of public services, returning to the relationship between tax, public spending and societal well-being. Social democrats fundamentally believe that individuals are part of a strong civic community where public goods contribute significantly to quality of life. There is a legitimate debate about the size of the state in any democratic society, but proposing that civic 'platoons' fill the void vacated by public sector retrenchment is misguided. Economies with high levels of self-sustaining community provision, such as the US and the Nordic countries, draw on deeply rooted values and norms that have endured for centuries. It is hard to envisage how this might be replicated during a single parliament, particularly in the absence of capacity-building by state institutions, which the 'big society' seeks to replace.

Nonetheless, the strategic backdrop to the next election will be one where there is little appetite among the public for traditional 'tax-and-spend' remedies given the squeeze on living standards, downward pressure on real wages and increased burdens among families, including university tuition fees and the cost of social care in older age.[12] The opposition will seek to portray Labour as the party of high taxes and incontinent spending that cannot be trusted to manage the state prudently and efficiently. More government cannot be the answer to every problem. Labour needs a new strategy which re-casts the terms of public debate.

## Towards transparency

The debate about public services too often separates funding and provision, as the Plant Commission's *Paying for Progress: A New Tax for Public Spending* acknowledged over a decade ago.[13] Research on the tax system and public provision exposes a deep, underlying psychological 'disconnection' between the taxes citizens pay and the services they receive. This reflects not only the incomprehensibility of the UK tax system, but uncertainty as to where taxes are going and whether government uses the money well. The paradox is that the public does not perceive that services have improved, even where its own experience was far better than anticipated. Not only does the state have to deliver improved services, it must also convince the public this is the case.[14]

The most intriguing finding is that if citizens are relatively certain that additional money will improve services then they are prepared to countenance additional taxes. The priority for the centre-left is to ensure people feel better 'connected' to the taxes they pay. The legitimacy of taxation and sustained support for additional spending will only be achieved when the public better understand how their taxes are spent and feel confident they are being used well. This should be achieved by 'earmarking' taxes more directly for specific purposes, despite concerns that 'hypothecation' reduces the flexibility with which governments can use revenues:[15]

- A hypothecated NHS and social care insurance fund would merge income tax with National Insurance, renewing the contributory principle. Transparency may help to loosen 'tax resistance', guaranteeing that higher sums are focused on citizens' priorities. Both health and social care are universal needs which are inefficiently allocated by markets, as well as 'superior goods' for which demand rises as incomes increase;
- The use of time-limited levies for special capital expenditures such as investment in transport infrastructure,

especially at the local level, where local referenda might be held to agree the specific proposal. These levies are removed when sufficient funds have been raised;
- The use of tax and public service pledges where governments set principal rates of tax such as income tax. Ministers must set out what additional revenues are designed to achieve and, where possible, the auditable improvements that will be delivered;
- The earmarking of environmental taxes for designated tasks such as improvements to public transport infrastructure, alongside incentive-based taxation that seeks to reduce adverse social and environmental impacts;
- Grant the power to vary basic and higher rates of income tax by a maximum of 3p in the pound to local authorities in England, subject to a popular mandate through a local referendum; and enable local councils to levy a supplementary business rate to fund specific improvements in consultation with local businesses;
- Reform council tax, which remains highly regressive and penalises the poorest households hardest. There is a case for introducing a new set of property value bands in order to achieve a fairer, more progressive local taxation structure.

This is not to imply that the burden of taxation in the UK ought to rise. Given the squeeze on real incomes, a future Labour government should seek to take more citizens out of the tax system, progressively reducing the tax burden through fundamental reform of the tax system as outlined in the Mirrlees Review.[16] This called for widespread changes, allowing the tax system to 'go progressive and go green', to direct and indirect taxation, environmental taxes, business taxes and taxes on savings.

The measures proposed in this chapter are intended to make the tax system more transparent, irrespective of overall levels of taxation. The purpose is to make public investment more sustainable for the long-term. Another example of transparency is the use of co-payments in public services. The co-payment approach in higher education will no doubt continue, though the government's reforms pay insufficient attention to the contribution of stakeholders, imposing a larger burden on the individual recipient without properly considering the obligations of employers and society at large.

Central to the notion of redistributing power should be the principle that citizens should not only have a greater say over how public services are funded, but that, via enhanced transparency, they should also be able to make informed decisions about how their taxes are spent, and to what effect. Thus while public services must be effective and efficient, they must also be seen as such, enabling citizens to better understand what is being done with the taxes they pay. This should include giving every household an annual citizen's statement, which sets out clearly how the tax system works and how public spending is allocated, as the Plant Commission initially proposed. It should also include an expert audit of government performance, undertaken by an independent fiscal authority accountable to Parliament, which advises government on tax and spending decisions, and provides transparent information to citizens.

Under Labour, the notion of public investment underwent a modest rehabilitation, but the public's confidence and willingness to pay taxes must never be taken for granted. The priority should be to improve the quality of services and 'connect' the public better to taxes and government spending. This reflects a wider debate about how the civic contract between citizens and government ought to be renewed in contemporary society. The Conservatives have a political strategy as well as an economic one: to secure a landslide victory at the next election with a little over 40 per cent of the vote by adopting a tax-cutting agenda. Labour must confront this, not least by reminding voters that it will merely recreate the decrepit and underfunded public services that so troubled them in the early 1990s. More intellectual and political self-confidence will have to be displayed than in the New Labour years.

Nonetheless, the short-term and long-term pressures on public spending are significant and Britain has a large structural deficit; it also needs a strategy to make the state more efficient. This can be achieved partly through making tough choices in policy terms: for example, developing a defence procurement strategy in conjunction with Britain's European allies, and reconsidering the efficiency of spending in the criminal justice system where there is little evidence that custodial sentences for less serious offences reduce long-term offending.[17] It is also necessary to contain increases in public sector salaries, especially 'top pay', while ruthlessly auditing annual baseline departmental expenditure. Labour must never again concede the mantle of public sector efficiency to the centre-right. The challenge is to make the state more accountable and responsive rather than removing it altogether, reforming centre-left statecraft rather than abandoning the terrain of government working in the public interest.

### A new settlement for public services

The argument of this chapter is that the financial crisis and the counter-reaction to New Labour's agenda of mechanical reform have heightened the importance of decentralisation and the redistribution of power through public services. To square the circle, the tax base which sustains high-quality services needs to be reconnected with the public. The next progressive agenda must think afresh about the role of markets and the public interest, including the future of the New Public Management paradigm, which sought to make the public sector operate more like the private sector via the embrace of market-oriented reform and privatisation that evolved in the 1980s.

In recent years, the case for insulating service delivery

from political interference has also grown in salience.
'Depoliticising' the entire NHS is hardly sustainable, given
that the NHS constitutes almost 10 per cent of the British
economy. But public bodies such as the National Institute for
Clinical Excellence demonstrate the advantage of allowing
experts to take decisions about the availability of drugs and
medical treatment.

The devolution of power in Britain is an important prerequisite towards building a fairer, more equal society. Giving
individuals and communities control remains empirically
important in increasing subjective wellbeing, constructing a
deeper bond of allegiance between citizens and public services.
In the past, centre-left governments failed to entrench enduring support for the public domain. Labour became increasingly
associated with the unresponsive and incompetent state. Public
services were apparently insensitive to the needs of individuals
and the wider community, making it harder to generate intrinsic support, paving the way for the firestorm of Thatcherism.
At the heart of today's debate is the appropriate balance of
responsibility between individuals, the community and the
state. Citizens who contribute to public provision should have
the ability to influence and shape institutions, instead of being
merely passive recipients of what the state provides.

This reflects two fundamental principles of democratic
empowerment that should inform the future social democratic agenda. The first is that power should be spread widely:
self-government means diffusing power as widely as possible.
The second principle is that the ideal of self-government
entails a politics of pluralism, power-sharing and negotia-
tion. From the constitution to public services, power cannot
be concentrated within an over-mighty central state. For, as
Tawney said, 'A society is free in so far as, within the limits
set by nature, knowledge, and resources, its institutions and
policies are such as to enable all members to grow to their
full stature.'[18]

1. See YouGov polling on Trust in Centre-Left Parties and Politics undertaken between 18 and 22 March 2011: www.policy-network.net.

2. It is important to acknowledge that in the context of devolution, national governments define divergent reform pathways. Nonetheless, the insights contained in this chapter can be applied to public services in England, Wales, Scotland, and Northern Ireland.

3. For a measured assessment of Labour's achievements, see Polly Toynbee and David Walker, *The Verdict: Did New Labour Change Britain?* (London: Granta Books, 2010).

4. The concept of moral and mechanical reform is elaborated by Peter Clarke in *Liberals and Social Democrats* (Cambridge: Cambridge University Press, 1978).

5. Amartya Sen, *The Idea of Justice* (London: Allen Lane, 2009).

6. David Riesman, *Crosland's Future* (Basingstoke: Palgrave Macmillan, 1997).

7. Geoff Mulgan and Nicola Bacon, 'Promoting Well-Being and Neighbourliness', in *How Equality Shapes Place: Diversity and Localism* (London: Solace Foundation, 2008).

8. The UK's ethnic minority population is no longer characterised by homogenous 'black' communities, and there is no longer a simple division between 'minorities' and 'the majority'. According to the Office for National Statistics (ONS), 42 per cent of London's workforce is foreign-born. Changes are marked in the younger population. In England, 19 per cent of schoolchildren in maintained schools are from 'non-white' ethnic groups while in London the figure is 53 per cent.

9. John M. Keynes, *The End of Laissez-Faire: The Economic Consequences of the Peace* (London: Prometheus, 2004).

10. See HM Treasury, Budget 2011.

11. Howard Glennerster, *Financing the United Kingdom's Welfare States* (London: 2020 Public Services Trust, 2010).

12. The Centre for Economics and Business Research recently estimated that UK household disposable income will fall by two per cent this year, the largest decline since 1921.

13. Raymond Plant, *Paying for Progress: A New Politics of Tax for Public Spending* (London: Fabian Society, 1999).

14. Matthew Flinders, 'The Future of the State', in Varen Uberoi et al., *Options for Britain II: Cross-Cutting Policy Issues – Changes and Challenges* (Oxford: Wiley-Blackwell, 2010).

15. These proposals draw on recommendations made by the Plant Commission. See Raymond Plant, op. cit.

16. See the Mirrlees Review: *Reforming the Tax System for the 21st Century* (London: Institute for Fiscal Studies, 2010).

17. Ministry of Justice, *Compendium of Reoffending Statistics and Analysis*, October 2010.

18. Richard H. Tawney, *Equality* (London: George Allen & Unwin, 1931).

# Breaking the link between demography and destiny: how to restart the engine of social mobility

*Alan Milburn*

The pursuit of social mobility has become the new holy grail of public policy. Intractable levels of social inequality and, until recently at least, flatlining social mobility have seen parties from across the political spectrum pin their colours to the meritocratic mast. The Conservatives and Liberal Democrats in government have followed New Labour's lead in making one of their key tests of success the creation of a fairer, more fluid society. That is a development progressives should welcome.

The proof of the pudding is, of course, in the eating. It is not intentions that count in politics. It is actions and, above all, outcomes. I believe that making social mobility happen requires a new New Labour approach to social change in which the state both plays an active part and actively empowers citizens and communities to play theirs.

## Demography and destiny

Social mobility is about ensuring that each individual, regardless of their background, has an equal chance of progressing in terms of income or occupation. The task of breaking the transmission of disadvantage from one generation to the next is a long one. Britain seems to have lower levels of mobility than other comparable countries and our society has become more ossified, not less, over time. When social mobility stalls, social disadvantage becomes entrenched. There are clear correlations in our country between where you start out and where you end up. If you grow up in poverty the chances are you will live your life in poverty. If you end up in a low-achieving school the chances are you will end up in a low-achieving job. If you miss out on university the chances are you will miss out on a professional career. When people feel the aspirations they have for their families and communities are unfairly thwarted then social responsibility and individual endeavour are undermined. Poverty of aspiration then kicks in; social resentment builds up. If Britain is to avoid being a country where birth determines fate, we have to do much more to break the link between demography and destiny.

The last Labour government made much progress towards that goal, through policies like the minimum wage and the primacy accorded to education. Children who received free school meals had faster improving GCSE results than those who did not. Similarly, some ethnic minority groups, such as African-Caribbean boys, began to close the attainment gap. Primary schools in the poorest areas improved almost twice as fast as those in the most affluent. In secondary education, city academies improved results at four times the national rate despite having twice the number of pupils on free school meals.

The truth, however, is that the glass ceiling was raised but it was not broken. The education attainment gap between rich and poor narrowed but, as Leon Feinstein's work demonstrates so graphically, low-ability children from wealthy families still overtake high-ability children from poor families during primary school. Similarly, child poverty fell but was not eradicated. The gender pay gap narrowed but the top jobs still go to men, not women. The long-running decline in social mobility was halted but it has not reversed.

In good part, New Labour did not get as far as we would

have liked because unfreezing British society is a project that will take decades to achieve. But we compromised our own efforts by a fundamental inconsistency in approach. My experience in government of making change is that clarity and consistency are the foundation stones on which progress is built. For all our good intentions – and many groundbreaking initiatives – Labour in government did not have sufficient of either. At some points the priority was social mobility, at others the eradication of poverty. Tony Blair spoke to aspiration, Gordon Brown spoke of equality. Of course, we were always on the terrain of fairness. But we failed to accurately define what we were trying to achieve – in part because we seemed to be pursuing two notions simultaneously and sometimes independently: one was equality of opportunity, the other equality of outcome.

The problem with equality of outcome is self-evident. It would need to be imposed by a central authority and determined irrespective of work, effort or contribution. It would deny humanity, not liberate it. The problem with equality of opportunity is, in the words of R. H. Tawney, that the invitation for all to come to dinner takes place in the sure knowledge that circumstances would prevent most people from attending.

### Future challenges

Today's world is a very different place from Tawney's. A globalised capitalist economy and welfare state social democracy have successfully combined to eradicate many of the social evils that gave birth to progressive politics. Thankfully, poverty today is a stranger to most families in countries like ours. Laws protect workers and uphold gender and racial equality. It is not that disadvantage has been eradicated – it has not – but that it takes different forms. As Amartya Sen has noted, families and communities can suffer not only economic disadvantage but social, educational and cultural disadvantage as well. A more holistic agenda is needed. In my view, its focus needs to be on how we narrow the gap in life chances between the less well-off and the better-off so that those who have the aptitude and aspiration to do so get a fair opportunity to progress – regardless of their starting point in life.

Labour should make fairness in life chances our new progressive cause by empowering individual citizens and local communities to progress. The goal we should be aiming for is to reduce the extent to which a person's class or income is dependent on the class or income of their parents.

That will require us to be far sharper at pursuing a differentiated public policy approach to social mobility, one that recognises the fact that different groups in society have different starting points in life. One approach will need to focus on those, such as the 1.6 million children living in absolute poverty, who might be a minority in Britain but who are a scar on a wealthy modern society like our own. Sharply targeted interventions – including income transfers and financial incentives – will be needed if those families are ever to get onto the first rung of the social ladder. The other approach, however, is for the majority who are on the ladder but still encounter barriers that prevent them from moving up it. Here there is a need for a wider opportunity-creating agenda. These are distinct, although, of course, intimately related approaches. It is sometimes suggested that we have to choose between an economics-led or an opportunity-led agenda to social justice. The truth is both are needed. The trick is to avoid confusion between them. When that happens the result is not only poor public policy, it can also result in poor politics with the needs of lower-income families seemingly in conflict with the needs of middle-class ones. At the end of Brown's premiership that, sadly, seemed to be where we ended up.

So in future we need to be explicit that a society where opportunities are frozen rather than fluid hurts more than those at the very bottom end. It hurts the people Bill Clinton once famously called the 'forgotten middle class'. You can see that already with internships. They tend to go to the few who have the right connections, not the many who have talent. Yes, we need to beat poverty, but social progress – if it is to be for the many, not the few, in our society – also has to be based on unleashing aspiration.

## The role of government

We will need to accept that governments and others can do more to equalise opportunities throughout life, but in the end social mobility relies on individual drive and ambition. It is not something that can be given to people: it has to be won through their efforts and endeavours. Many of the things that determine life chances are, in any case, way beyond the reach of government: individual temperament, family life, social attitudes. And there are many questions that other institutions in civil society – employers, professions, universities to name but three – have to answer if social progress is to be achieved.

None of this is to suggest that government – the state – has no role.

When it comes to social change it is inconceivable that poverty or disadvantage can be overcome without the state playing its part. Poor people are hardly able to spend their way out of poverty. They need help with education, housing, training, childcare. That is why those on the new right of politics who continue to reject the role of the state are an ideological blast from the past, not a progressive politics of the future. The challenges of the modern world call for the state to play its part. They also call, however, for the state to know its place. It is only the state that can equalise opportunities throughout life and empower its citizens. Equally, only citizens can seize those opportunities and realise their own aspirations to progress.

So, if we are to make faster progress towards a more open mobile society in Britain, we will have to be far clearer about what governments can do and what they cannot. At the simplest level it is parents who bring up children, not governments. What parents do holds the key to what their children can do. Parental interest in a child's education has four times more influence on attainment by the age of sixteen than does socioeconomic background. Improving children's life chances means improving support for parents, building on the progress achieved by Sure Start, but reforming it so that it more actively empowers parents to make informed choices that are right for them and right for their kids. And since we know that children's self-esteem and expectations are in part shaped by the areas that they grow up in, and the social networks they take part in, empowering communities to develop will also help children to develop.

History suggests that social progress is made more from the bottom up than the top down. It is time to apply that lesson. Too often governments – including New Labour – have fallen for the fallacy that once the commanding heights of the state have been seized, through periodic elections, progressive change automatically follows. In truth this works neither for citizens nor for governments. People are left confused and disempowered. Governments end up nationalising responsibility when things go wrong without necessarily having the levers to put them right. In the future, progress depends on sharing responsibility with citizens so that they become insiders, not outsiders.

Such a change is in-keeping with the times. In a world of massive insecurity and constant change people are looking for greater control in their lives. At the same time public expectations have rightly moved up a gear. People nowadays are more informed and enquiring. Consumers are getting a taste for greater power and more say. The problem is that, while people may have become more empowered as consumers, they do not yet feel empowered as citizens. Ours remains a 'them and us' political system. It was framed in an era of elitism. Rulers ruled – and the ruled were grateful. Economic advance and universal education have swept aside both deference and ignorance. Now the internet redistributes knowledge and offers us the chance to be active participants rather than passive bystanders. Representative democracy worked for the last century. It is a more participatory democracy that will work in this.

And equity demands that it should be so. The sense of hopelessness that clouds the poorest communities grows out of disempowerment. Of course, beating crime, creating jobs, and rebuilding estates can help. But I believe that this cloud of despondency can only be dispelled through a modern participatory politics which allows both local communities and individual citizens to share more evenly and directly in power.

One example: as a teenager I lived in the west end of Newcastle upon Tyne. It is slap-bang in the middle of a decades-long failed experiment in urban regeneration. It is not through lack of effort, whether from local councils, development agencies or national governments. It is certainly not through lack of resources. In the last thirty years this four-mile stretch of urban Britain has received £500m in regeneration monies, much of it from the public purse. It almost breaks my heart to see what has gone wrong. I have seen houses rebuilt and refurbished only to be knocked down, and then seen the process repeated in a bewildering array of projects and programmes. Some achieved successes but overall they missed the mark. The population has fallen by one-third. One-quarter live with a limiting long-term illness, four in ten adults have no qualifications and one in two women are economically inactive. It is officially classified as among the most deprived communities in Britain.

There is no single reason why it all went wrong. Thatcherite recession broke the relationship between employment and housing that had conceived west Newcastle in the first place. As jobs left the area so did families, attracted by better schools and new homes springing up in more desirable parts of the city. And as the housing market slumped – at one time you could buy a flat there for £1 – landlords moved in. They lived off the housing benefit system and many cared little for who their tenants were or how they behaved. Meanwhile, the battery of successive government initiatives too often left skills, schooling and support for families playing second fiddle to rebuilding or refurbishing housing. But, most importantly of all, they failed to secure the buy-in of the community. There were, of course, worthy attempts to involve local residents. The complaint is not so much a lack of consultation – people complain of feeling consulted to death – as a lack of a sense of ownership of what is being done to their communities. The people who were supposed to benefit from these schemes were never fully involved either in their formulation or their implementation. It is a myth that such communities lack social capital. They are rich with voluntary groups and community leaders – often women – whose expertise could be far better harnessed in running housing estates, local parks and childcare centres.

The tragedy of west Newcastle graphically demonstrates that the old top-down agenda has run its course. In any future New Labour government the whole thrust of policy should be to empower people and their communities. Both local police and health services should be made directly accountable to local people through the ballot box. Local councils should be freed from much central government control by moving their system of financing from national taxes to local ones with local communities having the right through referenda to determine locally decided tax rates. As in the US, Canada, Australia and many other countries, locally elected bodies would be able to borrow either from the markets or through local bond issues. The aim would be to get local services better attuned to the needs of local communities. Where local services are failing, communities would have the legal right to have them replaced. Community courts and restorative justice should spearhead a reinvigorated effort to deter and prevent antisocial behaviour. Community-run mutual organisations could take over the running of local services like children's centres and housing estates.

### Education and employability
Empowerment should not be limited to communities. It should extend from the collective to the individual. Education policy is a case in point. Of course, there is no single lever on its own that can make Britain more socially mobile. No single organisation can make it happen either. It is far too complex an issue for that. It is as much about family networks as it is careers advice, individual aspirations as school standards, career development opportunities as university admission procedures. But the key is employability and education.

Social mobility speeded up in the 1950s thanks to a big change in the labour market: the shift from a manufacturing to a services economy drove demand for new skills and opened up new opportunities for professional and white-collar employment. More room at the top enabled millions of women and men to step up as a consequence. Social mobility has slowed down in the decades since, primarily because of another big change in the labour market: the move to a knowledge-based economy. Since the 1970s technological change has been skills-biased. People with higher skills have seen large increases in productivity and pay while those with low skills have experienced reduced demand for labour and lower average earnings. Today we have a segregated labour market. Those with skills and qualifications enjoy greater job security, higher levels of prosperity and better prospects of social advance. Those without skills find it hard to escape a world of constant insecurity, endemic low pay and little prospect of social progress.

Bridging this divide is the key to healing social division in our country. Study after study has come to the same conclusion. Time spent in education – including the vital early years – is the most important determinant of future social status and success in schools is the most important factor determining mobility. So aligning education policy with a broader approach to social mobility policy is key. The trick is to get the right balance between the state acting and the state activating. A future New Labour education reform programme should aim to do so.

First, since there is such a strong correlation globally between higher levels of education spending and higher levels of social mobility, education must remain top of New Labour's policy and political priority list. Whatever the short-term pressures for public spending reductions might be, education must remain a long-term priority for investment. A commitment to invest more of our national wealth, particularly in schools and early years, is a prerequisite for any government or party serious about making a reality of social mobility.

Second, since the chances of a child who is eligible for free school meals – roughly the poorest 15 per cent by family income – getting good school qualifications at age sixteen are less than one-third of those for better-off classmates, the twin objectives of New Labour's future education policy should be to raise educational standards and narrow educational inequalities. The one without the other will doom Britain to lasting social division. So any future government should sign up to explicit five-year targets for reducing the gap in attainment between children from less well-off and better-off backgrounds.

Third, since aspiration often has to be nurtured New Labour should commit to embedding social mobility programmes across all schools. Many are already doing so, but without a strong national drive it will remain a lottery as to which pupils get the chance to participate. A national 'raising aspiration' programme would build on the best practice of the Aimhigher (which raises awareness about higher education options and opportunities among school children) and the Gifted and Talented programmes, and involve professions, voluntary groups and universities in providing new opportunities for pupils with potential to visit universities (including with their parents); to take part in professional work taster sessions and summer schools; and to benefit from personal mentoring and school alumni support.

Fourth, since schools nowadays need to help students build up a CV of soft skills – because that is what employers and universities are increasingly looking for – all state schools should ensure every child is able to participate in a range of extracurricular activities. Of course, schools need to be judged on their success in delivering good GCSE and A-level results but they should also be assessed by Ofsted on the quality of their soft-skills programmes and on the progress pupils make between starting school, leaving school and their destinations after school. And since New Labour reforms in other parts of the public services saw performance improve where rewards follow results, we should find ways of incentivising schools financially to improve pupils' overall outcomes.

Fifth, since greater autonomy – in the shape of city academies, trust schools and the first parent-run schools – has produced better results, New Labour should guarantee that all schools have the chance to become more autonomous. There need be no single model. They could be academies or trusts, parent-owned or community-controlled, run by social enterprises formed by teachers or by chains run by voluntary, or for that matter, private sector bodies. The aim should be to make greater autonomy the norm not the exception among all schools.

That brings me to a final area for reform – empowering parents to choose good schools. Here we need to be especially candid. Selection by academic ability may have largely gone from our schools system, but selection by social position still lingers. There might not be an overt marketplace in education but there is a covert one. Look at the financial premium on house prices in areas served by the best-performing state schools. Better-off parents can afford to move house to get their children into a good school. They can afford extra tuition or private education. The more wealth you have the more choice over a good education you can buy.

No one should decry those parents. They are merely doing what all parents want to do – get their child into a really good school. The problem is that, despite all the progress that has been made, there still are not enough of them and poorer parents, because they lack the market power of their better-off counterparts, invariably find themselves at the back of the queue. That cannot be right and it has to change. There is more than one way of doing so. Both parent-run schools and the pupil premium, if implemented well, could make a big difference. But while they empower parents collectively, they do not empower parents individually. Neither policy gives the poorer parent a right that is readily available to the wealthier parent: the right of exit, the ability to take their child out of a poorly performing school and into a better one. None of the political parties have been prepared to grasp this nettle. It is time they did.

The next Labour government should accord individual parents with children in schools where performance is officially assessed as consistently poor – often in the poorest parts of the country – a new right to choose an alternative state school. Those parents would be given an education credit weighted to be worth perhaps 150 per cent of the cost of educating the child in their current school. They could then use the credit to persuade the better-performing school to admit their child. The admitting school would have a positive financial incentive to do so. Indeed, for children holding an education credit the alternative school would be free to go above its planned admission numbers – although of course it could decide to cap its expansion at what it considered an appropriate level.

The losing school would also face a sharp financial incentive to improve. It would not only lose a pupil, it would also lose the cash it cost to educate them. I know some will find this unacceptably harsh. And, of course, the education credit would need to be properly piloted, but it is simply not right – and we should no longer tolerate the fact – that too many children, invariably those from less well-off backgrounds, are still not getting access to the best education. Correcting that injustice means shifting the balance of power to put more choice in the hands of parents who the system currently disempowers. If education really is to be the motor of social mobility, then poorer parents, not just wealthier ones, need the power to fulfil their aspirations for their children.

We will not create a mobile society unless we create more of a level playing field of opportunity. My contention is that it is not ability that is unevenly distributed in our society, it is opportunity. The core purpose of any modern progressive government should be this: to break down barriers of entrenched privilege and vested interest; to open up avenues of advancement so they are available to all, not just some; to redistribute power and opportunity in our society; to narrow the gap in life chances in our country. That is what New Labour should be working in in its next phase to achieve.

# Eliminating 'power failures': a new agenda for tackling inequality

*Liam Byrne*

When Tony Blair made his first speech as Prime Minister, he stood on an estate in Southwark and said concentrations of poverty and unemployment represent 'the greatest challenge for any democratic government'. How prophetic those words turned out to be. We are a party that is terrifically proud of our record and we become prouder every day we see the damage this government is doing.

One of the reasons for that is that our record of fighting poverty was, quite literally, one of the best in the world. When the Organisation for Economic Cooperation and Development studied its members in 2008, the UK was one of the only countries where median household income continued to rise – and income inequality declined.[1]

However, by the end of 2009 my work at the Treasury was beginning to uncover the problem that came to be called the 'squeezed middle'. We can now date the problem back to 2004–5; yet even so, for the lion's share of Labour's time in office we could point to rising productivity growth, rising wages and median family incomes up by a quarter over our time in office – an almost unprecedented achievement.

The numbers, the headlines, the lines to take, never quite seem to do justice to the material transformation of lives in Britain, but nonetheless, they are worth recalling:

- 2.8 million more people in work than there were in 1998;
- 500,000 fewer children now in income poverty. Indeed, new figures show that in the last year of the Labour government (2008-9–2009-10) 200,000 children were lifted from relative poverty. Between 1998 and 2010, the percentage of children in relative poverty fell by 6 per cent – or 900,000;
- The poverty rate for pensioners down by one-third;
- A doubling of the annual growth rate of the income of the poorest 20 per cent.

Is that a big deal? Well, compare our record to the policies of a neoconservative administration across the Atlantic, the government of George W. Bush. After the progress of the Clinton–Gore years, American families have gone backwards since 2000: real median household income actually fell by over $1,200 year as the link between rising productivity and rising wages snapped.[2] America was getting richer – but the wealth was simply not shared among ordinary people. As Paul Krugman recently put it: 'The value of output an average worker produces in an hour has risen almost 50 per cent since 1973. Yet the growing concentration of income in the hands of a small minority has proceeded so rapidly that we're not sure whether the typical American has gained anything from rising productivity.'[3]

So, yes, our achievement was a very big deal. But there is always a 'but' for the Labour Party. 'Progress,' said Nye Bevan in the only book he ever wrote, 'is not the elimination of struggle, but rather a change in its terms.'[4] The work that there is still to complete is staggering – and now, as we look ahead to 2015, it is already clear that we will have huge global forces ranged against equality and a very different political climate in which we have to build a new kind of consensus for a Labour vision of the welfare state.

## The global economic challenge

Let me start with the politics. When Labour was at its strongest, we governed on the basis of a simple premise: that economic efficiency can go hand in hand with social justice. The challenge for us, however, is that by the end of our time in office, people saw something rather different: economic injustice and social inefficiency. Bankers and corporate chieftains running off with massive salaries and bonuses on the one hand, and rising welfare bills on the other.

At the heart of this problem was the simple fact that while we got the economics of globalisation right, we got the politics wrong. Globally, the greatest achievement of the progressive left over the last two decades was to act as co-authors of the globalisation which has transformed the wealth and prosperity of the world, and in turn lifted hundreds of millions of people out of poverty.

But, at times we looked too comfortable, too cosy you might say, with the newly powerful that this new globalisation created. We did not do enough to stand alongside the newly powerless. We were basically too optimistic about the financial markets' ability or ambition to regulate themselves well, and too optimistic that the undoubted gains from global growth would distribute themselves fairly. There is no better emblem of all this than the banking sector, which became the most dangerous new concentration of unaccountable power.

By the end of the twentieth century, globalisation had set the stage for the greatest 'capital flow bonanza' in economic history. After the Asian crisis of the late 1990s, surplus nations like China exported hard and saved harder. Some $7tn of foreign exchange reserves were amassed, and much of it headed towards US Treasury bills.[5] Faster international capital flows helped make sure that most of the West's banking system had a stake in America's 'financial innovation', generally known by its better moniker 'subprime debt'. Indeed some 40-60 per cent of securities generated by US financial institutions ended up

in portfolios of foreign investors.[6] In turn, these flows underpinned a banking system that took on dramatic amounts of
new debt. In the US, financial sector debt rose from 22 per
cent of GDP to 117 per cent. By June 2008, leverage ratios at
European banks had grown gigantically; Credit Suisse stood at
three to one. ING stood at forty-nine to one. Deutsche Bank
stood at fifty-three to one. Barclays stood at sixty-one to one.
As Mervyn King recently pointed out, UK bank balance sheets
were, until the Second World War, stable at around 50 per cent
of GDP. But over the last fifty years, they have ballooned to
five times the size of our economy, and alongside them has
grown a shadow banking system $7tn in size.[7]

When this system crashed it destroyed one million jobs,
and £400bn of UK net wealth – most of it household wealth.[8]
So, as Ed Balls has argued, we did not challenge or control
that new private power effectively enough. We got the politics of globalisation wrong.

While this banking boom was gathering pace, wages
for ordinary workers were coming under huge pressure. In
Labour's first five years in office, between 1997 and 2001,
workers' share of national earnings rose from 68 per cent to
around its post-war average of 73.5 per cent.[9] But then the
trend went into reverse. Productivity kept on rising – by over
9 per cent between 2001 and 2008 – but workers' share of
national earnings fell, from 73.5 per cent to 69.6 per cent.
Over the same period, corporate Britain saw its rate of return
soar – from 11.8 per cent in 2001 to 14 per cent in 2008.

What did that mean for workers? In 2009, workers' share of
national earnings was around £768bn. Yet if workers' share of
the national economic pie had matched the post-war averages,
an extra £23.4bn would have ended up in people's pay packets.

This new inequality – of power, of reward – fuels a sense
among most voters that they no longer get out of government
what they put in. Most still feel that government is important. A majority prefer a government that tries to tackle our

national problems than a government that simply leaves the pitch. But, voters feel there would be a lot more help available for the responsible, for those who do the right thing, if we stopped subsidising the irresponsible who do the wrong thing. That is why we have to modernise the welfare state to restore a sense of the 'something-for-something' deal.

If we look ahead to the economics of 2015, global growth is likely to be weak. The eurozone remains beset with trouble. Business leaders in Germany are highly cautious about the prospects for sustaining German growth. America is still to publish, never mind implement, a deficit-reduction plan of its own. Regional integration in Asia – a key objective of China's new five-year plan – may fuel a faster and faster 'race to the bottom' as production is relocated from the overheating coastal areas to cheaper inland China, Vietnam and Bangladesh.[10] The fiscal latitude of any future Labour government will be narrow. If we suppose that George Osborne persists with his deficit-reduction plan, and removes the structural deficit entirely in five years, we will still have debt as a proportion of GDP at 60 per cent.

These are the political and economic realities of the world in which a new Labour government will have to think about reversing inequality. I think we can conclude the old methods are unlikely to be available – even if they still worked. So I would like to propose a renewed approach. It is not really inspired by Whitehall, or Westminster, but by Hodge Hill, the constituency I have served for the last seven years.

### Fighting poverty from the bottom up
Like much of the Midlands, the ancient history of my constituency is lost history; it is a place that was forged in the Industrial Revolution. Its life was animated by the great entrepreneurs of the nineteenth century; industrial and civic giants like Joseph Wright, William Morris and Lord Norton.

But its life has been changed by their modern successors; the entrepreneurs in the wider story of globalisation who have moved industries, firms, jobs and livelihoods elsewhere and left behind a legacy of unemployment and poverty.

Today, Hodge Hill has the second highest unemployment rate in the country and the highest youth unemployment. These are the circumstances which have shaped my political life, priorities, outlook on the future and my determination to see the fight against poverty as a cause we in our party take the responsibility to lead.

And, it is my constituency that has taught me that if we want to roll back inequality, we have to roll out power. This means moving beyond our old argument that equality of opportunity is enough. It is not.

Why do I say this? A couple of years ago, we marked the 150th anniversary of J. S. Mill's *On Liberty*, the founder of the liberal tradition. It is a tradition of freedom, in my view, inestimably improved in more recent times, first by John Rawls and now Amartya Sen.

It has been Sen, in particular, who has argued that for freedom to be truly meaningful we must deliver a far better equality in '"substantive freedoms" – the capabilities – to choose a life that one has reason to value'. This argument takes us beyond the idea that poverty is simply the absence of income – beyond the notion that equality of opportunity is on its own enough. It tells us that both income and opportunity might get you to the starting line in life, but without capabilities – what I would call 'powers' – you will only get so far down the track, stopping perhaps a long way short of your ambitions, or indeed your potential.

This emphasis on capability or power is absolutely vital. It recognises that we must break out of a confined and contorted debate about simply 'equality of outcomes' and the thin notion of an equal place at the starting line of a race that is ultimately fixed. Crucially, it takes us beyond the idea that poverty is simply the absence of income.

Not long after it was published, I met Sen at Harvard to talk about his book, *An Idea of Justice*. He summarised for me the problem of talking simply about opportunity: 'If many things are open to me I have opportunity to do them if only I could, but if I'm illiterate and education has been neglected [then] I might not be able to use that opportunity ... without the help of the state and the society, which allows me to acquire the education, which allows me to use the opportunity, I won't have any great use of that opportunity.'[11]

This argument stresses the reality that a fair distribution of power is something that cannot be frozen in aspic. We do not fix it and then stop. We do not get people up to a fixed threshold of power or capability and then halt. Rather, the capabilities or powers that people need to thrive, to live that life that they have reason to value, is something that has to advance as society advances: 'Human life consists of doing certain things ... to be able to take part in the life of the community, to be able to talk about subjects that interest me – in all kinds of ways there are different freedoms that affect our lives and you assess what our lives are like by looking at the various freedoms we have ... These freedoms ... are the human capabilities that we are looking at. Capability is just looking, saying, don't try to assess society in a way that is detached from the lives and freedoms of the people.'[12]

This argument corresponds very much with what I witness in Hodge Hill, where the thing that troubles me most are the 'power failures' which stop my constituents moving up in life. The lack of power to walk where you might chose for fear of crime. The lack of power to go to college even though you have the dreams, the talent, the grades. The lack of power to get a job even though you want a better life for you and your family. The lack of power to be able to lead a life that you have a reason to choose.

## The power to work

This perspective is important because it reminds us that, in the battle for equality, a simple measure of equality of income does not mean enough. A more basic equality of power would mean far more. This takes us to a far more sophisticated and meaningful agenda for action against poverty. Crucially, it tells you that if you want to tackle poverty you have to give people the real power to work: to get a job, to advance and not to worry constantly about being laid off, or losing a shift.

A simple illustration. If we raised the employment rate of just one ward in Hodge Hill to the national average, we would bring in £100m of extra wages each year. No government regeneration programme could ever match that. That is why Labour is, and always will be, the party of full employment.

But to give people the power to do the big things often means giving them the power over the small things: skills, transport links, childcare. To this picture we have to add real action to boost the supply of jobs, which is why John Denham's work exploring ways of backing small and medium enterprises and entrepreneurs, and making the UK a more attractive place to invest, is so important.

But fixing power failures is about more than just work. If you want a community to do better, then the community has to act as the authors of its own shared future. However, communities cannot function properly and people cannot work together if they fear leaving their homes at night because the community is riddled with crime, drugs and distrust. What we found in Hodge Hill is that we were going to make no progress in building an alliance of citizens for a richer place unless we got crime sorted out first.

That is why this was my first campaign. Meeting after meeting with local residents spent literally mapping the hot-spots, grot-spots and places where the drug dealers dwelt. Building the dossiers for police action. So, neighbourhood policing and community justice are not simply community safety issues. They are fundamental to the fight against poverty. Respect, I came to learn, is the ground-floor of renewal.

Further, if we want to fix these power failures for the future, then we need young people to have the self-confidence and savoir-faire to actually pursue their ambitions beyond school. For five years I have worked with young people, local second-ary schools, the University of Birmingham and the Templeton Foundation to study why so few of our young people go to university – when my work with young people told me that their top priority for new investment was learning a new skill. I found no shortage of aspiration. Some 80 per cent of our young people want to go to college.

But what we found is that these young people lacked a sense of how the world works. What James Arthur, who led our Templeton Foundation-funded research, described to me as the lack of a 'mental map' of how to get on in life. This is a roadblock for our young people. It is a power failure. To break it down our young people want to develop, not only their understanding of the things around them, but an understand-ing of the things inside them, self-confidence, self-esteem, ambition, motivation and nerve. These are things that some, but not all, of us were lucky to get from our parents; things that a small few often get from the finest public schools.

My point here is that to roll back poverty we have to roll out power and it is an agenda that stretches far beyond the boundaries of a debate about simply the future of the welfare state.

So what is needed? When I met with Sen he left me with an intriguing idea. That if we want to answer the question of what powers people need today, you need something of a national conversation. So, in the interests of getting that conversation going, here is a first list of just what capabilities or powers a centre-left government in the UK might wish for its citizens.[13] It was drawn up by a team in the Treasury and

Cabinet Office, which I asked to examine all of our public service targets against a handful of basic powers we want to see in the hands of citizens.

Some capabilities are difficult to measure and deliver such as 'family life' and 'aspirations' – but as a set of objectives which we should strive to achieve, it is not a bad place to start:

- To survive and have good health;
- To be skilled and knowledgeable e.g. to be able to read, write, communicate, be numerate;
- To have a good job which brings in a sufficient income;
- To have a decent place to live;
- To be free from fear or attack;
- To have a strong, supportive family life;
- To be part of a strong, active community;
- To have a healthy, sustainable natural environment;
- To be able to move around and access different places easily;
- To have aspirations for the future.

## Renewing the welfare state

The challenge now, though, is to build a political consensus for the kind of arguments made here. Reform of the welfare state is one of the starting points. Right now the Tories are speaking to the country's sense of pessimism. They are happy to play into a dialogue of the depressed.

Sometimes, when I listen to the rhetoric of this government, I am reminded of Ronald Reagan and his attack on 'welfare queens' thirty years ago. Reagan was determined to dismantle Lyndon Johnson's Great Society. Running for the presidency in 1976, he told the story of a woman from Chicago's South Side who he alleged had eighty names, thirty addresses, twelve social security numbers and was claiming social security, food stamps and welfare under every alias. Reagan never named her, but his myth inspired a movement that started with a call to responsibility and ended by ignoring cries for help as he set about the biggest attack on the measures to promote equality in American history.

We have to hope this government will not repeat Reagan's mistake. The signs, however, do not look good. The Chancellor has proposed a budget that puts 200,000 more people out of work, puts the benefits bill up by £12.5bn, and borrows £43bn more than planned to pay for it all. The result is a stealth squeeze of people's tax credits, help with childcare, university bills, travel bills and an attack on the most vulnerable people in our society.

We have to offer a different vision for the welfare state that rejuvenates a sense among the majority that government can do good. This is far from impossible. While it is true that the public feels that governments waste a lot of money, a large majority of people still feel that the solution to the problems we face today is not less government but a different kind of government; a government that restores a 'something-for-something' deal, and a sense of just deserts and reciprocity.

Franklin Roosevelt once spoke passionately of the democracy of opportunity: a place where everyone, no matter who you were or where you came from, if you worked hard you deserved to do well. Today, people want alongside that democracy of opportunity, a democracy of responsibility. Where we do not subsidise those who break the rules whether they are in the boardroom or on benefits, and where we instead reward those who do the right thing.

That means that we have to renew the welfare state so that it more clearly combines an attack on poverty with a rejuvenation of those 'social insurance instincts' that helped forge it in the first place. This is not easy – as some commentators have already pointed out. [14] The contributory principle only covers about 10 per cent of working age benefits today.

But we can make progress by exploring three ideas.

First, is the idea of looking at reward for contribution in the widest sense. That is why Ed Miliband has said we should explore the way we reward those who do the right thing, for example by looking again at the way we allocate social housing. These are ideas that innovative local authorities, like Newham and Manchester, are now exploring. In essence, your place in the queue is affected by whether you are doing the right thing, getting a job, paying taxes, being a good tenant and neighbour, and so on.

Add to this the trend for more and more people to become self-employed – not least as firms push down fixed costs and move the risks of variable demand onto a more self-employed work-force. Nearly 750,000 more people have become self-employed in the last decade. Thus as more and more higher earners face the uncertainties of unemployment, we need to examine whether there is a way of protecting people's income in the first period they are out of work, as they do so successfully in Denmark. And this is an approach that could have widespread public support: 67 per cent of people in our private polling say that people with a history of paying into the benefits system should get a higher level of support if they lose their job.

Third, we need to look at the new 'lifecycle of savings'. Young people now can expect to have many more jobs in their lifetime than their parents. Our polling shows that the public is really worried about how hard it has become for young people to earn enough to pay off their college debts, save for a deposit for a house and then save up for a pension. Today, families face a radically new lifecycle for savings – with tuition fees to pay back, big mortgage deposits to save for, and the cost of social care and a pension that needs to nourish them far longer in old age. We have to ask how the welfare state is helping ordinary working people face new risks.

To this picture of new risks, we have to look at whether there are new ways in which welfare services can be delivered in a way that strengthens relationships in society. How can we do more to encourage mutuals, co-ops, social enterprises, organisations that are powered by the value of human relationships, to help deliver a stronger welfare system in the future?

If we can propose reforms that speak to these instincts, we can build far bigger alliances for progressive politics. Why? Because, quite simply, an approach that puts the rejuvenation of social relationships and mutual obligations centrestage is more likely to command a wider political consensus. It connects to a different tradition of freedom which takes account of some of the legitimate criticisms made by the new right of old-fashioned welfare programmes.

Samuel Bowles and Herbert Gintis, developing the work of Robert Axelrod and others, underlined how absolutely central this notion of reciprocity is for retaining support for progressive values: 'The welfare state is in trouble, not because selfishness is rampant (it is not) but because many egalitarian programmes no longer evoke, and sometimes now offend, deeply held notions of fairness, encompassing both reciprocity and generosity, but stopping far short of unconditional altruism towards the less well-off.'[15]

This approach speaks not to 'unconditional altrusim' but a 'something-for-something' deal. Nick Pearce of ippr recently put the argument like this: 'In focusing almost exclusively on outcomes, reform strategies may miss important insights about how the procedures that govern public services – and in particular their fairness – elicit particular responses from the public.'[16]

## Capabilities for all

I think we can roll back poverty by rolling out power, and I think we can build a political consensus for the kind of values we support, by reforming the welfare state to restore a sense of reciprocity and mutual obligation.

But this argument about power has wider importance for the left.

We should be the party that tells an optimistic account of our national renewal and our prospects in a world that is going to be transformed again in the next thirty years. By 2050, China, India, Brazil, Egypt, the Philippines, Indonesia, Iran, Mexico and others will account for 60 per cent of global GDP in a surge of growth that could push two billion people into the global middle class – around 70 per cent of these in India and China.[17] That could create incredible demand for the kind of things we make and sell.

The challenge for Labour is to make sure that this new wealth is not wealth concentrated in the hands of the few. Reform of our welfare system and a new agenda for a determined rollout of power in our country is the best guarantee that we will succeed.

1.  OECD, *Growing Unequal? Income Distribution and Poverty in OECD Countries* (Paris: OECD, 2008).

2.  Analysis courtesy of the Centre for American Progress.

3.  Paul Krugman, *Conscience of a Liberal* (New York: Norton, 2007).

4.  Aneurin Bevan, *In Place of Fear* (London: Heinemann, 1952).

5.  Such was the wall of demand for Treasury bills, that by August 2005, Alan Greenspan was pondering a 'conundrum'. The Fed had raised interest rates from 1 to 3 per cent. But the long-term rate on US Treasury bills was not rising, it was falling, from 4.9 per cent to under 4 per cent. As the Fed raised the headline interest rates between 2004 and 2006, from 1 per cent to 5.25 per cent, long term rates and mortgage rates barely moved.

6.  Nouriel Roubini, *Crisis Economics: A Crash Course in the Future of Finance* (London: Allen Lane, 2010). Roubini estimates that half of the collateralised debt obligations and mortgage backed securities created in America were held by foreign investors.

7.  Mervyn King, Second Bagehot Lecture, Buttonwood Gathering, New York City, 25 October 2010.

8.  Office for National Statistics, *Economic Review*, August 2010.

9.  Analysis commissioned by Liam Byrne from the House of Commons library reveals that broadly speaking, since 1948, British workers have laid hands on around 73 per cent of our national earnings.

10. See, for example, Cheng Siwei, speech to the Pacific Economic Cooperation Council's General Meeting, 13 May 2009.

11. Liam Byrne, interview with Amartya Sen at HM Treasury, 3 September 2009.

12. Ibid.

13. Martha Nussbaum has also had a crack at drawing up a similar list. Martha Nussbaum, *Women and Human Development: The Capabilities Approach* (Cambridge: Cambridge University Press, 2000).

14. Nick Pearce, 'The limits of the contributory principle', ippr, 14 June 2011. www.ippr.org

15. See Samuel Bowles and Herbert Gintis, 'Is Equality Passé? Homo Reciprocans and the Future of Egalitarian Politics', *Boston Review* (1998) vol. 23, no. 6, pp. 4–25.

16. Nick Pearce, 'Fair Rules: Rethinking Fairness', *Public Policy Research* (2007) vol. 14, no. 1, pp. 11–22.

17. See for example Goldman Sachs analysis.

# Securing social justice:
## savings and pensions for all

*Rachel Reeves*

In Britain today the distribution of wealth is fundamentally unequal, with the top 1 per cent of people holding nearly one-quarter of all assets. We have a persistent problem of undersaving among Britons – 13 per cent of people have no savings at all and out of the G7 countries only the US saves less. As a proportion of GDP, Germany and Japan save almost double what we put away. And we now have a government that – by scrapping child trust funds, the Saving Gateway and through its treatment of savings in its reform of the benefits system – does not recognise the contribution that assets make in terms of empowering people and families.

Savings and assets make a huge difference to our opportunities. They provide options – to go into further education, rent or buy a house, perhaps start a business, buy Christmas presents for the family or go on holiday. They determine options on redundancy, whether an individual is able to change jobs or end up in debt in an emergency like a car breakdown or illness. It can also mean the difference between drawing on savings and borrowing from high-cost lenders. Pension savings might make the difference between taking on part-time work or taking early retirement. And they can then determine whether individuals are able to keep their home and, for example, provide for social care.

Undersaving and asset inequality form a collective problem too: without sufficient private resources more people will rely on welfare in tough times and poverty, including pensioner poverty, is a greater risk.

Crucially, savings and assets can act as a springboard or safety net throughout our working lives – removing insecurity around unexpected payments and providing the platform on which social mobility is based. Asset-based welfare, or asset-based empowerment, sees the role of the state as a facilitator, building the framework in which individuals can make their own decisions and choose to live the life they want.

Therefore, when we return to power an asset-based approach to social policy must be at the heart of Labour's strategy for improving equality and opportunity. The welfare system is a crucial tool for realising social justice and equality – it provides a minimum quality of life and is a floor upon which individuals can build their lives, as the Beveridge Report set out at the creation of the welfare state. As David Blunkett has said in his writings on asset-based welfare 'individuals must have the opportunity to accumulate and control assets in order to have equal life chances. We must ensure that assets, such as savings, are spread widely through society.'

### A nation of undersavers

We are not talking just about emergency or 'rainy day' situations, but for retirement, too. The average monthly income for couples in retirement is £564. This compares with over £2,000 for the average UK family. Though that is a significant increase from 1997, it is still not enough to give people meaningful options. According to research from Scottish Widows, 20 per cent of people are not saving for their retirement and only 51 per cent are making sufficient provision for their retirement.

And there are significant distributional issues: undersaving is most acute among the lowest earners, and this is the case across both the public and private sectors. The highest proportion of those without pension savings is among employees with the lowest earnings. That means that across all employees 87 per cent of those earning less than £5,200 per year have no non-state pension provision. This compares with 73 per cent of those earning between £5,200 and £10,400 per year; 68 per cent of those earning between £10,400 and £15,600; 55 per cent of those earning between £15,600 and £20,800; 44 per cent of those earning between £20,800 and £26,000; 35 per cent of those earnings between £26,000 and £31, 2000; and just 23 per cent of those earning above £31,200 per year. In the private sector, over 60 per cent of employees on average earnings have no non-state pension provision. That number rises to over 70 per cent for people earning just less than £20,000.

These low levels of personal savings are not a new phenomenon. For the last thirty years we have been saving less than 20 per cent of GDP, but the share of income saved has gradually fallen from over 18 per cent in 1980 to just 12 per cent in 2010. Research from the Institute for Fiscal Studies has shown that the run-up to the financial crisis saw families accumulating very little liquid wealth between 2000 and 2005, and that this was particularly stark among 'younger families and those on the lowest incomes'.

The IFS also estimated that, in real terms, incomes fell by 3.8 per cent in 2010–11, and that household incomes will continue to fall in real terms over the coming three years. The immediate outlook does not look good for households addressing their lack of savings.

In addition to the immediate challenges in a world of squeezed living standards, a substantial part of the problem is a result of more fundamental – and complex – structures.

First, the pension system that we have today was designed in the 1940s for the 1940s. This was a time when men made up almost 70 per cent of the workforce, part-time workers accounted for just 4 per cent of the workforce and most people entered the workforce into what they considered to be a 'job for life'. We have seen a huge change over the last sixty years: in 1951, 40 per cent of women aged 15–64 were economically active, compared to 71 per cent today. And in 1951, virtually no men worked part-time, compared with 13 per cent today, and for women, the proportion has increased from 25 per cent to 44 per cent. Labour made inroads into reforming the pension and savings system to reflect these changes – particularly recognising the role of women as mothers and carers for the state pension – but problems persist, including for occupational pensions.

Second, while Labour began to experiment with the idea of an asset-based welfare system when in government (explored in further detail in the next section), thanks to the coalition government we are returning to a welfare state that does not recognise the role that assets and savings play in building opportunity and empowerment. And, worryingly, the idea of savings for lower-income earners is being implicitly discouraged in its reform of the welfare system, with the introduction of a £16,000 savings cap on eligibility for universal credit, which will ultimately punish – or disincentivise – low-income working families who want to save for the future.

Third, the tax relief structure is fundamentally flawed and, one could argue, unfair, acting as a significant factor contributing to the distributional problems of saving: the incentives to save offered to low-to-middle income families through the tax relief system are very limited. HM Revenue & Customs estimate that around £19.7bn of tax relief was given to pension contributions across all taxpayers in 2009–10, and within this total an estimated two-thirds of the relief was on contributions made by higher-rate tax payers.

### Labour's record in government
Against the backdrop of very low rates of saving and a period where incomes grew substantially, but financial wealth, at least for most households, barely increased at all, Labour set out on a series of reforms, and it is important to understand what

we achieved in order to lay out the priorities for empowering people through assets and savings when we return to power.

*Pension system*

When Labour came to power in 1997, the immediate priority was tackling unacceptable levels of pensioner poverty. Between 1997 and 2010, 1.1 million pensioners were lifted out of poverty, and pensioner poverty now stands at its lowest level for almost thirty years.

In addition, the Labour government recognised the need to instigate reform of the state pension system. So in 2002, Labour established the Pensions Commission to look into the undersaving problem in the context of 'a new pension settlement for the twenty-first century'. The result was the Turner Report, which, among other things, recommended the introduction of automatic-enrolment whereby every employer is required to enrol their employees (earning above a minimum threshold) into a pension scheme and to pay into that scheme.

Labour legislated for this in the Pensions Act of 2007 and 2008 and auto-enrolment will roll out from 2012. The result will be up to seven million people who previously were not saving, now putting something aside for their retirement. In the pensions bill, the coalition government is in the process of watering down the scheme, characteristically pulling the scheme away from up to 1.5 million people – mostly women – by raising the earnings threshold at which employees will be auto-enrolled and by introducing a three-month waiting period before employees are enrolled.

*Welfare system*

In government, Labour also recognised the role that assets have in welfare policy. It understood the reality of what social research had been telling us, specifically, as an ippr report in 2006 put it, that 'an asset can act as a springboard, working not just to alleviate immediate poverty (as income assistance can do), but also to transform the opportunities available to an individual.'[1]

A number of Labour reforms were designed to enable increasing numbers of people to share in the benefits of asset ownership, the biggest of which was the child trust fund. The child trust fund acts as a long-term tax-free savings account designed to ensure that all young people can have access to assets and a financial foundation at the start of their adult lives.

The fact that a new mother leaves hospital with forms to easily access a platform for saving from day one of their child's life was a significant nudge to save: 73 per cent of eligible parents took advantage of this baby bond, creating 5.8 million accounts. £700,000 a week was put away with child trust funds in 2010 according to the Children's Mutual, and up to 50 per cent of families who opened accounts for their children were saving every month. Using the full tax-free allowance of £1,200 a year, savings could be built up to cover the cost of university, set up a small business or provide the deposit for a house by the time the child is eighteen. Savings of around £50 a month from birth would potentially generate a pot of some £20,000 on the child's eighteenth birthday. That is potentially life-changing.

In addition, the Labour government introduced the Saving Gateway, designed to match the savings of people on low incomes with public funds. It was aimed to get the poorest saving, by adding 50p to every £1 saved in the programme, and aimed to reach eight million people on benefits and on tax credits. The Saving Gateway would have provided up to £300 a year in matched funding for people putting away money for the future. The Saving Gateway and child trust fund offered tangible financial benefits for those who traditionally have the fewest assets, as well as building a habit of saving among low-income groups, parents and children alike. But these benefits were not recognised by the coalition government and were scrapped.

Before their abolition, these schemes saw the government's role increase as an active supporter in encouraging savings. By putting forward some direct support such as the child trust fund, and tying other support to long-term savings, the government created steps to overcome the barriers to savings. But with nudges like this towards individual saving, and soon through Labour's policy of auto-enrolment into pensions, attitudes can be slowly modified and saving can become a habit rather than an exception.

## A future agenda for Labour

The big question for the next Labour government is how it will maintain and build on the momentum that was created between 1997 and 2010, as well as tackling what else is needed to address the structural barriers to saving that exist. Critically, what can be done to help empower people to build up assets and to save to empower them to expand their options? In this section, I set out three priority areas: ensuring automatic-enrolment is a success; renewing the asset-based welfare system, including finding ways to get at the normally hard-to-reach groups such as through credit unions; and reform of the tax relief system for saving.

### *Ensuring automatic-enrolment is a success*

We must ensure that automatic-enrolment is a success and that it achieves what it sets out to do. That is, ensuring that the auto-enrolment framework gets people on modest-to-middle incomes, often in small businesses, saving for their retirement.

The watering-down of the pensions bill will be a retrograde step, but we must be clear that the priority will be to let the rollout get under way in 2012. There will inevitably be teething problems that will be identified and dealt with, but equally as important will be the review planned for 2017 in the next parliament. This review must revisit some of the questions that are raised by auto-enrolment now, in terms of who is excluded, and we must also be extremely aware of any further rises in the earnings threshold as the income tax threshold rises.

There are some other core questions that must also be addressed in the review in order to make auto-enrolment the success that it can be. Currently, those with multiple jobs with no one job earning above the earnings limit are not automatically enrolled – and this should be looked at so that these people are also entitled to be automatically enrolled, recognising that, increasingly, people have more than one job and more volatile work patterns.

The industry must also address the question of 'annuitising' small pots of money – i.e. turning a pot of money into an annual income when they retire. This is something that will become increasingly important as the first of those to benefit from auto-enrolment start to retire. Many people are likely to have very small pots after just a few years in the workplace under automatic-enrolment and, at the moment, due to the relative cost of annuitising small pots of money, pension providers are often reluctant to annuitise amounts below £5,000. This will need to be addressed, including making it easier to merge small pots to ensure people can get meaningful pensions out of their savings.

Alongside automatic-enrolment, the previous government also set out the proposals for the National Employment Savings Trust, an occupational pension scheme which was set up to ensure all employers have access to a simple scheme for the employees that they will need to auto-enrol. There will be issues here that need to be addressed too. In particular, the cap on annual contributions into NEST accounts that currently exists will need to be reviewed if we want people to build up adequate retirement incomes, as will the restriction on savers' ability to transfer amounts of money in and out of the scheme. This could also help significantly with the challenge of annuitising small pots of money and of excessive charges in some occupational pension schemes, especially for people with lots of small pots with different providers built up in different jobs.

*Renewing asset-based economics*

Second, and perhaps a much bigger challenge, is that of renewing the asset-based welfare system that the Labour government embraced through the introduction of child trust funds and the Saving Gateway. The government has scrapped these on the grounds that they are unaffordable, but in doing so it has missed the point that it is the infrastructure – for example, of each child having a unique account number created for them at birth – that counts as much, if not more, than the actual sum of money given by the government to be invested. For example, in principle, the 'nudge' and success of the child trust funds work with only a very small contribution from government, because it is the framework that is given to parents that is the key to encouraging saving.

However, as we renew our approach it is right to look at how we could improve it. Even though the child trust fund encouraged saving for children in many low-income households it would be wrong to say it reached all those it was intended to reach, and the next Labour government will need to develop new and innovative ways of reaching those for whom the conventional ways of saving, through for example banks and building societies, do not work.

One way to achieve this is through credit union networks, which can assist in broadening and widening savings on a local, community basis. Credit unions are cooperative financial unions owned and controlled by members that lend within the union. And on a personal level, I have seen the difference that credit unions make to neighbourhoods when they are local and active.

In my area of Leeds two credit unions are available and provide a stable footing for savings for people otherwise at risk of turning to loan sharks and entering dangerous spirals of debt. Leeds City Credit Union operates from one-stop centres, the location where benefits, libraries and advice are delivered, while Bramley Credit Union works from a community centre, church and school in a small area within west Leeds. These credit unions know the needs and priorities of their members, and can tailor their solutions to the communities they serve.

If we can tie the Saving Gateway and child trust fund mechanisms to local community-based solutions in this way we can empower individuals, and free communities from the ties of debt and welfare. It is something that the mutual sector and credit unions can offer which the state cannot. Current schemes for financial education – funded by the financial services industry and government – could be delivered effectively by funding schemes led by credit unions at the community level and linked to the success of building assets, while decreasing the reliance on high-cost credit.

There are other areas where credit unions and mutuals are better placed than the state to provide the most appropriate solution to the problems we face. Many people are simply unaware that they are chronically undersaving, and are unaware of the consequences this will have on their lives further down the road. Because credit unions and mutuals are embedded within their communities, they are uniquely placed to take the role of trusted information distributor to address the information gap which exists across large segments of the population. They can provide localised and individualised information, informing people of the long-term benefits of saving, helping them achieve realistic objectives.

If credit unions are to expand into this much larger role we also have to address the barriers which currently limit their size. One of the main challenges that credit unions face is building up and sustaining a strong branch presence due to the significant costs associated. Against the reality of declining numbers of local branches of high street banks, the historic underserving of rural communities and poorer areas by banks, and the importance of face-to-face interaction to successfully engage those with less experience of financial services and savings, building up a strong local credit union presence in communities across the UK has to be a priority if the objective of widening access to savings and assets is to be realised.

A partnership between credit unions and the Post Office could provide a solution to this problem, expanding credit unions' availability and visibility, and helping to maintain the viability of the valued local Post Office branch network as well. The Post Office has an unrivalled high street presence, with one located in almost every community. In the post-financial crisis era, when trust in the banking industry has been eroded, people's trust in the Post Office has remained high. As the Association of British Credit Unions highlights, allowing credit unions' products to be made available via the Post Office network 'would provide a much needed revenue stream to the Post Office, greatly boost the availability and visibility of credit union services and significantly expand the level of competition in the financial services industry'. In the context of empowerment it could greatly expand the reach of products to those with the least savings and help engage those who have been hardest to reach through traditional models of encouraging savings.

Grasping the nettle of undersaving is an opportunity for us to draw on the cooperative and ethical socialist roots of our movement, unleash the benefits of mutualism, emphasise the local credit union and, most of all, to ensure that everyone, particularly those with the fewest resources, has their own savings on which to rely and build. Cooperatives, friendly societies and trade unions are examples of where people have come together to insure against risk and ensure that they have made provision for unexpected expenses. Credit unions and mutuals provide savings provision that the government cannot match, with community-based products on a micro scale.

They should be emphasised as a core part of the solution to undersaving and the importance of assets in providing opportunity and equality. For example, taxpayer-owned banks, particularly Northern Rock, could be utilised as the hub of the Saving Gateway, potentially as the facilitators of building savings as the building society and mutual model were originally created to do, forming partnerships with local credit unions to bring savings to the heart of our community. And, most important, they work from the community centres and churches within our communities, rather than the banking halls. A building society model, plugged into our communities through the network of credit unions, could transform our poor record of saving, particularly among those on most incomes.

### Restructure the tax system

Pensions tax relief must also be reformed. Tax relief and employers' National Insurance relief significantly improve employers' incentives to remunerate employees through pension contributions and, as the Turner Report pointed out, 'under reasonable assumptions, an individual's pension is increased by 8 per cent over that which could be obtained by saving out of post-tax earnings into an ISA, and by 17 per cent over that which could be obtained if they saved out of post-tax income into accounts subject to the normal rate of tax on investment income'.

But the Turner Report also highlighted that if people could also persuade employers to contribute to pensions funds, reducing cash wages but keeping total pay the same, they could be 40 per cent better off than saving in a non-privileged tax form.

However, the reality is that the benefits of tax relief are skewed towards higher-rate taxpayers who have the biggest savings pots already. In 2009–10, two-thirds of the £19.7bn given in tax relief went to those paying the highest rates of income tax. Figures by income decile from the Department for Work and Pensions have shown that 75 per cent of tax relief went to the top two income deciles, whereas those in the lower five deciles totalled less than 10 per cent of the total tax relief between them. Hardly surprising, then, that the Pensions Commission concluded that the benefits of tax relief are 'extremely unequally distributed, and do not flow primarily to those most in danger of undersaving'.

It cannot be right that those on high incomes paying 40 per cent tax only have to save £600 to generate £1,000-worth of pension savings, while those on middle and low incomes have to save £800 to generate the same amount.

The government has taken some steps to address the issue by limiting the annual tax-free savings threshold to £50,000, from a previous level of £255,000, while limiting the total pensions pot to £1.8 million for tax-relief purposes. Eighty per cent of the 100,000 people affected by this move have incomes of more than £100,000 a year. But this does not go far enough.

The next Labour government must be bolder. It must remove the 50 per cent rate of tax relief and it must find ways to create a more progressive system. The problem is that those on the lowest incomes are undersaving, yet they have to pay 80p to save £1, compared to those on the highest incomes earning over £150,000 who only have to pay 50p. Replacing tax relief with matched contributions, or a system that was even more progressive, offering higher relief to those on lower incomes than those on higher incomes, should be explored. At present, the pensions tax relief rewards those who already have the highest savings and can most afford to save. This seems to be a very inefficient use of the £20bn spent on pensions tax relief and is in urgent need of attention.

### Empowerment through assets

We know that we undersave in Britain. A phenomenon that has grown over time has been thrown into stark relief during the recession when families have struggled to cope with stagnant incomes, rising prices and a jump in unemployment. Increasing longevity and more flexible and insecure labour markets have at the same time made savings more important, both as a buffer in hard times and as an income stream in retirement.

The last Labour government sought to get to the heart of the problems of inertia and myopia with automatic-enrolment into occupational pension schemes, the creation of the child trust fund and plans for the Saving Gateway. While the coalition government seeks to undermine that progress, Labour must look to the future. We recognise that fiscal constraints make further subsidies difficult, but we also recognise that an asset-based approach to social justice and social mobility must be at the heart of our welfare and taxation agenda.

To meet these challenges more targeted tax relief to boost the savings of those on middle and modest incomes would be a much more efficient use of scarce taxpayer resources, while making automatic-enrolment work for those on such incomes and those in multiple jobs will also be key.

But we must also recognise that, if we are to truly empower people, assets play a core role, and it will be important to those who most need support to encourage savings, financial education and advice with a tailored and local approach. Harnessing the power and reach of credit unions in all of our communities to deliver personalised support as part of lifetime savings accounts, and a more targeted and reinvigorated Saving Gateway, would draw on Labour's cooperative and mutual roots, and help achieve the objective of empowering those people who most need a buffer against the shocks that life throws at them. That should be Labour's progressive and empowering approach to building savings and pension provision for all.

---

1   Dominic Maxwell, Sonia Sodha and Kate Stanley, *An Asset Account for Looked After Children: A Proposal to Improve Educational Outcomes for Children in Care* (London: ippr, 2006).

# Restoring Labour's moral economy: the role of National Insurance

*Frank Field*

Every action of government – as with all institutions – embodies values. Governments teach their values by the very act of governing. It has always puzzled me that left-wing activists see government as a powerful weapon in positively changing people's habits, with respect to smoking for example, but recoil from judging the negative impact that means-tested welfare has on behaviour. As welfare is by far and away the largest single government budget it necessarily powerfully influences our behaviour, whether for good or ill. It can, for instance, encourage thrift, saving and work, or it can appear oblivious to its effect on such values.

The Attlee government's welfare state embodied core Labour values about fairness and reciprocity, reflecting the central belief of Labour voters that welfare should be earned by contributions. The system Clement Attlee adopted paid out benefits based on individuals' contributions. Welfare was very largely awarded on the basis of contributions and public housing was allocated to those who had waited longest and who were best-behaved. Later, however, these values came under increasing pressure. And, in 1997, without any discussion within the party or the wider country, and with only a passing reference in the manifesto to a review of taxes and benefits, Tony Blair and Gordon Brown tore up this established welfare contract. In place of Labour's traditional, contributions-based contract they put means-testing at the heart of New Labour's strategy, entirely disregarding the fact that the values it instils, and its impact on behaviour, are totally the opposite to what had gone before.

By simply concentrating on the levels of poverty (as defined by income) New Labour stripped out the wider providential role welfare plays in working-class budgets. Fairness ceased to be based on contributions and reciprocity and was supplanted by a single mechanical calculation of supposed need. This fundamental change in direction amounted to a war of attrition against working people's moral economy.

It cannot be stressed enough that this enthusiasm for means-testing is a recent phenomenon. The whole party had historically held a much stronger opposition to means-testing than St Augustine took on chastity and continence. In his famous quip, the saint expressed the desire for chastity – but not just yet. Like St Augustine's view on sin, the party has known the difficulties of entirely eliminating means-testing: there are always a number of people who, for various reasons, do not qualify for insurance benefits. But its resolution was to minimise the role means-tests would play in welfare.

After 1997 New Labour warmly embraced means-testing – under the euphemistic cover of tax credits – as though it was a crucial building block in the new society. The number of people whose minimum income was determined by means-testing grew from 13.7 million to 22.4 million during these thirteen years.

Moreover, Labour's means-tested welfare left power decidedly in the hands of the Chancellor of the Exchequer, who decides each year who gets help, but extends that help only on the condition of partial serfdom; trying to free yourself from this serfdom results in massive financial penalties. Not only are marginal tax rates way beyond the level imposed on the very richest, a partner's income is also taken into account.

National Insurance, by contrast, builds a floor underneath families so that the family, apart from the claimant, is free to add to the family's income without penalty.

This means-tested strategy was central to Labour's attack on poverty among pensioners and families. Although it gained less public attention, the drive on pensioner poverty was the more impressive of Labour's welfare achievements if we are to consider only short-term, immediate outcomes. The numbers of poor pensioners were cut by 1.1 million over the 1997–2010 period down from 2.9 million and at a cost of £86bn.

The record in reducing family poverty is more disappointing. After spending over £150bn the number of children living in poor families has been reduced by only 800,000 – from 3.4 million to 2.6 million. Worse still, the tax credit payments have, like immigration, held down the wages of the lower paid. Under current rules, the system makes it nigh on impossible for most claimants ever to earn enough to free themselves from means-tested assistance. We have thereby created a new benefits serf class whose economic behaviour is largely determined by the eligibility rules.

**Moral hazards**
Labour's means-tested strategy to combat pensioner poverty involved far less moral hazard when compared with that for working-age poor people, and therefore parents, but it still came with a pretty big political price tag. Far fewer pensioners will be affected by work incentives for the simple reason that most of them will have given up work anyway. But the unfairness of the pension credit system rankles with pensioners whose savings disqualify them from help. 'Clearly the government views me as a fool. I should have blown every penny I had and then claimed benefits just as all too many people in this road have done', is a refrain all too many decent working-class elderly voters tell those canvassers who wish to listen. Moreover, no studies have been conducted on the

impact of the offer of pension credit on the savings that lower-paid workers make while employed.

The violence that means-tests inflict on the working-class moral economy is in a different league when considering its impact on people of working age. Means-tests have a major impact on incentives to work: tax on each additional £1 of earnings plus the loss of means-tested help imposes marginal tax rates of up to 95.95 per cent, and with the new universal credit just under 20 per cent of the working poor will still face a tax-and-benefit loss rate of 50 per cent or more. But means-tests have also fundamentally changed the attitudes and character of all too many claimants.

The argument that 'it doesn't pay me to take a job; I would only be £15 or £20 a week better off' marks a sea-change in working-class attitudes. Means-tested benefits, designed as a temporary safety net, have been turned into a pension for life for all too many claimants: we have, in effect, created a class of dependents, as addicted as anyone on crack cocaine. The change has meant that not all claimants see work as their ultimate goal: too often they balance their extra income against the required effort and judge the rewards insufficient. It is difficult to exaggerate how fundamental this change in attitude has been and the size of the political challenge it throws up for working out a new strategy for the next Labour government.

During my time as MP for Birkenhead I have come to the conclusion that there needs to be a fundamental change in the attitude of many claimants. Too often the safety net that benefit claimants are offered today is seen as an income for life, and particularly by young adults. We cannot afford to let this view take root any more deeply.

There are, therefore, two strategies that governments can adopt to bring the values of welfare back into line with the sense of decency that characterises not only working-class culture but also society more generally.

The first is to continually tighten up the eligibility rules for the main income support benefits, such as means-tested jobseeker's allowance, with the aim of forcing reluctant workers back into the labour market.

The alternative is to begin again, emphasising why work is so crucial to an individual's fulfilment and as a mainstay for the family, and to reflect this new emphasis in an insurance-based welfare system. Welfare would then begin again to play a virtuous role. It would emphasise Labour's traditional values, and by so doing help develop a self-policing system as an ever-growing proportion of voters begin to see a direct link between how well the scheme is run, and the rules abided by, and the premiums they pay.

Both strategies, of course, need to be employed. But there would be greater support and understanding, and a wider sense that justice was being done, if both approaches were pursued together. So what shape should a major rebuilding and repositioning of insurance take in a twenty-first century welfare state, which simultaneously shifts power away from the centre?

## Reinventing insurance-based welfare

First, we need to decide what the aims of the system should be. This needs to reflect the uncertainties that a global economy places on the budgets of ordinary families and how these can best be countered by an insurance-based system.

Too much is made of how obsolete William Beveridge's five war-time 'evils' are. Unemployment was then the chief cause of poverty. It remains so today if we consider the numbers who are genuinely unemployed and who lodge in the incapacity benefit (now employment support allowance) queues. Let me illustrate the form an insurance-based welfare scheme could take by examining one element of it: that against unemployment.

Newly means-tested unemployed claimants often explode with anger when told, after paying in to an insurance scheme for decades, that the only help they are entitled to is a six-month, time-limited derisory insurance-based benefit of

£67.50 per week. After six months a partner means-test is applied, and often working wives' or husbands' income disqualifies the unemployed person from any help whatsoever.

But where an individual has played by the rules, and built up an exemplary contribution record, a new insurance system should surely 'reward' this. A National Insurance scheme would seek to provide unemployed claimants with a fixed income relative to the insurance premiums each claimant has paid. The scheme, as noted earlier, would provide claimants with a floor income on which they could build. Individuals would, furthermore, make their own decisions as to how good their contribution record is. The system would, of course, be backed up with a tough system of moving people into work, including time limits on benefits.

Similarly a new system should encourage claimants to be less risk-averse when re-entering the labour market by supporting them with a fast-track re-eligibilty criterion. Facing an often insecure range of job prospects, our current system rewards the faint-hearted who do not take risks to get back into work, yet being in work is the best place to find better job opportunities.

We would be wise, in the first instance, to propose a salary-based insurance system that is one where the higher the salary the higher the contributions, but so too are the level of benefits. Workers entering the labour market for the first time, or immigrants, would not qualify until they had made a minimum number of contributions. Those who had not met this criterion, or had not gained credits for being carers, would be dependent on a less generous means-tested system of allowances.

These two moves would not only draw immediate political support, they would also set the framework for how the reshaping of welfare would progress. It would also open up the possibility of extending insurance cover to new areas of need, such as long-term care.

It would, for instance, be sensible to include long-term

care, where only one in six of us will need to spend significant extra costs – currently £24,000 on average for a woman – as part of a new insurance-based welfare system.

While no sensible person would deny the difficulties there are in policing eligibility to 'benefits', private companies already run schemes for higher-income groups, and such a task should not be beyond a universal scheme.

## Owning welfare

Two further issues must be dealt with. The first is cost and the second is ownership. I tried to deal with both these issues in papers before the 1997 election.

At that time the government actuary costed the schemes I was proposing. These numbers are now out of date, but they underscore a crucial point that must not be ignored. Better welfare is not going to come cheap. It has to be paid for and this will involve fundamental political questions: how the costs fall on individuals and which other sources of revenue or the withdrawal of which tax allowances might be used to finance both the transition to, and then the regular costs of, the new system. Moreover, there will also be questions about how quickly the scheme can realistically be introduced.

Hence the importance of salary-related contributions and benefits if a wider coalition of support is to be rebuilt for welfare reform. In his first budget Brown talked of the 'National Insurance tax', for reasons best known to himself. Voters have never viewed their contributions as a tax, as the present government will soon learn as it tries to combine taxes and National Insurance.

The scope for reform along these lines was inadvertently initiated by the National Insurance change the last government made specifically to bring NHS funding up to the European average. When the then Chancellor was cornered into changing the rules to introduce a specific National Insurance contribution for the NHS he was met with overwhelming support. Not only in increasing by one percentage point all National Insurance contributions, but in lifting the cap which currently limits the size of all contributions from those on higher incomes. These two changes increased the National Insurance revenue by around £75bn over the last eight years.

There is a further major change that should be embraced. National Insurance must be converted from a state-run scheme to one which is mutually owned by its members. Here this policy fits further with *The Purple Book*'s theme of redistributing power.

Before 1997 I posed the question as to how the Bank of England's governance model – of being responsible to, but possessing a high degree of independence from, government – could become more democratic, and form the basis for voter ownership of what would clearly become a member-owned, insurance-based welfare state. It is clear to me that the Bank of England is the ideal place to house a new National Insurance system although it will need to become more accountable to Parliament.

New Labour's means-tested strategy has done enormous harm to the moral order of working-class families. It has cost huge sums in revenue and it has failed to reach its single goal of halving child poverty.

Reshaping welfare along insurance lines in a scheme which is owned by the contributors will appeal to working- and middle-class voters alike. It will begin to reshape the public finances, with voters owning their scheme and having a say on both contribution and benefit levels. Such a reform would therefore be seen as a staging post to voters having a more direct say over what they pay and to what services they contribute. And, most importantly, it sends out a clear moral message that benefits are to be earned and that reciprocity will sit at the heart of the welfare society.

# Putting families first: universal care from cradle to grave

*Liz Kendall*

Families matter. They help make us who we are as individuals, give us love and support, teach us how to behave and shape our values, beliefs, confidence and self-esteem.

Families are also the building blocks of our communities and society as a whole. The ability of parents and carers to work and financially provide for their families is critical in improving living standards and tackling poverty and inequality. The quality of the home environment and parents' involvement in their children's learning has a profound effect on how well children do at school. Families also make a huge contribution to the health and wellbeing of our increasingly ageing population, through the care and support they provide for elderly relatives.

So families are central to creating opportunities and life chances, and providing wider emotional, social and financial support, which is why family policy must be at the heart of any progressive vision for the future.

Families also matter politically. Winning the 'family vote' has long been a key battleground in British politics. At the last election, Labour promised to help 'hard-working families', championed our record on family-friendly working, childcare and tax credits, and promised to support families of all shapes and sizes.

The Conservatives claimed they would protect Sure Start

(a pledge they have since broken), reward marriage in the tax system and make Britain the most family-friendly country in the world. The Liberal Democrats opposed tax incentives for marriage and promised to allow mothers and fathers to share parental leave.

That all the main political parties put childcare and family-friendly policies at the heart of their 2010 manifestos is testament to the huge strides Labour made when we were in government.

We introduced free nursery places for three- and four-year-olds, established 3,500 Sure Start children's centres, and helped families with the costs of childcare through new tax credits. We produced the first-ever national strategies for childcare and for supporting carers. We also increased maternity pay and leave, introduced paid paternity leave for the first time, and brought in a new right to request flexible working. Many of these changes faced considerable opposition, including from the Conservatives, and were achieved in no small part due to the efforts of our women MPs.

Yet, despite our very real achievements, too many families at the last general election felt we were out of touch with the reality of their daily lives. In my own constituency, many families – too 'rich' to get help from the state yet struggling to make ends meet – told me they felt let down by Labour. And our 'offer' to families at the last election was not clear enough or bold enough to convince many voters we were still the best party to help them through difficult times.

In order to win again, this must change.

Labour must once again show we understand the pressures and anxieties families face in the here and now, and that we will offer them a positive alternative for the future.

This will require us to more clearly articulate Labour's view of the relationship between individuals, families and state.

The role of government is not to tell families what form they should take or how they should live their lives, but to create genuine opportunities within which families can themselves determine how to build a better life.

Making these opportunities real means ensuring a range of resources are available to families, including services, financial support and, crucially, time. Securing these resources is not something that can be left to markets alone – it requires an active role for the state.

The way these resources are provided also needs to change to redistribute power between the state and individuals and to give families more control. In order to retain support in the long run, public services must respond to wider changes in society, where people want and expect to be given a greater say. There is also increasing evidence that the quality and outcomes services achieve can be improved if users play a more central role.

Of course, families come in very different shapes and sizes. They face different circumstances and have different views about the help and support they need. So there is no one single policy or initiative that will secure the 'family vote'.

However, many families face similar pressures and have similar hopes for the future. These pressures and hopes are influenced by profound social and economic changes that have shaped family life in Britain in recent decades, and will continue to do so in the years ahead.

### Family structure and demographic change
The structure of Britain's families is changing. While marriage remains the most common form of partnership – figures show that in 2006 half the adult population were married – it is now less common than it has ever been.

More couples live together before getting married. One-fifth of all couples are expected to be in a cohabiting relationship by 2021, compared to 12 per cent of couples in 1996.

Divorce rates rose steadily throughout the latter part of the twentieth century, stabilised in the mid-1980s, and then declined: in 2007 divorce rates were at the lowest level since 1981.

According to the last 2001 census, 5 per cent of all families are 'stepfamilies' – a figure which is likely to have increased over the last decade.

The number of lone-parent households has increased too: around a quarter of all children are being brought up by single parents, compared with one in fourteen in 1972. Women are having their first child much later, in part due to their increased participation in the workplace. This in turn is affecting the size of families, with parents having fewer children than in the past.

The ageing population is also changing family life, bringing new caring responsibilities. There are 1.7 million more people aged sixty-five now compared to the mid 1980s. At the same time, the percentage of the population aged under sixteen has decreased, a trend that is set to continue. By 2034, 23 per cent of the population is projected to be aged sixty-five and over compared to 18 per cent aged under sixteen.

**Living standards**
Living standards have risen steadily over the last fifty years. During the immediate post-war period, these increases were driven by greater educational opportunities and technological change. In the 1970s and 1980s living standards continued to rise as more women went out to work. In the late 1980s and 1990s rises in living standards were fuelled by financial deregulation and the credit boom; and in the 2000s they were boosted by the introduction and expansion of tax credits for people of working age.[1]

Average incomes continued to grow during the recession in 2008–9 and 2009–10, even after taking account of inflation and in spite of the increase in unemployment. However, average incomes will be more than unwound in 2010–11 as the long-term effects of the recession are felt and higher inflation erodes living standards.[2]

Furthermore, there is no guarantee that increasing prosperity will be fairly shared among all sections of the population when Britain's economic growth returns.

Living standards for those on low-to-middle incomes stagnated even before the 2008–9 recession. While productivity has continued to grow, the gains have not fed into pay packets, particularly of low-to-middle income earners. There has been a stronger increase in top wages than those at the middle or bottom and the balance between wages and profits has also changed, with workers getting a smaller slice. There has also been a deeper and more fundamental shift in the way technology is driving jobs growth. Instead of displacing jobs at the bottom and replacing them at the top, today's technologies are displacing jobs in the middle.[3]

Other trends have had a profound effect on living standards, particularly for those on low and middle incomes. Inflation has hit these families disproportionately hard and prior to the financial crisis mortgage repayments for families owning their own homes were actually rising, despite falling interest rates.

### Working patterns and caring responsibilities
The last fifty years have also seen major changes in working patterns.

Mothers' employment tripled between the 1950s and late 2000s, and two-thirds of mothers are now employed. Forty-four per cent of women now work part time, and there has also been a significant increase in the number of men working part time, with the proportion doubling from 7 to 14 per cent.

Ninety per cent of families where both parents are employed work at least some atypical hours (outside 8am to 7pm). Eighty per cent of working fathers in couple families, and half of all working mothers, including single mothers, work atypical hours.

Our ageing population is also leading to significant changes in working patterns. As people live longer, they are working for a longer period of their lives. For example, between 1975 and 1995, the economic participation of men fell as many took early retirement. From 1995 to 2005, this trend was reversed.

The increase in mothers who work and our ageing population is putting family time under increasing pressure. The 2007 British Social Attitudes survey found that 84 per cent of full-time women workers and 64 per cent of part-time women workers want to spend more time with their families.

It is not just mothers who are feeling the squeeze on their time: half of all fathers say they are not spending enough time with children. This is partly due to the number of hours men have to work, but also because they are much less likely than women to live in the same household as their children.

A recent survey by the National Family and Parenting Institute found that the greatest concern about family life is caring for elderly relatives. Worries about caring for elderly relatives are likely to increase, particularly as the 'baby boomer' generation reaches old age and more people in their fifties face caring responsibilities.[4]

## Squeezed incomes, squeezed time

The consequences of the financial crisis and public spending cuts combined with longer-term changes in family structure, living standards, working patterns and caring responsibilities, are having a profound effect on family life in Britain today. Many families are anxious about their jobs. They find life a constant struggle to make ends meet financially as the cost of living rises. Families are also worried about finding enough time to look after their children and elderly relatives. Their incomes are being squeezed, but so too is their time.

This is particularly true for families on low-to-middle incomes. These families cannot afford for one partner to stop work or go down to working part time. At the same time, they often cannot find the formal care services that would help them strike a better balance between their work and family life. Even when formal care is available, it is often too expensive for ordinary families to afford.[5]

Childcare costs across the UK are high, with annual price

increases outstripping wages. The cost of childcare in England for a child aged two and over increased by 4.8 per cent last year, with similar increases for children aged under two.[6]

This is a major barrier to parents getting work and escaping the low pay/no pay cycle. Lack of flexible childcare in the evenings, at the weekends and during school holidays is a particular problem.[7]

The costs of social care are also very high. The latest evidence from the Personal Social Services Research Unit has shown that the average total cost of residential care for over 65-year-olds who use it – including both accommodation and care – is £50,000. One in ten people over sixty-five years old who need residential care face costs of £100,000, and one in a hundred face costs of over £300,000.

### The challenge for progressive politics

The anxieties and pressures on Britain's families raise two key challenges that Labour must address when developing our future family policy.

First, while a return to economic growth is absolutely critical, it may not be sufficient to ensure increasing prosperity is fairly shared among all families, particularly those on low and middle incomes. Childcare and elderly care look set to become even more important than before in helping these families increase their earnings through work.[8]

Second, increasing incomes alone will not be enough to help families secure the kind of life they want to lead. Time is an increasingly precious but rare commodity in family life, particularly for those on low-to-middle incomes.

This presents Labour with a huge opportunity, but also a challenge.

The opportunity is that providing universal, high-quality and affordable childcare and elderly care and boosting family time through more flexible working cannot be left to markets alone. It requires an active role for government, which is something progressive political parties are best placed to achieve.

The challenge is how Labour can achieve these goals during uncertain economic times, when growth is at best fragile and when public spending and services are being cut.

Since the election, Labour has rightly opposed the government's public spending cuts for going too deep and too fast, risking the jobs and growth our economy urgently need, and threatening the public services on which families depend.

However, Ed Miliband and Ed Balls have made it clear that Labour will not oppose every cut. This is crucial, particularly as we approach the next election, as it would risk raising expectations that every cut will be reversed if Labour regains power, which is neither convincing to the electorate nor realistic for a party that is determined to demonstrate we are a government-in-waiting.

There is a strong case that protecting early years services and care for the elderly should be a priority for Labour, as cutting these services will have long-term consequences for individuals, families and taxpayers.

Reducing early years services and closing Sure Start children's centres will make it harder for parents to find work. It will also reduce children's later life chances, leading to increased costs for other public services. Yet the government is cutting the early intervention grant, which includes funding for Sure Start, by 11 per cent this year, and 7.5 per cent next year. Two hundred and fifty children's centres are set to close this year, affecting 60,000 families.[9]

Cuts to social care will also harm the health and wellbeing of older people and end up costing taxpayers more in the long run, as many older people end up in hospital or requiring more intensive and expensive residential care. Spending on older people's care is set to be £300m lower over the next four years. Real spending on older people will be £250m lower in 2010–15 than 2004–5. At the same time the number of people over eighty-five has risen by two-thirds to 630,000.[10]

So Labour should continue to make a strong and powerful case against these cuts. But we will not win again on an anticuts agenda alone. We must offer a clear and positive vision for the future, and an alternative agenda for government.

Political debate about public services has long been dominated by the core services of education and the NHS. When Labour was in government, we championed investment and reform in schools and hospitals. This was urgently needed after eighteen years of neglect by the Conservatives.

However, there are compelling reasons why Labour should now place a greater emphasis on championing childcare and care for the elderly.

The experience of countries like Sweden and Denmark suggests the provision of universal, high-quality childcare helps promote higher employment levels among women. Increased female employment is crucial to supporting the long-term sustainability of the welfare state as the population ages, to reducing the gender pay gap and to allowing more women to provide for their own old age.[11]

Childcare is also critical to tackling child poverty, improving life chances and promoting social mobility.[12] The Joseph Rowntree Foundation estimates that getting early years services right could move between a sixth and half of all children out of poverty.[13] High-quality early years provision benefits all children, but particularly boys, children with multiple disadvantages, and those with special educational needs.[14]

It is also likely to produce net economic gains in the long run by reducing expenditure on the costs of 'failure', such as welfare benefits and the criminal justice system.[15, 16, 17]

A similar case can be made for prioritising care for the elderly. Services that promote the health, wellbeing and independence of older people, and which prevent or delay the need for higher intensity or institutional care, have been shown to improve the quality of life of older people and deliver significant savings in reduced NHS spending.[18] Fully integrating health, housing and social care, and shifting the focus of both these services towards prevention and early intervention could lead to even greater benefits, with some reports suggesting savings to the NHS of £2.65 for every £1 spent on integrated care.[19]

Improving support for informal carers would also help the wider economy. Carers UK has shown that one in six unpaid carers gives up work to care. This not only harms their own living standards but the economy as a whole, as their skills and talents are lost to the workplace, and through increased spending on welfare benefits.

## Universal care from cradle to grave

The profound impact of the very earliest years of a child's life on their later life chances, and the clear benefits of high-quality, preventative social care, suggests childcare and care for the elderly should move to the top of Labour's agenda. Our ambition should be to secure high-quality care from cradle to grave, transforming childcare and elderly care into universal public services that are as integral to our country and the social fabric of our communities as schools and the NHS.

This will mean difficult decisions about Labour's priorities for future public spending.

These decisions should be informed by the work on 'capabilities' developed by Amartya Sen. Sen argues that material wellbeing is not an end in itself, but the means to a better life. Income and economic resources are important because of the capabilities they endow people with – the ability to achieve certain aspirations and to participate in the social life of the community.[20, 21]

In other words, people's ability to choose the life they want to lead is shaped by their opportunities in the widest sense – their health and wellbeing, and their skills, educational and social opportunities – as well as their income.

This suggests Labour needs to consider how to strike a

better balance between funding for tax credits and benefits, and funding for services like childcare and care for the elderly.

These services play an absolutely crucial role in helping families work and increase their living standards, in tackling poverty and inequality and in improving outcomes for young children and older people. They are also more visible and tangible than other types of family support, which arguably makes them harder to reduce or remove, particularly during uncertain economic times and when public spending is tight.

The report of the Commission on the Funding of Care and Support, led by Andrew Dilnot, provides a particularly important opportunity to develop a secure and sustainable system of funding for older people and their carers in future.[22]

The Commission proposes to increase the current means-tested threshold above which individuals have to pay for their residential care from £23,250 to £100,000, and to place a cap on the overall amount they pay of between £35,000 and £50,000. The Commission also calls for an end to the postcode lottery in the eligibility for social care so that local councils meet the 'substantial' needs of individuals, rather than the present situation where many local authorities are meeting only the needs of those assessed as 'critical'.

Labour has taken a bold stance on this issue by offering to work with the government in taking the Commission's proposal forward. Our ambition must be to develop a system of funding for social care that is both fair and affordable and which has broad-based support, to ensure sustainability over the long term.

Alongside decisions about how best to fund early years services and care for older people, Labour must also develop a clear plan to improve the way these services are delivered in future.

A full set of policy proposals on how this should be done is beyond the scope of this chapter. It instead focuses on a central issue: redistributing power to give staff, users and carers a greater say and greater control through the greater use of mutuals, social enterprises and the voluntary and community sector.

The Conservatives are attempting to claim this territory through their plans for the 'big society'. Labour should treat the coalition government's supposed conversion to supporting voluntary, mutual and cooperative organisations as a sign of the strength of our enduring principles and values, and not a threat.

However, the reality is that the government's 'big society' aims to roll back the state and leave volunteers to fill in the gap. The Conservatives fail to understand that a key ingredient in helping local people and communities take on real power and control is a democratically elected, enabling state.

There is a huge opportunity for Labour councils to champion new ways of delivering childcare and care for older people, demonstrating how this can be achieved in practice, even when we are not in power nationally.

One of the key challenges in social care is improving the quality of the workforce. Social enterprises have shown they can help increase skills and training opportunities for staff, which in turn help improve the quality of care for older people.

For example, Sunderland Home Care Associates is an employee-owned organisation with 300 staff who deliver 7,000 hours of care to older people a week, including washing, bathing and showering, preparing meals and supporting carers. Staff have a vital role to play in making decisions about how the organisation is run, such as helping set budgets, pay and conditions. They also have extensive opportunities for training and study to NVQ levels two, three and four. As a social enterprise, any profits made are spent on improving services or rewarding staff.

Labour must also consider how to improve the quality of the childcare workforce. One option would be to learn from the experience of the Teach First model in schools.

Teach First was established as a charity in 2002, with funding from government and the corporate sector. It has been a huge success in recruiting 800 high-achieving graduates to work in Britain's most challenging schools. By recognising that government does not always know how best to solve problems, Labour helped create an innovative scheme – run by the third sector, with backing from the state and business – to improve children's life chances.

Labour should consider piloting a Teach Early Years First scheme to attract the best and brightest graduates into childcare. This could help increase the quality, skills and motivation of the early years workforce and improve the life chances and aspirations of children in disadvantaged areas.

Another way that voluntary and community groups can help improve the quality of services is by better engaging and involving families.

Charities like Home Start train volunteers who have parenting expertise themselves to visit families in their own homes, offering friendship and support to deal with issues like post-natal depression and practical help, such as encouraging breastfeeding. The Peers Early Education Partnership helps parents in deprived communities understand the importance of the very earliest years for their children's learning, and how they can make the best of everyday activities to develop children's literacy and numeracy skills, their self-esteem and their propensity to learn.

Involving members of the wider community can also help improve support for older people and their carers.

For example, time banks are not-for-profit organisations that allow people to 'deposit' one hour of their time to help other members of the local community, such as offering lifts, accompanying people to the shops, providing companionship and checking up on people after hospital discharge. When they need help themselves, people can 'withdraw' one hour of time and support in return.

Time banks have been shown to help isolated older people remain independent and stay in their own homes by providing them with much-needed practical help and support.[23] Greater use of time banks could also make a real difference in supporting the UK's six million informal carers, four million of whom are of working age.

## Boosting time to care

Boosting time to care should be at the heart of Labour's family policy agenda. Time should be seen and treated as an integral social value – crucial to helping families and communities choose the kind of life they want to lead.

There is also a strong business case for family-friendly working, as it helps companies retain the skills and experience of parents and carers, boosts staff morale and productivity, and helps save time and money on the costs of recruitment.

The UK has a very different system of parental leave compared to other countries, with the gap between what mothers and fathers can take among the highest in OECD countries.

British mothers are entitled to twelve months' maternity leave, nine of which are paid at the statutory rate and fathers get two weeks' paid leave around the birth of a child. Other countries have a shorter period of statutory maternity leave, followed by a reserved proportion of leave for fathers, then extended parental leave entitlements, which can be shared.

Labour should learn from international experience about the benefits of redistributing time more fairly between mothers and fathers. Some countries have pioneered the use of 'daddy quotas': a period of leave that only fathers can take – they have to 'use it' or they 'lose it'. For example, in 2000, Iceland divided leave into three blocks: three months' non-transferable maternity leave, three months' non-transferable paternity leave, and three months for parents to determine. This has led to a significant increase in the amount of time fathers take overall, and on how joint leave is shared, with dads now taking one-third of the shared entitlement.

A separate and increased entitlement for fathers in the UK could help change cultural norms, including at work so employers see fathers' time with their children as equally important to that of mothers. It could also help improve child outcomes. There is increasing evidence that time spent by fathers with their newborn children is crucial to securing lasting bonds and that this can help fathers stay in contact with their children even if they are separated from the child's mother.[24]

As well as time off around the birth of children, Labour should build on our record in government in championing flexible working.

Labour introduced a right to request flexible working, initially for families with young children and then all children under eighteen and carers. However, some studies have suggested that the right to request is overly complex and that its effectiveness could be improved.[25] Labour should consult with businesses about how family-friendly working can be strengthened in future. This could include offering the right to request flexible working to all employees (not just parents and carers of older relatives); extending it to agency workers who are currently excluded; and starting entitlements from day one, instead of after twenty-six weeks as at present, so that employees and employers can be clearer about their needs from the start.

**Putting families first**
Childcare, elderly care and time to care should now be at the top of Labour's future policy agenda. Our ambition should be nothing less than to transform support for families from cradle to grave.

In uncertain economic times, this will mean difficult decisions about the balance of funding for different public services, and between the amount of money spent on these services, tax credits and other family benefits.

The way we deliver childcare and elderly care services also needs to change. We need to draw more deeply on Labour's mutual and cooperative tradition to give users and carers a greater say and control over their services – as individuals and members of the wider society. This will require a fundamental redistribution of power between the state, individual families and the community as a whole.

Labour has a huge opportunity to show families we are the party best placed to help them live the life they want to lead and to support them through difficult times. It is an opportunity we must seize with both hands.

1. James Plunkett, 'Growth Without Gain? The Faltering Standards of People on Low to Middle Incomes', Resolution Foundation Commission on Living Standards, 2011.
2. 'Long term effects on living standards yet to be felt', Institute for Fiscal Studies, 13 May 2011.
3. James Plunkett, op. cit.
4. Stephen A. Hunt (ed.), *Family Trends* (London: National Family and Parenting Institute, 2009).
5. James Plunkett, op. cit.
6. Daycare Trust, *Childcare Costs Survey 2011* (London: Daycare Trust, 2011).
7. Ronald McQuaid et al, *How Can Parents Escape from Recurrent Poverty?* (York: Joseph Rowntree Foundation, 2011).
8. James Plunkett, op. cit.
9. '250 Sure Start children's centres face closure within a year', Daycare Trust and 4Children, 28 January 2011.
10. Age UK, *Care in Crisis, Causes and Solutions* (London: Age UK, 2011).
11. Gøsta Esping-Andersen, 'Towards a New Welfare Equilibrium', Report to the Progressive Governance Conference, July 2003.
12. Kathy Sylva, *The Effective Provision of Pre-School Education (EPPE) Project: Final Report* (London: Institute of Education, University of London, 2004).
13. Jane Waldfogel and Alison Garnham, *Eradicating Child Poverty: The Role of Key Policy Areas* (York: Joseph Rowntree Foundation, 2008).
14. Kathy Sylva and Fiona Roberts, 'Quality in Early Childhood Education: Evidence for Long-Term Effects', in Gillian Pugh and Bernadette Duffy (eds), *Contemporary Issues in the Early Years* (London: SAGE, 2010).
15. Gøsta Esping-Andersen, *The Incomplete Revolution: Adapting to Women's New Roles* (Cambridge: Polity, 2009).
16. James J. Heckman, 'Policies to Foster Human Capital', *Working Paper 7288* (Cambridge MA: National Bureau of Economic Research, 1999).
17. Pedro Carneiro and James J. Heckman, *Human Capital Policy* (Cambridge MA: National Bureau of Economic Research, 2003).
18. Department of Health, *PSSRU National Evaluation of Partnerships for Older People Projects*, 2007.

19. Turning Point, *Benefits Realisation: Assessing the Evidence for the Cost Benefit and Cost Effectiveness for Health and Social Care* (London: Turning Point, 2010).

20. Amartya Sen, 'The Living Standard', *Oxford Economic Papers – New Series*, 1984, vol. 36, Supplement: *Economic Theory and Hicksian Themes*, pp. 74–90.

21. Amartya Sen in Geoffrey Hawthorn (ed.), *The Standard of Living* (Cambridge: Cambridge University Press, 1987).

22. Department of Health, *Fairer Care Funding*, 4 July 2011.

23. New Economics Foundation, *The New Wealth of Time: How Timebanking Helps People Build Better Public Services* (London: New Economics Foundation, 2008).

24. Dalia Ben-Galim, Family Policy: *Where Next for Parental Leave and Flexible Working?* (London: ippr, 2011).

25. Ibid.

# The authors of their own lives: stronger communities and the relational state

*Tessa Jowell*

The 'task before the Labour Party', wrote R. H. Tawney in 1931, is 'not to pretend that change is smooth. It must promise less and demand more, say less of what it will do but more of the responsibility that rests with the public. Seeing the public as partners in a common enterprise to achieve its goals it must be less of an electoral machine, more of a movement and a crusade.'[1]

In today's context 'seeing the public as partners' would mean allowing local residents to commission their own services; giving local communities the opportunity to identify the priorities for local spending; or putting people in need in touch with local residents with skills and time to give. Stronger communities will be built through stronger relationships, not through pseudo-commercial transactions between the provider and receiver of services. A new role for the state will need to be conceived – the relational state, committed to developing people's relationships rather than the technocratic language of outputs, targets, and value-for-money.

We need to build on local examples of citizen action to make them the rule, not the exception. Rather than trying to rebuild society as it looked before the financial crisis, we need to use this opportunity to reshape the communities we live in so that the most disadvantaged also hold power. To quote Tawney again, 'the practical thing for a nation which has stumbled upon one of the turning-points of history is not to behave as though nothing very important were involved … but to consider whether what it has done hitherto is wise, and, if it is not wise, to alter it.'[2]

The post-war settlement of the 1940s and 1950s established universal solutions to problems that were experienced nationwide. The post-financial crash settlement needs to address problems that are unique to people's experience street by street. Even if the challenges are similar in Brighton as in Bradford, the best solutions will come from locally conceived action and tailored state support, as opposed to nationwide monolithic government.

The role of the state needs to move with the changing demands of the times and, therefore the role of politicians in Westminster and the town hall will need to change too. In the future, politicians will need to be able to combine the robust nature of national politics with a more grounded, humane approach to local representation. People rising to the challenge of local activism should feel that they are the leaders, while the politicians harness ideas, nurture fledgling civil action and, when necessary, guide their local leaders through the maze of central government.

David Cameron's 'broken Britain' narrative and the response of the 'big society' in return is the Tories' best shot at meeting this challenge. It fails because it is a confusing blend of sepia-tinged nostalgia akin to John Major's 'warm beer' speech, a noblesse oblige approach to philanthropy and naked hatred of state intervention. It is significant that their slogan is 'big society, not big government'. They don't want a smaller state, or even a cheaper one. They want a nugatory state – one that does not impinge on the lives of people to any great extent. This is a hopelessly inadequate formulation to cope with the huge pressures created on society by globalisation and the attendant job and family insecurities. Instead of being inspiring, the Tory 'big society' leaves people to fend for themselves creating more insecurity, not less.

The left, though, must find ways to give communities the means to solve problems in their own ways and, in doing so, to create their own futures. The accruing benefits to individuals and communities who will discover their own agency will be worth the risk of difference caused by decentralisation. Truly putting power in the hands of the many not the few could form a radical alternative to the Conservative vision of a little platoon society and define the next stage of Labour's transformational purpose.

## New Labour's legacy

The accusation that in government New Labour never fully embraced the need to steer, not row, as David Osborne and Ted Gaebler suggested in their book *Reinventing Government*, has some merit. But in recognising some of the missed opportunities of our thirteen years in power, we should not overlook the real transfers of power to communities which did take place.

As Tony Blair said in his speech to the National Council for Voluntary Organisations in 1999, 'history shows that the most successful societies are those that harness the energies of voluntary action, giving due recognition to the third sector of voluntary and community organisations'. Under New Labour, it is estimated that the size of the third sector almost doubled and received £12.8bn from statutory sources in 2007–8. The creation of new mutuals in public services personalised and shaped provision around the needs of individuals, as well as promoted democratic accountability. Mutuals make our communities stronger by putting more democratic power in the hands of users, enabling decisions to be made by representatives of the community rather than unelected appointees.

The biggest expansion of mutualism took place in the NHS, with the creation of more than 130 NHS foundation trusts with nearly two million members. Of the forty-two trusts ranked as 'excellent' in the 2008 Healthcare Commission annual health check, the vast majority – thirty-eight – were foundation trusts. The Labour government also launched over 100 cooperative trust schools, which involve the wider community in the running of the school, including local people, businesses, voluntary groups, charities, parents, pupils and staff through membership of a council or forum.

But while a greater role for mutual and other community organisations did drive improvements and made services more responsible to people, the way in which commissioning operates means that this transfer of responsibility for services did not meet its full potential. Too often services failed to cut across the silos of government departments, and the emphasis was too often on the old Beveridge institutions rather than the character of communities and the needs of people.

The operational dimension of procurement and performance meant that voluntary and community organisations have been made subject to the processes of the way the state governs. The emphasis on market mechanisms in public service delivery, and the adoption of technocratic terminology and measures, has been found to alter the way in which voluntary and community organisations behave.[3] Accountability has therefore flowed upwards to its funders, rather than to members, service users or trustees – the guardians of the values on which the organisations are founded.

None of this should deny that public services got better. Public service reform in government was an evolutionary process starting with investment in the first stage, moving towards greater accountability and measurement of efficacy in the second, and personalising services in the third. Thirteen years of governing may have led us to a technocratic place, but it was necessary to raise standards in public services to their current levels. Our mission for public services, however, must be to build on this third stage of greater community and individual control of public services. We know that stronger communities are formed by individuals pursuing relationships with a common purpose, and we must find ways of building on the progress we made in government if Labour is going to grasp the next stage of the unending process of transforming public services.

## The Conservative alternative

The 'big society' should be Labour's territory. As an idea, it speaks to Labour's principles of solidarity, mutualism and collectivism. Labour also understands that the third sector has always played a complementary role to the statutory sector, campaigning and agitating for improvements, rather than just taking over failing services as in the Conservatives' view. The failure of the coalition to pursue the 'big society' through progressive principles means that the bonds of community are likely to weaken over the course of the next parliament.

According to a recent NCVO survey of charity leaders, 55 per cent of charities plan to cut staff and 35 per cent plan to decrease the amount of services they offer.[4] These are hardly conditions from which a blossoming of community life and organisations will grow. At the very moment expectations are being raised, public sector cuts are damaging the capacity to expand the sector.

This is because the Conservatives' stance is first and foremost ideological – you have either civic action or government support, but not both. They wrongly believe that the presence of local or national government intervention inevitably enervates flourishing communities. This doctrinaire obsession with a smaller state defeats the objects of the 'big society'. Under the indiscriminate impact of public sector cuts, the essential elements of community life are being starved of sustenance. What the sector loses in the next two years may become impossible to rebuild in the next ten.

## The relational state

Even if there were miraculously large increases in the amount of money for public sector spending in the next decade, there will not necessarily be the public appetite for the state to spend it. A study by Demos, which looked at the attitudes of voters who switched from supporting Labour at the last election, found marked dissatisfaction with the role of the state. Almost one in five (19 per cent) agreed that 'central government interferes too much in local services' while more than one in four (27 per cent) of the voters that Labour lost said they saw government as 'part of the problem, not the solution'. Only one in three former Labour voters considered government to be 'a force for good' improving their lives and the lives of their family.[5]

This requires Labour and the left to develop a new theory of government intervention. Government must move away from the 'delivery state' to a 'relational state', as Geoff Mulgan argues.[6] 'Conceived as a production line,' Mulgan suggests, the delivery state 'has repeatedly hit barriers. Even if the targets are met they may miss the point. The public may not be grateful. They may not share in any sense of achievement. And they may resent the tools used to achieve success.' The goal of government is to constantly seek legitimacy, but ironically the tools it uses can help to divorce people from its aims almost as much as if it had none in the first place.

Instead, Mulgan suggests government can succeed better by 'directly addressing the quality of its relationships with the public, rather than doing so indirectly through promises and their delivery'. Both market logic and an overly bureaucratic approach may achieve narrow outcomes, but they miss out on the crucial dimension that allows doctors to heal, teachers to teach and carers to care. A relational state would value the relationships they build with their patient, pupil or client, and the successes and failures they experience together.

We need to give greater recognition to the humanity of

people who serve the public. Whether it is the carer who dresses an older person in the morning, or the health visitor who gives a young mum the confidence to breastfeed, or the social worker who brings a young person out of their shell; our approach to politics needs to value the quality of their relationships more than established or conventional performance measures. There is a reason why patients cite the kind attention they receive from nurses as a key indicator of whether they are satisfied with their NHS experience, because it is the quality of human relationships that shapes their views of the success of the treatment.

New Labour often talked of the need to devolve power to the individual and pursued this through a number of successful measures – for example, individual budgets and the expert patient programme. But the way it measured success was still through numbers rather than the quality of the person's lived experience. Even the most commendable programmes failed to recognise the importance of individual or community buy-in. The closure of Accident and Emergency departments to make way for polyclinics, for example, while based in efficacious medical evidence, failed to recognise the loyalty users had to local institutions and the role they played in supporting their sense of local security. Little effort was put into tapping users' allegiance for the old and converting it to enthusiasm for the new.

It is no surprise, therefore, that people react with mistrust when the state announces changes or closures when they have no stake in the resulting structures. They campaign to keep what they have because they don't believe it will be replaced with anything better. But if people are put in charge of service design and, crucially, delivery, it will make it easier for the transformation of public services to take place, and ensure that the nature of public services are constantly changing in order to meet the changing needs of the population.

A relational state would recognise that the process of building community change is almost as important as achieving the change itself. This will require the state and politicians to value individuals more than bureaucratic institutions. It will need us to put far more trust in people's ability to create change for themselves, find the tools and capacity building to support them, and be less nervous about the risks of taking decisions out of the control of public servants. In doing so, we build more confidence in the case for change, in turn embedding the legacy of investment in communities.

### 'Community where possible, government where necessary, partnership always'

Too many local initiatives are stifled by the high barriers the state has erected to provide accountability for public money and ways of minimising risk. While it is essential that services which are based on reciprocity, or community relationships, are held to account, we need to have a bigger debate about what measures are necessary for the safety of the public, and those that make true community engagement impossible.

One good example of this in practice is the system of universal Criminal Records Bureau (CRB) checks. These were introduced in reaction to the Soham murders and the universal public anxiety about the safety of children. Seven years since their inception, these are widely seen to be onerous and bureaucratic. Sometimes the rigmarole of needing to go through checks, just to volunteer for an hour a month, puts off more good people than it catches bad. In particular, the length of time these checks take mean that short-term volunteering projects cannot reach out to a wider pool of people in the community without a huge undertaking.

Such complexities need to be addressed through a debate about how we recalibrate the relationship between communities and the state. The coalition has announced that it is changing the rules relating to criminal record checks for people with time to give who wish to work with children or vulnerable adults, so that organisations have the option of asking for a check or managing the risk of allowing that person to give time without one. This may address the obstacles that CRB checks have created, as long as local organisations keep best practice in mind (for example, by continuing to require checks for volunteers who are unknown to the project leaders) and ensure that the public are not exposed to unnecessary risk.

If we are to expect greater community involvement, it is right that risk management is placed with local organisations rather than the national state. Often the leaders of local community organisations will have built relationships based on trust which allows them to take a legitimate risk. The state's responsibility should be, however, to ensure that any organisation that wishes to check someone's background can do so in a timely way. Online technology opens up the opportunities to streamline checking systems, and it is hoped that the coalition's ambition to 'retain the benefits' of the online vetting and barring system will be seen through. The key here, however, is to divine the right role for the state which is to protect the public against unnecessary risk in the voluntary sector while ensuring that people's opportunities to transform their communities for the better are not stifled.

Another of the main barriers people cite that stop them giving time is their work. Fifty-eight per cent of those interviewed in the 2008–9 Citizenship Survey said that their work commitments prevent them from giving time while 31 per cent said that caring for children at home takes up their spare time.[7] As pressures on time and home life have become greater, this is likely to form the key problem for building stronger relationship-based communities. Therefore, negotiating stronger links with local employers and gaining their commitment to activity in the community will be important. We should consider incentives for businesses to give staff opportunities to volunteer to enable those people who can prove they want to make a difference in their community to do so.

Often those communities which need to build the strongest bonds are those in which it is most difficult to find people with time to give. According to the Citizenship Survey, people living in big urban areas (particularly London), with poor qualifications, who are out of work or on low pay, who were not born in the UK and who feel unsafe in their neighbourhood, are least likely to give time in formal and informal activities. It is instructive that they are also more likely to feel they cannot influence decisions in their local area and, when asked their view about other people, they agree with the statement 'You can't be too careful' rather than 'People can be trusted'.

Until now, giving time has been seen as a good addition to the health of our society, rather than something we see as a necessary part of being a good citizen. If we are seriously to redistribute power to localities, it will be very important for all residents – particularly those from lower-income backgrounds – to be involved to avoid those with the loudest voices and sharpest elbows from monopolising things. Part of the problem has arisen with the nature of the welfare state, which has created a sense that it is 'not my problem' or 'someone else will fix it'. This was not the aim of William Beveridge or the early ethical socialists such as Tawney, who saw the role of the state as to liberate people to help themselves.

Indeed, release from Beveridge's 'five giants' was on the prerequisite that recipients of the state's largesse played their part in creating the conditions for moving forward. Want would be defeated by out-of-work security, but the individual had to both seek work and pay National Insurance to receive the benefit. The new NHS would help combat disease, but people had to maintain their own health. Ignorance would be defeated through the extension of secondary education, but young people would have to work hard to get their exams. Squalor would be eradicated through a combination of new social house-building and house-proud tenants. Finally,

idleness could be challenged through a goal of full employment, while the task of the person who was unemployed was
to keep themselves 'fit for service'.

The right to state support was matched, every time, by
individual responsibilities. If genuine community engagement
is to get off the ground, a sense of human agency must be our
starting point. The role of the state is therefore to open doors
and create possibilities, but the obligation should be on the
individual and their community to find the answers to their
destiny. Labour's new maxim should be 'community where
possible, government where necessary, partnership always'.
Our expectations of human endeavour should be high and
the universal assumption should be that our duty is to play
an active role in our communities. We are all responsible for
making society what it is.

## Bringing power back to the community

The relational state seeks to create 'public value' rather than
just efficiency. By focusing on the quality of relationships
with people, rather than the quantity of outcomes, the state
can improve public service performance more effectively than
managerial methods. One of the ways to do this is by making
processes 'über-local', as Mulgan has argued. That means
pinpointing those activities which are best carried out by the
community for the community and which have the greatest
opportunity of developing relationships. Mulgan suggests
prioritising systems which encourage citizen feedback and
one-to-one relationships; treating public sector employees
and people as participants, not bystanders; viewing public
services as a platform, rather than a deliverer.[8]

The following examples show how a relational state could
work in practice to empower communities, but by its very
nature, these solutions cannot form a programme for national
governance. Each community will have its own smörgåsbord
of options and it should be for each community to determine

what is best for them. Local government is, in any case, in the best position to provide the support and direction for redistributing power since it operates at the closest level to people. Labour's councillors in local government should be the standard bearers for injecting a sense of community leadership in their wards, not by telling people what to do, but encouraging them to take control for themselves.

National government's role is to agitate on behalf of community empowerment, provide the funding to build capacity – particularly start-up and transition costs – and to incentivise local authorities who are not doing enough by providing funding for pilot projects. So how could community empowerment work in practice?

First, for services that are best provided collectively – for example, integrated health and social care – there is a strong case for community-led commissioning. At the moment too much of the state's role is about commissioning services for people. Community-led commissioning would require the state to commission services with people. It recognises that, often, local people know more about their needs than commissioners do and that, with support, they can help commissioners to build smarter solutions to local problems. The relational state would support this because it helps to build relationships between decision-makers and service users.

Turning Point is a social enterprise which runs a community-led commissioning model called Connected Care, which enables communities to become involved in the design and delivery of health and social care, as well as other support services. Working in ten deprived communities across the country, their model has reduced costs by shifting the emphasis of services towards prevention; helped commissioners develop a better understanding of the needs of the local population; and developed communities' capacity to engage in service redesign.

Indeed, community-led commissioning can also help to strengthen social networks. It is sometimes the little things in life that stop people from finding a new job or getting better. Mostly it is local social services which try and pick up these cases, but as the government cuts spending, local authorities are increasingly focusing their spending on the most acute cases. Initiatives such as Southwark Circle provide an answer to the gap that could be left by the state's retreat from such areas. It works with over 250 older people and matches them with local 'neighbourhood helpers' who volunteer to take care of households tasks, forge social connections and find new directions in life.[9]

In this instance the relational state would encourage social enterprises and the voluntary sector to run programmes like this with different sections of the community, by instituting stronger voluntary and community organisation commissioning practices.

Thus the role of the state in this respect is to encourage local authorities to build community-led commissioning into as much as it can do. Using organisations such as Turning Point to learn from, local authorities need to recognise the value of involving the public in making decisions about services. It helps local people to understand the pressures public services are under and gives them a stake in creating better services – an important spoke of the relational state.

Within the commissioning community, there is clear recognition that making users commissioning partners is good practice, but there needs to be a stronger steer from government that this should be the norm.[10] We should consider including a pro-social clause in every commissioning contract, placing economic value on positive social outcomes, therefore helping to shift commissioning values towards the community and away from strict performance measurements, which can miss the real difference community organisations make on the ground.[11] Such a clause will force commissioners to consider the extra community benefits voluntary and community organisations provide (for example, community involvement), over and above single outcome measures, and ought to lead to greater commissioning of organisations which involve users and the community as a matter of course.

Government should also require all public bodies to develop a voluntary and community sector commissioning strategy. This will ensure that bodies are required to meet with the local voluntary sector to show how community-led commissioning will work in practice.[12]

Second, participatory budgeting – which was pioneered in Porto Alegre in the late 1980s – is designed to give local people not just a say in how services are provided in their area, but to allow them to allocate money. Around 10 per cent of the city's population takes part in setting the budget which has led to a shift in the spending priorities of the city's council and is reported to have led to an improvement in the extent and quality of the provision of basic services to the city's disadvantaged communities.

An example in the UK can be found in Lewisham Council's eighteen 'local assemblies', one for each ward, which include ward councillors, council officers, voluntary and community sector representatives and local residents to deliberate on locally important issues. As people feel they have been involved in the decision to allocate funding to projects, their commitment to a project's destination grows stronger. Websites for each of the local assemblies track the decisions taken and keep people up-to-date with progress. This is another example of building relationships between people with a view to improving the outcomes of communities. By taking part in setting a budget locally, people feel more ownership over what happens to them.

In the National Evaluation of Participatory Budgeting it was found that people's sense of their ability to influence local decision-making improved through the process, greater capacity in the community was built, and people who participated had an increased sense of self-esteem and confidence.[13] By moving dry decisions about public spending from the dusty offices of the bureaucrat into the melee of the street, people feel more engaged with the decisions which directly affect them, and local representatives are more accountable for them too. By increasing transparency, there is also a good knock-on effect of greater scrutiny of poor decision-making by public bodies. All of this helps to improve community relationships and the sense that the community is in in charge. Therefore, we should consider giving local communities who wish to introduce participatory budgeting a right to request a pilot in their community, if money can be found from central government. This will ensure that those councils which are reluctant to have the extra scrutiny of the public are forced to allow dissatisfied communities to hold them to account. Most aspirational local authorities will see the inherent benefit in such schemes, however, as best practice spreads.

Third, credit-based time-banking. Edgar Chan created the concept of time-banking in response to frustration with social services in the US, which he felt were too top-down and failed to utilise the assets of the community to help people help themselves.[14] The UK only recently adopted time-banking, most notably with the Rushey Green Time Bank set up in 1999, which put patients suffering from depression and isolation in touch with volunteers in their neighbourhood. Time banks can provide opportunities for linking volunteers with many local projects including childcare, home repairs, befriending schemes, language lessons and many more skills which the community needs. Most banks operate on the basis that a person donates an hour of their time and can take an hour of someone else's time in return. Time-banking is a great relationship builder. It requires individuals to donate time in return for another's. It also puts local people in charge of finding their own solutions to life's little problems.

Credit-based time-banking goes one step further.

Lambeth Council is considering a scheme which would allow residents to give their time in return for credits that would give them to be rewarded with financial or other benefits. This follows a model in Wales which has been piloted by the organisation Spice, which hosts the time bank in a public sector agency and offers credits to time-givers such as free trips, recreational services or visits to local events.[15] Given the huge potential of time-banking and the role it could play in the 'big society', it is extraordinary that the national volunteering charity TimeBank has had its funding for core costs cut by the Office for Civil Society.[16]

The current government's cuts to the third sector and its ideological commitment to a state on sufferance will undermine, not replenish, our disjointed local communities. A return to an old command-and-control state, however well meant, is not the answer, either.

Only when we recognise that people and the quality of their individual experiences of public services are often more important than the service itself will the left be able to seize the 'big society' mantle. Community commissioning and budgeting, building the framework for local social networks and time banks: these are the tools the left needs to grasp if it is to find new meaning in the word 'empowerment'.

The relational state could help to shift the balance finally away from Whitehall to communities across our country. By prioritising relationship building, collaboration, user feedback and local decision-making, communities could be given a new lease of life.

The Tories' localism is a mask for cuts and contempt. Our localism has to be trusting people's instincts and their better natures. Labour's mission must be to support people to become the authors of their own lives. We have always been optimists, and we have the chance in the next few years to puzzle out not how to survive the cuts, but how to infuse Britain with optimism for the future.

1. Richard H. Tawney, *Equality* (London: George Allen & Unwin, 1931).

2. Richard H. Tawney, *The Acquisitive Society* (New York: Harcourt Brace and Howe, 1920).

3. 'Instituting the "Third Sector" as a Governable Terrain: Partnership, Procurement and Performance in the UK', *Policy & Politics* (2008) vol. 36 no. 2, pp. 155–71.

4. 'Charity leaders' confidence levels hit rock bottom', NCVO, 29 March 2011.

5. 'Poll shows Labour voters lost faith in the state', Demos, 3 August 2011.

6. Geoff Mulgan, *The Birth of the Relational State* (London: The Young Foundation, February 2010).

7. Department for Communities and Local Government, *2008-09 Citizenship Survey Volunteering and Charitable Giving Topic Report*, April 2010.

8. 'A Public Service Renewal Agenda for the 21st Century', The New Synthesis Project, United Kingdom Roundtable Report, London, 16-18 November 2010.

9. For more on Southwark Circle see www.southwarkcircle.org.uk.

10. National Skills Academy for Social Care, *User-Led Organisations and Commissioning: 18 Good Practice Learning Resources* (London: National Skills Academy for Social Care, 2011).

11. For more on this see BASSAC and DTA's response to the Government's Commissioning Green Paper: www.bassac.org.uk.

12. For more on this see NAVCA's response to Government's Commissioning Green Paper, 5 January 2011: see www.navca.org.uk.

13. Department for Communities and Local Government, *National Evaluation of Participatory Budgeting in England*.

14. Edgar S. Cahn, 'Time dollars, work and community: from "why?" to "why not?"' *Futures* (1999) vol. 31, no. 35, pp. 499–509.

15. See Timebanking Wales: www.timebankingwales.org.uk.

16. Timebank, 'Government Pulls the Plug on Timebank Funding': www.timebank.org.uk.

# A state in society for all: better homes in stronger neighbourhoods

*Caroline Flint*

Pollsters have told us over the years that housing is not one of the big four or five decisive factors at general elections. They will tell you that 18.7 million people own their homes, most without help from government. That the economy, crime, the NHS or immigration matter more to people. But try telling that to the 4.4 million people on a waiting list or the three million struggling to get a foot on the property ladder or the 1.4 million households in substandard housing in the private rented sector.

In the 1980s the Tories had only one policy – to sell council houses and shift the political debate by creating a million new working-class homeowners. Their flagship councils followed suit, selling off estates with vigour and even screening new tenants to ensure potential buyers were moving in. The denial of revenues from council house sales, a deliberate policy to reduce public reinvestment in social housing, reinforced by rate-capping councils, created the huge backlogs of disrepair that Labour inherited in 1997.

Today's Tories share their predecessors' scepticism and ideological suspicion of the involvement of the state in providing housing. Their only answer is to leave it to the market.

The consequences of this approach, and the challenges facing an incoming Labour government, are clear: an even greater residualisation of social housing, entrenching deprivation and other social and economic ills; an expanding but unregulated private rented sector, where too many properties are not decent and rent is perceived as 'dead money'; and the hopes of a generation of would-be first-time buyers going unfulfilled.

## More than a roof over your head

Labour's challenge is to fill this policy void; to rectify the hopes unrealised, the aspirations denied, the hardship caused by creating new relationships in the market and in social housing, which shift the balance of power and opportunity in the interests of individual security and advancement, and the common good. The case for using the power of government, then, is a strong one and the benefit of public investment in housing is clear.

But our answer to this challenge must be realistic, both about the complexity of the housing market and the limits of what the state acting alone can achieve, as well as likely future levels of public expenditure, not least because certainty for lenders and housebuilders alike is crucial.

Just simply providing more housing, vital though that it is, is no longer enough. We must be honest that for too long, and in too many places, our housing policy was too divorced from the creation of communities that people want to live in. A successful housing policy must be about more than a roof over your head.

That means thinking about housing in terms of people's relationship with their home and with their neighbourhood in a way that goes beyond just talking about tenure, which empowers individuals and neighbourhoods to take control over where they live, and where people are able to take advantage of decent public spaces and good local services, in strong, safe communities.

Our aim should be to redistribute power so that people have control over their home and their neighbourhood, so that everyone can enjoy the sorts of power and choice those with financial means already have.

But for our offer to the public to be credible, we have to be candid about our housing record when we were in government.

As a former housing minister, I know that during the last Labour government nearly two million more homes were built, including half a million more affordable homes. But it was not enough.

There are reasons why we did not do more. In 1997 we inherited a £19bn maintenance backlog and over two million substandard homes in desperate need of renovation. Our Decent Homes programme put that right and brought a million and half homes up to a decent standard.

But it came at the cost of not building enough new homes to keep up with demand. While local resistance to new housing developments suggests that the connection between the lack of housing supply and rising housing costs is not fully understood, there can be no doubt that whether it is a first-time buyer struggling to get a foot on the property ladder, or a family looking for somewhere to settle, or the housing benefits bill, what is at the root of all these problems is a lack of affordable housing.

To compound the problem, as housing has becoming increasingly unaffordable, public subsidy has shifted from the supply side to the demand side. Thirty-five years ago, 80 per cent of the housing budget actually went on bricks and mortar, on building new homes. Now, more than 85 per cent of the housing budget goes on helping people with their housing costs, because the lack of affordable housing has driven up rents and house prices so much. That is unsustainable. But it's also an inefficient use of a public subsidy; pouring money into private landlords' pockets neither gets to the root of the problem nor helps people secure assets of their own.

## A foot on the ladder

Today, the average age of a first-time buyer without parental help is thirty-seven, and this could rise to the mid-forties by the end of this decade. The number of first-time buyers is at its lowest level for forty years, the typical deposit on a property is more than half the average income and people are being forced to change or reorder important life decisions, such as when to marry or have children. Some research even suggests that couples are consciously delaying having children because of housing costs, potentially with long-term implications for their ability to conceive.

No one can doubt that the credit crunch has exacerbated the problems for first-time buyers, with mortgage lending plummeting, but the downward trend in the numbers of first-time buyers predates the global financial crisis. Even before 2008, during a period of easy mortgage finance, affordability problems were preventing many people from buying.

We should forget those who say home ownership is losing favour, penning articles from the comfort of owner-occupied leafy suburbs and country cottages. The desire to be close to family, invest, improve, move to the nice neighbourhoods, leave something behind for the next generation, or just have a few square metres all of your own – conservatory and all – is instinctive, and the drive to own is unshakeable. Crucial to Labour's agenda is enabling this aspiration to be enjoyed as widely as possible.

Limiting the opportunities for home ownership is more than just a cause of frustration for would-be first-time buyers; it fundamentally shapes the sort of society we live in. Giving people a stake in the property market and allowing them to build up an asset base is empowering because it gives people control over where they live. The shift to owner-occupation that took place in the twentieth century was crucial to creating a fairer society, where assets were more evenly spread, and helped to reduce inequality between the very rich and those on middle incomes.

That trend now appears to be in reverse, with housing wealth increasingly concentrated among existing owners and the older generation, creating a chasm between those able to rely on help from parents, and those with no parental resources to call on. Labour must have a positive offer for these people, especially those families who would not qualify for social housing, but who cannot currently afford to buy their own home.

That does not mean encouraging irresponsible lending to those unable to meet their mortgage repayments, as happened in the US with so-called NINJA (No Income, No Job or Assets) loans, because that does not empower people: it traps and eventually impoverishes them.

Instead we should be looking to new and underdeveloped models of home ownership. This can only be done if additional finance, particularly from institutional sources, is brought to bear on the task of increasing the supply of new affordable homes.

The single biggest problem facing potential first-time buyers at the moment is the level of deposit required. But the other side of the coin to struggling first-time buyers is an ageing society. The number of people over eighty-five in the UK is predicted to more than double in the next twenty-five years, and to treble in the next thirty-five.

Is it not strange that parents and even grandparents, whose mortgages may be paid off, see their children or grandchildren struggling to find deposits, when all the security a mortgage lender might require is locked up in their own home? We need to be more imaginative about the power of equity release, on fair terms, to transfer assets from one generation to the next. Equity release gained a bad name because of the fees and poor rates of return. But intergenerational transfers of assets would be easier if equity transfer was provided as part of a package by mortgage lenders, backed by government. A lender could, for instance, use spare equity in a parent's or grandparent's home as additional security against a mortgage. This would enable first-time buyers to get a more manageable mortgage, with a smaller initial deposit, without needing large cash transfers or increasing the risk to the lender.

Equally, the market is not good at enabling people to trade down in their later years, so that they can move to smaller or more manageable properties. Many older people want to stay close to friends, to family, to the church they know. But as a result, some stay put for as long as possible, even though they may struggle with a family-sized house.

Providing housing that better meets the needs of older people would not only be good for the people who live there, it could also potentially free up housing that may otherwise have been underoccupied, as older people choose to move from a larger home to something smaller.

We should examine whether a council, housing association or even a letting agency could offer a smaller rented property to an older person. In return, instead of having to sell their home, the housing provider could take a lease on it for a defined period, which they would then be able to rent out. The rental income from the larger property would more than cover that of the smaller, and potentially even provide an additional revenue stream, which could either be returned to the original homeowner, or kept by the housing provider to subsidise rents for low-income families, or invested in new affordable homes (or some combination of all three, as an incentive to the existing owner, as well as prospective housing providers and tenants).

This would offer the most efficient use of all properties, help to release finance in later life that would otherwise remain unused, while avoiding an unnecessary early sale and retaining the home as a family asset, which could then be handed down to children and grandchildren, so that they can begin to build their own asset base.

For the families renting the properties, given the lack of suitable family accommodation in the private rented sector, and the insecurity associated with short-term assured tenancies which often only last six months, it could also potentially provide better accommodation and greater security than is currently available.

But for first-time buyers without parental assets to rely on, the challenge of getting onto the first rung on the ladder remains.

Shared ownership schemes are ideal for young couples as they allow for joint ownership of a property. Nearly half of all buyers of shared ownership homes in 2008–9 had household incomes below £25,000, nearly a quarter had incomes below £20,000, and the average age of a shared ownership home buyer was thirty-two, compared to an average of thirty-seven for first-time buyers without parental assistance.

By purchasing as little as 25 per cent, paying rent on the remaining share, and with the option to build up a larger stake as and when circumstances allow, they allow first-time buyers without a big deposit to gradually move to full ownership. Rent-to-buy schemes also offer another way for first-time buyers, without the ability to raise large deposits, to begin to build up their own asset base. By offering a discounted rent, and in some cases even the return of a portion of rent paid, rent-to-buy schemes mean that tenants are able to build up a deposit, allowing them to access home ownership, often through shared ownership schemes.

Such schemes have already helped over 130,000 first-time buyers, but they have the potential to help many more. To date, they have been pioneered by housing associations, but to expand them we need to be looking at how we can get greater private sector involvement, from both developers and lenders, in shared ownership schemes.

Shared ownership lending is more complex than a traditional mortgage. But at the moment the way loan-to-value ratios are calculated (which determines whether, and how much, the lenders are prepared to offer) penalises shared ownership; the loan-to-value is calculated on the buyer's share of the property, rather than the value of the entire property, even though the lender is able to claim against the landlord's share too were the borrower to default on their mortgage. In this way, the ratio, and the level of risk it implies, is overstated for shared ownership models. Indeed, the risk to lenders, and the level of repossessions, is actually lower for shared home owners than for traditional home owners or even buy-to-let properties. Lenders need to understand this and become more familiar with shared ownership models. For that to happen Labour's housing policy review will be looking closely at whether clearer and fairer guidance is needed from the government, the Council of Mortgage Lenders and the Financial Services Authority.

Nor is it a huge leap to envisage the mortgage lenders retaining 10 per cent of the equity in a house to secure their lending, pooling the risk through industry-wide funds and thereby enabling smaller deposits to be required. Similarly, some local authorities, such as Sunderland, are looking at how they can stimulate their housing markets and support first-time buyers by providing mortgages. Sunderland offers mortgages of up to 90 per cent, but no more than three times the household income and up to a maximum of £200,000. Their mortgages are only available to people who are in secure employment, with a good credit history, but who have been unable to secure a mortgage elsewhere. While such an approach may not be viable in areas of higher housing demand or higher house prices, it is certainly worth exploring.

Equally, mutual home ownership offers another way to provide affordable housing. It works by making land available as a community asset held in perpetuity by a Community Land Trust, whose sole objective is to provide affordable housing to local people. Because the cost of the land is separated from the cost of the development, the housing is much cheaper and more affordable for people looking to rent or buy. And due to the fact that the housing is explicitly and permanently for local people, some of the most common objections to development can be overcome, not least the fear in some places that new housing will just be bought by outsiders, driving up the costs of housing for local people.

Birmingham Cooperative Housing Services are at the forefront of the mutual home ownership model. Co-op members effectively pool their resources to help the co-op to buy properties. Members build up shares in the housing development, allowing them to develop equity, which they can sell to the co-op or on the open market if they leave. This model shares power and promotes democracy and self-help in equal measure.

## Renewing social housing

Social housing is fundamental to a decent, civilised society. But it must be more than just a last-chance saloon or a refuge for the dispossessed. It should never entrench deprivation, reinforce dependence or hinder social mobility.

In the most obvious sense, that means giving people in social housing much greater influence over what happens on their street, in their estate or around their neighbourhood. The shift from councils managing their own housing stock to arm's-length management organisations was intended to improve the management of social housing and give tenants more of a say in decision-making. But we need to be honest about how well this worked, whether it went far enough, or if there is more that could be done to improve the nature of the relationship between social housing providers and their tenants so that, instead of being passive recipients of decisions taken by others, tenants have the right – and the ability – to actively shape where they live. The best housing associations already do this. And the evidence from cooperative and mutual housing associations shows that they can deliver high levels of resident satisfaction, as well as foster resilient, vibrant and engaged communities through self-management and mutual ownership.

Building on the 'right to manage' where stock transfer ballots are being held, we will look closely at the idea of giving them the option of a community-led mutual. Even where ballots are not in the pipeline, if there is demand from residents, there is a case to be made, in principle, that they should be able to petition for a ballot, where they could then vote to move to a community ownership model. For this to have effect, formal rights need to be backed up with capacity building, provided by either local authorities or housing associations, so that communities have both the right and the ability to take greater control over where they live.

Indeed, the ethos of the friendly societies – of mutual action, common values and empowering people to come together to improve their neighbourhood – is one that should be transplanted not just to social housing but to other types of tenure too.

But empowering social tenants goes beyond giving them greater control of their housing and means looking at how we can use social housing to give people greater control over their lives, their employment and their relationship with the community they belong to.

Allocation by need means that, where demand is highest, only the poorest, most vulnerable and most marginalised have any chance of renting a social home. Over time, the impact of right-to-buy sales and the failure to adequately replenish stock has led to a profound residualisation of social housing, with prospective tenants forced to clear ever-higher tests of need, creating estates characterised by a vicious cycle of workless-ness and deprivation, and neighbourhoods scarred by narrow horizons and low ambitions. We must seek to reverse this.

Labour councils like Manchester and Newham point to a different way of doing things. In Newham, they are looking to prioritise those in employment in their allocations policy, so as to support people in work. In Manchester, as well as helping the most vulnerable with housing, their allocation gives priority to those who contribute to their communities – what they describe as having a 'community connection'. That means more than just living or working locally. It covers people who have been involved with a community-based voluntary activity in the area for at least six months, as well as people who provide employment or a service in the area, which provides job for local people or a service for the local community.

Those systems reward good tenants and good neighbours. They are fairer because they look not just at what people receive but also at what they put in. And they encourage the kind of responsible behaviour that makes our communities stronger and safer.

Other than an innate conservativism, there's nothing stopping more local authorities doing this. Indeed, many are already looking to councils like Manchester and Newham for inspiration. But if priority for social housing allocation is, at least in part, determined by national laws which state which groups must be given reasonable preferences, it is certainly worth looking at whether the existing national guidance needs revisiting.

But if greater powers to shape the places people live in are devolved to local authorities, in return we must also empower local people to hold their council to account and ensure those powers are being used to maximum effect.

Labour's Together campaign, which brought communities into the process of tackling antisocial behaviour, supporting communities and tilting the balance of power away from their violent neighbours, is a model for future action.

One of the most effective police powers is the civil order to close a crackhouse. Where properties were reported for Class A drug dealing, the police obtained a closure order, moving in within forty-eight hours and boarding them up, searching and arresting the inhabitants where required.

What many people would welcome is an eviction order – call it the 'Hasbo' if you will – against antisocial neighbours: a simple mechanism for the police to employ where a household is reported repeatedly for antisocial or violent behaviour. The power for residents to petition the police, to submit complaints confidentially, leading to a magistrate's order could be a powerful tool. Imagine if the family most people fear is evicted and refused the right to live within five miles of the area, whatever their housing tenure? What a message that would send out.

Experience has shown how hamstrung councils are when they evict a family, only for them to rent a property privately 100 yards away and the problems and the fear continue. What does 'power to the people' mean if it is not on your own doorstep?

The crackhouse policy was so popular because people saw their complaints, their fears for their children, being turned into action, and the culprits dispersed or arrested. A central ingredient of Labour's neighbourhood empowerment is for residents to know that the state is on their side and that justice prevails.

**Empowering tenants in the private sector**
The fall in first-time buyers, and the government's failure to invest in social housing, means that the rapid growth we have seen in the private rented sector over the last two decades is likely to continue. Reversing the historic trend of the twentieth century, which saw private renting displaced as the most common tenure by owner-occupation, more and more people will be spending time in the private rented sector.

Most people living in the private rented sector are happy with their home. But to talk of a single 'private rented sector' belies its heterogeneity and complexity. Alongside mobile young professionals, students and those on high incomes in the choicest locations paying prime rents, is the housing benefit market, as well as immigrants, asylum seekers, and those in temporary accommodation.

And there is a serious problem, particularly at the bottom end of the market, with a minority of rogue landlords who exploit their tenants and fail to meet their responsibilities. Nearly half of all homes in the private rented sector, over a million properties according to the Chartered Institute of Environmental Health, would not meet the Decent Homes standard.

Our answer must be to empower people to hold their landlords to account and drive up standards in the private rented sector. When we were in government, work had begun on a register of landlords, and we will look closely again at how we could create the best possible standards regime with robust rights for tenants. We will look also at what bodies are needed to implement and, where necessary, enforce them, and how we communicate with tenants to make sure people know their rights. Such a system could empower not only tenants, but responsible landlords too.

But it would be naive to believe that such a system alone would be sufficient to drive up standards, especially at the bottom end of the private rented sector, not least for tenants currently living in poor quality housing, who would understandably be reluctant to report their landlords and risk jeopardising their home. So we must be prepared to look at the housing benefit system too and ensure it is more closely allied with our objectives for housing policy.

Housing benefit is paid towards 40 per cent of private rented tenancies, and 40 per cent of those properties would not meet the Decent Homes standards. I find it difficult to accept that the state should be subsidising substandard housing, or lining the pockets of irresponsible landlords, or indeed that the state has no sway over the market. By introducing a landlords' register you could ensure that housing benefit was only paid in respect of properties that met the Decent Homes standard. In this way you could empower people renting privately and drive up standards without requiring an overly burdensome regulatory system.

For young professionals and students, the flexibility of the private rented sector is its greatest asset. But we need a private rented sector that works better for young families. The short tenures that characterise private renting, and the high turnover of residents that it encourages, can be disempowering for individuals and communities. If people are spending longer in the private rented sector then we need to ensure they can do so with the security that is needed to raise a family, find stable employment and contribute to the community. Similarly, if we want to give people a greater sense of control over where they live, we have to appreciate how destabilising and difficult it is to build strong, resilient communities, with high levels of trust and social capital, when people find themselves with a new set of neighbours every six months.

In theory, there are no restrictions on longer tenancies being offered, but in practice they are rarely available. One of the reasons they are not is because, at the moment, many lenders offering buy-to-let mortgages stipulate that borrowers can only offer short tenancies of six or twelve months, for fear that if interest rates rise landlords would be saddled with tenants paying below-cost rent and left unable to service their mortgage. Our housing policy review will consider why a longer fixed tenancy of five or ten years could not contain some flexibility on rents. While it would need to ensure that rents could not be dramatically increased overnight, there could be a mechanism for rents to be periodically reviewed so as to reflect any changes in interest rates or other demonstrable costs. Longer tenancies of this nature could benefit not only tenants looking for stability, but also landlords looking for the security of a regular, guaranteed rental income. In turn, the risk to lenders would be reduced too, as the likelihood of gaps between tenants, with the landlord being left to pick up the bill, would be cut.

**Power for the many**
For two centuries, the great reformers have looked at housing as essential to the civilising of society, to creating stability and even to avoiding revolution. Government-led house building epitomised the British renaissance and recovery from the traumas of the Second World War. A decent home for all was the ambition then, and it endures today.

A badly organised or mismanaged housing system – whether private or public – can stifle aspirations, halt mobility, deny choice and reinforce dependency, without intending to do any of these. That is why we must get it right. In 2015, Labour can use housing to embody the best of Britain. We can demonstrate optimism, show empathy with those who strive to get on, and demonstrate our accord with the ambitions, hopes and dreams of every family.

Labour's vision must rebuild the concept of homes in real communities, not houses in dormitories: neighbourhoods where pride matters, where neighbours matter; where people live and enjoy, and do not simply exist. To do so, we must recast the relationships between tenant and landlord, mortgage holder and lenders, and resident and community. We must recast rights and responsibilities that go beyond paying the rent on time or stop at the front door. In so doing, we can build a stronger, fairer society where power, wealth and opportunity are in the hands of the many, not the few.

# Cutting crime and building confidence: empowering victims and communities

*Jenny Chapman and Jacqui Smith*

Crime and justice should always be one of Labour's priorities. Everybody is affected by it, but if people cannot afford security or to move away from antisocial behaviour, you suffer more. If you cannot afford insurance because there are many burglaries where you live, then having your house broken into is a financial as well as a personal disaster. It is not just partygoers who have to walk home late at night, but also low-paid, shift and female workers. Those with least financial clout and power suffer most from crime and antisocial behaviour. That's why tackling crime and supporting victims must be a central part of a progressive political agenda.

This chapter examines how to redistribute power to local communities in order to improve accountability in the criminal justice system. Crime intimidates victims and the wider community and makes people feel powerless. Giving people information and influence over how crime is tackled acts to redress this power imbalance and makes detection and prosecution more likely. We begin by reflecting on Labour's record in tackling crime and considering various approaches to involving communities, including some examples from the US. For us, this chapter is an opportunity to open a conversation about how Labour should approach crime and punishment. The role of the victim, the community, sentencing and the prison service are given particular attention. A common theme is a call for greater openness and transparency throughout the system, from reporting of crime to the completion of sentence.

We do not, however, focus on international or organised crime and counter-terrorism work in this chapter. That is not because these are not important. Globalisation impacts upon crime as well as the economy and there will continue to be real challenges for policing in tackling drugs, organised crime and terrorism in the coming decade. We note that the Serious and Organised Crime Agency (SOCA) had begun to make progress towards a more international and intelligence-led approach to tackling this type of crime. The government plans to replace SOCA with a new national crime-fighting agency in 2012. It will include organised crime, border policing and the Child Exploitation and Online Protection Centre. Labour should watch to see whether the planned replacement, the National Crime Agency, builds on SOCA's work or disrupts its progress through a needless reorganisation.

Labour home secretaries were often charged with populism by the liberal-left. Frustration with a criminal justice system that consistently failed to focus sufficiently on communities and victims led politicians – as the only directly accountable part of the system – to speak up for the views they heard daily on doorsteps and in their surgeries. Faced with the pain and impotence of victims and the tired resignation of local communities, it is not surprising that politicians try to gain the initiative with criticism of judges, public association with high-profile victims and tough words on reforming the system.

Prioritising the interests of victims is the right political instinct, but it needs to be turned into long-term reform. The appalling treatment of Milly Dowler's family during the trial of her killer earlier this year shows that there is still a very long way to go. Bob Dowler described the experience of gaining justice for his daughter as 'a truly mentally scarring experience on an unimaginable scale'.[1]

## Labour's record

In this chapter, we argue for a real shift of power to local communities, accountability of policing and the wider criminal justice system, and strong, statutory rights for victims. But we should not forget that there were notable successes in pushing reforms in this direction during our time in government.

Labour left government with crime lowered. There were fewer victims and the chance of being a victim was at a historic low. British Crime Survey data reveals that crime has fallen by 43 per cent since 1997.[2] Predictions of increases in acquisitive crime through the recession have so far proved false. The number of police officers increased. Workforce reform enabled the introduction of highly visible police community support officers, and the percentage of people reporting the police doing a 'good' or 'excellent' job rose from 47 per cent in 2003–4 to 56 per cent in 2009–10.[3] Police officers were freed to concentrate on the work that most needed their expertise and training by the civilianisation of support roles.

Neighbourhood policing teams were established in every part of the country. All forty-three police forces in England and Wales signed up to the Policing Pledge in December 2008. It laid down a minimum standard of performance for the 3,600 neighbourhood policing teams, including holding monthly 'beat' meetings with the public, and abiding by target response times, such as getting to somebody within fifteen minutes of a 999 call. In scrapping this, the current government mistakes a guarantee to the public for a centrally imposed target. In fact, all central targets and most central data collection was scrapped by Labour, leaving just one national target: to increase public confidence that the police were dealing with the issues that matter most to local people. This focus guaranteed that police had to engage locally, had to determine local priorities and had to communicate results. Labour also introduced local crime maps so people could check what was happening to crime in their neighbourhood.

Labour recognised that antisocial behaviour was not just a nuisance, but was having a devastating and sometimes even fatal effect on individuals and their neighbourhoods. Antisocial behaviour orders were starting to have an effect and we were wrong to play down our focus on antisocial behaviour towards the end of our time in government. Labour rightly focused on domestic violence and sexual abuse where victims are particularly powerless. Introducing new services, particularly independent advisers and advocates for victims, meant they had support through the criminal justice system. Support was also provided in dealing with the wider impacts of these crimes, such as financial, health, family and housing issues. We recognise that this support remains patchy across the country. This is unacceptable and must improve.[4]

Labour understood that supporting victims of crime, and preventing crime, involved changing public services beyond the criminal justice system. For example, preventing repeat offending among young people involved a number of agencies. Authorities gained the power to remove young people from the street to a place of safety and early intervention projects, involving multi-disciplinary teams, worked with families to prevent their young people going off the rails. This is not simply a police or social service function, but the business of professionals from education, health and housing too.

Local criminal justice boards brought together all the agencies involved to promote a more coherent approach, although they still lack real visibility or accountability. Stubbornly high reoffending rates were starting to shift. When controlling for changes in offender characteristics, the proportion of offenders reconvicted has fallen by 10.4 per cent since 2000.[5] Reducing reoffending remains the holy grail of criminal justice policy. Probation services were building

stronger partnerships with local authorities, the private and
voluntary sector to ensure effective ways of turning offenders
away from crime.

## A fair deal for victims

Home Office research suggests that four-fifths of all directly
detected offences had victims or witnesses able to provide
helpful leads.[6] The police know that they cannot tackle crime
alone and they certainly cannot achieve convictions without
support from victims and people willing to act as witnesses.
But there needs to be a fair deal here. If the public provide
information, sometimes at actual or perceived risk to themselves, the least they deserve is to be told what the result of
their contribution was.

Community confidence in the criminal justice system will
only grow if victims are treated properly, well supported and
well informed. Labour knows the needs of victims are not
adequately understood. We appointed Louise Casey as the
first commissioner for victims and witnesses, who agrees that
the system is balanced away from victims: 'Offenders have
rights within the criminal justice system to ensure their interests are protected. And rightly so. However, victims make do
with codes, charters and pledges, which are well intentioned,
but not enforceable.'

Labour must commit to legally enforceable rights for
victims – to support, to information, and to a say within the
system. In this way victims know what they can expect from
the system and have the power to challenge where services are
lacking. We will say more on victims' role in sentencing later.

## Empowered communities

Crime has an impact beyond the victim and their family.
In some communities, people feel that crime and antisocial behaviour has made them all victims even when they
are not directly affected. Labour understands that citizens

can improve their lives by getting involved in determining, designing and sometimes providing the services they need. Furthermore, evidence suggests that being able to take control and influence crime-fighting priorities does not just make communities feel empowered, it has a positive impact on levels of crime too. Home Office analysis suggests that people living in areas with strong informal social control, where residents think that neighbours are willing to intervene to stop minor crime and disorder, experience lower levels of crime and antisocial behaviour compared to otherwise similar neighbourhoods. [7]

There are several programmes already in existence at home and abroad that we believe Labour should examine more fully with a view to widening their use to empower communities throughout the country. But we do not have to wait for Labour to win the next election; the party in local government can begin piloting and implementing these programmes now.

First, we should begin by involving more communities in the Community Crime Fighter programme. Nearly 4,000 community activists have received training to help them challenge criminal justice agencies on the level of service they provide.[8] Volunteers are given training and act as a link between the police and the public. Similar approaches to community involvement are found in the US. Citizen police academies are used by many police departments to offer members of the public training and education about the structure and operation of the police. Evening courses generally run for a number of weeks with students visiting police stations and meeting officers. Students are encouraged to share their experiences with others and become an informal volunteer support network for the police. Critics argue that participants are already supportive of the police and rarely fully reflect the communities where they live. The truth is that all efforts to engage the public take time to become the norm and that, providing the professionals are aware of the need to make extra effort with under-represented groups, involving willing community activists is better than involving none at all.

Second, there is no doubt that careful planning of meetings and use of local intelligence is important in tailoring an appropriate approach which prioritises engagement of a cross-section of the community. In Houston, officers relied on existing community groups to assist in establishing and running community police stations. Volunteers are based in community venues and assist the police in conveying and receiving information. Volunteers do not replace police officers but support them at a very local and grassroots level. This is an interesting idea that should be piloted in the UK, with care taken to involve individuals from an appropriate range of backgrounds. In Houston, volunteers came predominantly from white middle-class backgrounds. The programme evaluation found that benefits such as a reduction in the fear of crime were restricted to this population and that poorer minority communities did not hear about, or benefit from, the work. Officers, councillors and community activists leading public meetings or coordinating activities need to be aware of the danger of excluding some groups from the benefits of their programmes. Nonetheless, it is important to remember that the 'usual suspects' can often become the most dedicated core of volunteers. Rather than putting off the most dedicated participants, enlightened practitioners find ways to harness their enthusiasm and availability while not excluding others.

Third, community engagement experts make the point that participants must be involved in a process to improve their lives, not simply used as a tool in a police initiative. Feedback, real-time information and a two-way dialogue are essential. Similar projects can have very different outcomes depending on the quality of the relationship between agencies and the public.[9] Getting the flow of information right is difficult but crucial and there are many ways of doing so. In Darlington, the Police and Communities Together programme is in its third year. Monthly meetings are held for residents, police and other agencies to share information. Up to three policing priorities are agreed. Police commit to returning to the next meeting and updating residents on what has happened, residents undertake to act as the 'eyes and ears' of the police and organise to support them. A typical example would be establishing activities for young people to assist in reducing antisocial behaviour. There are many similar approaches being taken around the country. We believe there must now be a thorough evaluation of the impact of these programmes so that lessons can be learned and implementation improved.

Success of such engagement initiatives is unlikely if communication fails. There are already examples of hyper-local websites enabling people to pool information about vandalism, fly-tipping, areas where drugs are being used and sold, or acute noise nuisance. Labour councils could lead the development of these in their areas and bring together agencies to respond through publicising their action on the websites too. Labour needs to understand that citizens want to communicate in ways that make life easier for them. This means providing a variety of methods.

Some areas have experimented with the use of Facebook as a tool for sharing local crime information. Previously a volunteer may have received information from the police and delivered a newsletter to neighbours. An alternative is to create a Facebook group, or similar online forum, where the police can communicate with residents, respond to enquiries, receive intelligence and provide information and reassurance quickly and cheaply. This allows for the engagement of those who might not come to a public meeting but are interested in the safety of their neighbourhood all the same.

The government is wrong to scrap ASBOs and replace them with either weaker injunctions or orders that require a criminal conviction. However, they are right to propose giving communities the ability to initiate action where agencies fail to respond. But a right to take community action without the capacity to ensure that it can happen is an empty promise. This is a good example of where Community Crime Fighters can support communities to make their voices heard. Police and local authorities should also have to report their response to this community call to the locally elected crime representative as well as directly back to those who made the complaint.

Crime maps were an important step forward in providing timely, local information on crime levels, but they stop at the reporting of the crime. We would like to show what happens next. Labour should ensure that crime mapping also includes 'justice mapping' so that information about what happens when a crime is reported is shared. This should include whether a conviction took place and what sentence was received. The golden thread running through our criminal justice system in the future must be transparency. This starts with the police working together with communities to prevent crime, but must extend to the easy accessing of sentencing information for those who have become victims.

Labour strengthened the confiscation of assets regime and ensured that a significant part of the proceeds of confiscation went back to police forces and other agencies. However, people rarely see what happens to them and there is little local say in how they are spent. Baroness Newlove, in her recent report on safe and active communities, proposed that where communities work together to reduce crime, they should be rewarded with money from confiscated assets to reinvest in crime prevention and they should decide how it is spent.[10] This is a good idea that Labour should support and, where possible, Labour councils and mayors should start to put it into operation now.

And there are other innovative Labour authorities that could be the inspiration for future national policy. As Steve

Reed and Paul Brant outline in their chapter, community-led commissioning in providing diversionary youth activities can be both more effective and more efficient.

As Reed has argued elsewhere:

> Many councils spend several hundred thousand pounds a year to steer young people away from gangs, but with success rates barely any different to what Mimi [the single mum and pastor leading the work] achieved. So why was this community-led initiative so successful? It's because the community itself understands the social networks, individuals, families and highly localised circumstances far better than any outside professionals could do. They use all this, driven by their urgent concern for their own children, to engage with the young people and divert them away from the ruinous path they are following. It works, delivering better results for the community but at a fraction of the cost of what the public authorities were spending.[11]

## Accountable policing

Our proposals encourage local police and criminal justice accountability to residents, but there is more we must do to deliver truly accountable policing. We will enter the next general election campaign in an era of directly elected police and crime commissioners. Labour cannot be arguing for a return to unelected and largely unnoticed police authorities. We must demand more, not less, direct accountability. In most areas of the country, a single force commissioner will be distant from the day-to-day crime concerns of most localities. To make an impact he or she will have to come into conflict with the chief constable – this is where the threat to operational independence will emerge. Labour should argue for direct election of crime commissioners to represent part of a force area perhaps coterminous with the areas covered by crime and disorder reduction partnerships – the multi-agency groups set up by Labour to tackle crime, drugs and antisocial behaviour throughout a geographic area – which could be chaired by the directly elected member. These representatives would then make up a force-level authority.

At a neighbourhood level, accountability depends on the existence of a neighbourhood policing team and the guarantee of regular consultation with local communities. Together with the reinstatement of the Policing Pledge already discussed, Labour should improve incentives to officers to remain in neighbourhood roles for longer. This reform, which has been recommended in a government review of police pay and conditions by Tom Winsor, must be delivered.[12] Furthermore, there should be dedicated training and recognition for this role – it must have the highest status, not just be a route to promotion to a more 'specialised' role. Just as our best teachers have been given special incentives and status in recognition of excellence in the classroom, our officers should be rewarded for providing top quality neighbourhood policing. Teachers no longer need to take management roles in order to gain additional rewards; the same principle should apply to policing.

Labour should restate its commitment to obliging the police and their partners to build the confidence of the local community. The coalition government has removed the requirement for police forces to report on their progress in delivering the British Crime Survey measure of local people's confidence that 'the police and local council are dealing with the antisocial behaviour and crime issues that matter in the local area'. The importance of this measure is that it focuses policing on how crime and antisocial behaviour can be reduced – how the police are working with local partners, addressing their priorities and communicating the results. It would drive the type of involvement and transparency that we want to see, and Labour should insist that forces publish their results on this measure.

### Victims, communities and sentencing

What happens after the police have done their job also matters to victims and the wider community. Most favour reparation and support rehabilitation as a means of safeguarding others. The public and the professionals share insights into the underlying causes of criminality. With regard to previously offending under-eighteens, 82 per cent of the population consider 'better supervision by parents' to be a 'very' or 'somewhat effective' measure in preventing further crime, compared to just 14 per cent who see it as an ineffective measure. Treatment to tackle drug addiction (77 per cent) or binge drinking (74 per cent), and better mental healthcare (73 per cent) are also considered successful measures in preventing under-eighteens reoffending.[13] But the public want to know that alongside effective rehabilitation comes punishment, and they do not want to pay for expensive prison sentences that leave offenders unprepared for life away from addiction or crime.[14]

Public confidence in sentencing is weak. It is difficult for victims to understand what a sentence means, how long will actually be served and how an offender will be monitored upon release. Politicians of all parties have made commitments to increase transparency in sentencing but little has changed. Labour needs to establish a sentencing framework where the victim's experience is put first.

The public are unconvinced by the use of community sentences, with 60 per cent seeing community sentences as 'a soft option' or 'weak and undemanding'.[15] There is greater support for community sentences where the sentence directly benefits the people who have suffered as a result of the crime. The public say they want community punishment that is visible, manual and where breaches are rigorously enforced. We think it is appropriate for victims to be allowed a greater say in determining the nature of a community sentence. The use of restorative justice as an alternative to conventional sentencing, or as an alternative to entering the criminal justice system at all, shows high levels of victim satisfaction.[16] Implementation of restorative justice is poorly funded and lacks a national strategy. We must learn from forces such as Lancashire and Durham where restorative justice and greater use of discretion among police officers is becoming commonplace.

We can go much further in integrating the courts and judiciary into local communities, ensuring they work with other agencies and give people a sight and say into sentencing and offender management. We know that victims of crime can differ in their attitudes to punishment. Judges already listen to the experience of victims in impact statements, but victims do not have any formal role in determining a sentence. We should explore the possibility of allowing victims the right to provide a recommendation, and whether or not this should be binding, on the length or type of sentence, within clearly defined ranges available to the judge.

In December 2004, Labour set up the first community justice centre in north Liverpool (based on experience from Brooklyn, New York). Different agencies under the same roof ensure joint working aimed at engaging the community, with a single judge bringing together a range of measures in sentencing to address underlying causes of offending. Early evaluations are cautiously positive.[17] The project should be piloted in other areas and evidence gathered with a view to replicating community justice centres across the country. All those passing sentences need to become better acquainted with the true nature of community sentences and undertake regular training to help inform their decision-making.

### Holding prisons to account

It is not just transparency in community sentencing or length of sentence that matters to victims – what happens inside prison is important too. Using time behind bars to challenge offending behaviour, educate, rehabilitate and help prepare people for a non-criminal life is the desire of any prison governor or justice secretary. This frequently fails because programmes are ineffective, resources inadequate and release not properly planned. Labour needs to consider how to make better use of the resources that already exist within prisons.

Prison officers are the largest professional group working in our prisons, with thousands of others including teachers, psychologists and probation officers supporting inmates to become law-abiding citizens upon release. We believe prison officers are an under-utilised resource within the criminal justice system. Rehabilitation needs to become a 'whole prison' objective involving all staff. Prison officers spend more time with prisoners than any other professionals. They form the most influential relationships with inmates and have the greatest opportunity to alter the beliefs and values of the incarcerated. Labour needs to ensure more prison officers are trained to act as Personal Support Officers, with the duty of becoming the key figure in the rehabilitation of a number of inmates. Personal Support Officers can negotiate regime regulations to ensure timely access to courses, act as a role model in demonstrating good interpersonal skills and write informed reports on inmates' progress.

If prison officers are to have an increased role in the rehabilitation of offenders, we need to examine recruitment, training and remuneration policies. As more officers fulfil duties beyond security alone, different personal qualities and higher levels of qualification should be required. The government cannot leave rehabilitation to the third sector or specialist services and neglect the most influential people in the lives of inmates.

If the job of prisons is to rehabilitate offenders, then the performance of prisons needs to be assessed according to how successful they are in improving outcomes for the community. Aside from maintaining security, the reoffending rate should become the most important measure of how well a prison is doing its job. Ways of ensuring all staff benefit and share the incentive to make preventing crime central to their daily work need to be considered. Currently, government Inspectorate visits and reports from organisations with an interest in prisons, such as The Howard League, provide detailed qualitative insights into practice, but comparison of outcomes by establishment needs to be extended. Governors, prison officers and others working in a prison do not know how well they have done their job in rehabilitating, and are not rewarded or recognised when they succeed.

Poor conditions, cruelty, violent incidents and security breaches are investigated and measured, but all prisons need to be accountable for their outcomes, not just their practices. Recidivism information for inmates previously held at prisons of a similar security category, across both the public and private sector, should be available for comparison and to provide feedback to prison officers and others. Currently, those working with offenders rarely find out whether their efforts have been successful or have failed. Good outcomes should be recognised and rewarded through the pay structure and also through allowing successful prisons greater freedom to innovate.

From preventing crime to completion of sentence we have argued that victims of crime deserve greater status in the criminal justice system and that empowering communities will help to reduce crime and to catch and convict criminals. It has not been possible in this chapter to focus on all crime or all the agencies and professionals involved in criminal justice. We have deliberately highlighted those areas where redistributing power to communities, victims and professionals is likely to bring the greatest gains in cutting crime and building confidence. Some of this work is already under way in Labour local government. But only a Labour government can ensure that it will happen everywhere.

1. Caroline Davies and Karen McVeigh, 'Milly Dowler family say Bellfield trial was "mental torture"', *The Guardian*, 24 June 2011.

2. Home Office, *British Crime Survey* 2009–10, 2010.

3. Home Office, 'Crime in England and Wales Quarterly Update', *Home Office Statistical Bulletin*, April 2011.

4. Polly Rossetti and Ellie Cumbo, *Victims' Justice? What Victims and Witnesses Really Want from Sentencing* (London: Victim Support, 2010).

5. Ministry of Justice, 'Adult Reconvictions: Results from the 2009 Cohort', *Ministry of Justice Statistical Bulletin*, March 2011.

6. Louise Casey, *Green Paper Response: Commissioner for Victims and Witnesses*, Ministry of Justice, 2011.

7. Home Office, 'The Drivers and Perceptions of Antisocial Behaviour', *Home Office Research Report 34*, 2010.

8. Baroness Newlove, *Our Vision for Safe and Active Communities*, Home Office, 2011.

9. Mike Maguire and Tim John, 'Intelligence-Led Policing, Managerialism and Community Engagement', *Policing and Society* (2006) vol. 16, no. 1, pp. 67–85.

10. Baroness Newlove, op. cit.

11. 'Taking on crime cooperatively', ProgressOnline, 21 May 2011.

12. Home Office, *Independent Review of Police Officer and Staff Remuneration and Conditions*, March 2011.

13. Natalie Hart, *Parents not Prison* (London: YouGov, 2010).

14. Louise Casey, op. cit.

15. Blair Gibbs (ed.), *Fitting the Crime: Reforming community sentences* (London: Policy Exchange, 2010).

16. Giselle Cory, *Summing Up: A Strategic Audit of the Criminal Justice System* (London: Victim Support, 2011).

17. Katharine McKenna, *Evaluation of the North Liverpool Justice Centre*, Ministry of Justice, October 2007.

# One Nation Labour: tackling the politics of culture and identity

*Ivan Lewis*

For the centre-left now, as through history, the politics of culture and identity poses the ultimate challenge. Our instincts to be internationalist, liberal and champions of multi-cultural societies jar with the growing insecurity of citizens buffeted by rapid economic and social change. To those who urge no compromise with the electorate I say not only is that a political cul-de-sac, but it would be an admission that our politics has nothing to offer people whose legitimate concerns can be dismissed as neither reactionary nor bigoted. That does not mean we should pander to racism or collude with those who would have our country retreat to a mythical bunker where 'Little England' can somehow be protected from the realities of change.

But if we are to be a credible alternative government we must offer positive answers and not vacate territory that the mainstream right seeks to monopolise and the far-right to exploit. Mistrust about our instincts and values on identity and culture-related issues is one of the key reasons why voters have rejected social democratic parties across Europe. In an age of austerity that suspicion will remain unless we are willing to break free from outdated comfort zones. Ed Miliband has made it clear that Labour will confront and tackle these issues as we build a new agenda for a fairer Britain in a rapidly changing world.

Over the past forty years we have seen the National Front

become the British National Party and, more recently, the emergence of the English Defence League. Far-right movements have gone from mobilising around 'the nation', to Britain and now to England. As Jon Cruddas constantly reminds us, the resurgence of English national identity raises big questions for Labour, questions which are magnified by the impact of Scottish, Welsh and Northern Irish devolution. But, paradoxically, as Richard English wrote in his recent paper for ippr, the resurgence of English cultural identity has not been accompanied by assertive nationalism.[1] Therefore there is real scope to both respond sensitively and seriously to this resurgence of English identity while seeking to build a new sense of national mission and commitment to the United Kingdom.

In Scotland, despite the Scottish National Party's recent political success and the need for Labour to learn lessons, a significant majority of the electorate remains steadfastly opposed to Scottish independence. The government at Westminster is pursuing policies and a too-fast, unfair cuts agenda which will divide Britain. This will fuel resentment and alienate an increasing number of people, further eroding their weak political support in the north of England, Scotland and Wales.

This political environment provides Labour with an opportunity to demonstrate that we have the values and policies to be the UK's authentic 'one nation' party. By addressing the electorate's cultural and economic insecurity with an ambitious and credible vision for the future we can begin to regain the confidence of both 'heartland' voters and voters in the south, west and east of England: One Nation Labour, listening to and speaking up for Britain's 'silent majority'.

I write this chapter from the perspective of someone whose life has been rooted and enriched by a strong sense of cultural identity, growing up in a tight-knit Jewish community located in a north Manchester suburb, where I continue to live and which I represent as one of the three towns that make up my constituency. My life, and that of my children, is inextricably tied up with a faith community which remains vibrant, a multicultural suburb which has a very strong sense of community identity, distinct from its host local authority, and a Britain which has given me the opportunity and privilege to serve my community and country. For me these anchors have been a source of strength. But I know that a diminishing number of people in today's society live their lives in one place or identify with a faith community, that their sense of identity and cultural affiliation is more complex and less settled.

The global market, mass migration, the terrorist threat, climate change, advances in science, technology and communication, intergenerational aspiration and an ageing society all make perpetual change in Britain inevitable. We live in an age of serious and growing personal and collective insecurity. People feel less able to control their own lives and the destiny of their families, and worry about their government's capacity to exercise control in areas where they expect stability and fairness. This summer's outbreak of looting and criminality in some of our cities has left people feeling angry, but also bewildered.

Today, in an increasingly globalised world, people yearn for a sense of identity and belonging. Some find it through family, work, community networks, good causes, sport or faith. Others live isolated, atomised lives or, worse still, in a permanent state of siege, with poor opportunities and low aspirations or a distaste for change fuelling fear and, for some, hate. This siege-like mentality has been reinforced by a combination of the failures of politicians and sections of the press, who understand the potency of insecurity and fear among their readership.

The centre-left should be change-makers, leading and embracing change in the pursuit of progress. But we should also be acutely sensitive to people's need for reassurance, their expectation of state intervention where change leads to undesirable or unintended consequences, and a natural human desire for an oasis of calm amid the surging waves of change. Citizens must have a stake in change, feel they can exercise control and rely on public institutions to preserve enduring values. To use a human analogy, people's anxiety and sense of disorientation grows when they feel their life is spiralling out of control.

## Appraising the past

To build a better future we need an honest appraisal of our past.

New Labour's modernising zeal was good for the country and the party. For the country it promoted a sense of renewal and confidence. And, until our latter years in government, we were the political party in Britain strongly identified with change and the future. This was undoubtedly positive and a major reason we achieved a historic three successive election victories. It is far too easy for some of our opponents to rewrite history about many of our positive achievements. 'Compared with a decade ago, this country is more open at home and more compassionate abroad. That is something we should all be grateful for.' Not the words of a Labour supporter, but the words of David Cameron in his speech on the steps of 10 Downing Street on the day he became Prime Minister.

But there was also a reluctance, a hesitancy to face up to the fact that too many people on low and middle incomes felt they were being left behind, with their sense of injustice fuelled by a system which, to some, appeared to favour people receiving benefits and choosing not to work, migrants who were being helped but had not contributed to Britain, and irresponsible senior bankers who caused the financial crisis but continued to receive excessive payoffs and bonuses while everyone else was paying the price for their recklessness. Others felt migration was changing the nature of our society and undermining Britain's way of life. The new threat from global fundamentalist terrorism put the spotlight on radicalisation and extremism in Britain.

The impact of globalisation meant we should have pursued an active industrial policy to protect and create jobs and build a more balanced economy as an integral part of our strategy, not simply a response to the financial crisis. We could have introduced a points-based system earlier to better control immigration. We underestimated the scale and impact of the influx of eastern Europeans and should have done more to address the effect this had on local communities, public services, and the jobs and wages of UK workers. We should have done more to increase the supply of decent affordable housing and continued our programme of welfare reform. Labour and previous Tory governments should have acted earlier to tackle radicalisation in some Muslim communities by adopting a zero-tolerance approach to anyone, including religious leaders, who preached hate, and by refusing to legitimise organisations unwilling to condemn extremism or the use of violence. When devolving power to Scotland and Wales we should have devolved more power to English local authorities and communities. As market forces reshaped high streets and closed Post Offices we should have given communities greater support to take over facilities and community assets. Too often it was the state, the market or nothing. What about the community?

The positive elements of the 'big society', such as enabling community organisations and local people to have greater control, should have played a greater part at the heart of New Labour's agenda, alongside the active state that did so much to renew our public services and reduce the inequality which, unchecked, would have further degraded our society. That combination would have transformed, not simply improved, Britain. The tragedy of Cameron's 'big society' is that as an antidote to a withered state it is destined to fail and be a 'lightening rod' for public scepticism about the government's motives. However, it is vital that we do not allow this to give succour to those on the left who favour a paternalistic state and seek to marginalise the importance of citizen and community empowerment.

None of this means that we did not take steps in the right direction. We did, but it took too long for us to adopt a coherent strategy. Some of the positive changes we introduced, such as incapacity benefit reform, the points system for immigration and the requirement to learn English and pass citizenship tests, were lost in a 'fog' of public cynicism.

## The politics of insecurity

Before we address how Labour should respond, it is important to examine the causes of that insecurity and acknowledge that it did not arrive solely with the election of the current government. The course they are set on will slow down our economic recovery, choking off not only growth but hope, and increasing fear and division. We need to understand how large numbers of our fellow citizens feel removed from the cosy consensus of Britain's elite and a Labour Party activist base that, while becoming more diverse, still does not look sufficiently like Britain. A recent survey undertaken by anti-fascist organisation Searchlight concluded that a new politics of identity, culture and nation has grown out of the politics of race and immigration. Two groups now make up what could be described as the middle ground of British politics. One group is insecure and pessimistic about the future, likely to be working class, live in social housing and view immigration through the prism of its economic impact on its opportunities and the social impact on its communities. Interestingly, this group includes a significant representation from BME communities and identifies with Labour politically. The second group, which largely identifies with the Tories, is generally older and is or has been professionals and managers. It views immigration as a cultural issue, with concerns about the impact of immigration on national identity and immigrants' willingness to integrate.[2]

To be more specific, increasing numbers of people work hard for diminishing returns. Capped or reduced wages and rising bills mean treats for the kids, the family holiday and the night out with friends can no longer be taken for granted. Resentment, even anger, follows. The costs of higher education, shortage of jobs and affordable housing creates not only anxiety among young people but parents and grandparents too. And in some areas this insecurity is compounded by seeing their neighbourhood change with concentrations of new migrants. We also see alienation among other groups. In some inner-city areas parents live in fear of a gang culture which threatens to ruin their children's lives. Some young people grow up with no positive parental or adult role model, are influenced by negative forces and trapped in a cycle of intergenerational deprivation where there are few opportunities and no sense of responsibility. Christians feel angry when liberal secularists do not see the irony of their anti-faith bigotry, and are infuriated when they hear of employers banning workers from wearing crosses while people of other faiths are free to dress in accordance with their religious beliefs. Some young Muslims feel alienated from their community, strongly oppose British foreign policy and are victims of racism. Many communities are experiencing rapid change. Most of the pubs have gone, the neighbourhood Post Office is no more, and the mix of small independent shops has long been replaced by a supermarket and array of charity shops.

Blue Labour has raised some of these issues in its critique of New Labour. While I cannot pretend to share Maurice Glasman's analysis or views on all issues, he and others are right to unsettle us with some home truths about our failure to take seriously people's disquiet about some of the changes which took place on our watch, as well as pointing out that our managerialism sometimes failed to take sufficient account of the nature and value of relationships which are so important to every aspect of life. Equally, blue Labour has to acknowledge in its contribution to the debate about the future that the forces of globalisation and modernisation bring good as well as bad changes, and we will only regain public support with policies and values which speak to the aspirations of people both for a better standard of living and a better quality of life.

This malaise in our sense of identity is taking place at a time when public confidence in the pillars of the establishment is at an all-time low. The MPs' expenses scandal, the reckless behaviour and excessive bonuses of senior bankers, the crisis engulfing parts of the national press and Metropolitan Police reinforces a public view of an unaccountable elite which lives in a parallel universe and is detached from their anxieties. For too many, Labour was seen as a party which looks like, and speaks on behalf of, an urban metropolitan elite. We are not that, but we will only prove that this is not the case through our style of politics, community campaigning and the audacity and boldness of our ideas and vision for the future.

The role of the state and affordable public investment is important. But we should put people and communities at the heart of our future offer, redistributing power from Whitehall to the town hall to local residents, from the City square mile to towns, cities and regions across the country, responding to people's insecurity by giving them greater control and a strong stake in decisions which affect their lives.

Our overriding vision should be to adopt a policy agenda which puts integration at the heart of a strengthened, one nation United Kingdom – integration which respects devolution of specified powers and the diversity of different cultures and faiths with a strong aversion to forcing everyone to be the same. But this would also be integration which asserts common values and rules which, alongside the law, are non-negotiable, have no opt-outs and are applied without fear or favour.

I believe these are some specific proposals which would help to build a stronger, more united, country consistent with Labour values.

## Opportunity, aspiration and responsibility

We should be explicit about the rights and responsibilities of citizenship in a modern Britain, a new covenant which binds together not only state and citizen but families, employers, local government and communities. A covenant which offers people fair access to early years support, high-quality education and childcare, the NHS, apprenticeships, jobs, affordable housing and dignity in retirement. In developing this new covenant we should be clear that fair access includes reasonable standards of personal and family responsibility, a much greater correlation between contribution and benefit in a reformed welfare system and, where appropriate, co-produced, locally developed projects rather than top-down, state-run programmes. Affordability underpinned by fiscal responsibility will require us to achieve the right balance between state, private, philanthropic and personal financial contributions.

In every community priority should be given to fighting the antisocial behaviour and crime which can blight communities and prevent people from escaping a vicious circle of low aspirations and low expectations.

The most innovative projects often come from community leaders, parents, mentors, voluntary organisations, faith groups and local authorities who know their communities best and can secure value for money. In communities where positive role models are in short supply, we should place a much greater emphasis on the potential role of mentors to transform people's lives. In the aftermath of the recent violence and criminality on our streets it is time to listen more to the local innovators and pioneers, the unsung heroes who sometimes, in small ways, have shown that change based on both opportunity and responsibility is possible even in the most challenging of communities. Programmes dictated by ministers and designed by officials in Whitehall should be a last resort and only deployed when local solutions have failed. Central government should play a much greater role in identifying, disseminating and supporting best practice.

All citizens, irrespective of their personal circumstances, should have a right to information about benefit and public service entitlements. This would be a way of both empowering people and also busting some of the myths which surround this topic.

**Patriotism and national pride**

This year's royal wedding showed the strong patriotic feeling which endures in every part of the UK. This is to be celebrated and not mocked. Some people on the left are all too willing to be selective when promoting the importance of community and solidarity. The same applies to reclaiming the flag on St George's day from the far-right and ensuring public buildings fly the flag throughout the year. Those who challenge Labour's patriotism should be reminded that the pursuit of a fairer, more united, country where every citizen is given the chance to pursue their potential is patriotism in action. This does not mean people of other political affiliations are not equally patriotic but they should not be allowed to claim moral superiority. The 2012 Olympics promises to be another historic occasion which will strengthen national pride, but we need to do more than express our patriotism around one-off events.

I am attracted to the idea of a new rite of passage for teenagers which would involve them undertaking an educational project focused on learning about British history, their local and family heritage, culture and family tree. This could enable young people to explore their personal 'roots' and strengthen their knowledge of our history. Graduation ceremonies would celebrate student achievement but also act as a focus for local and national pride.

Three institutions which showcase Britain at its best and enjoy overwhelming public support are the NHS, the BBC and our Armed Forces. Yet public engagement and involvement in these is limited. They are run by a managerial and professional elite. We should review how we can bring these institutions closer to the communities they serve, turn citizens and communities into 'shareholders', active participants and cheerleaders for their contribution to our society. We should, therefore, give serious consideration to a proposal, first floated by Tessa Jowell, that the BBC could become a mutual organisation, so that all those who pay the licence fee become its members and owners with, for instance, rights to elect the trustees who oversee its operations and direction. In the future we should also consider strengthening the BBC's role and duty to contribute to the economic, social and cultural wellbeing of every region.

In terms of the NHS, future health reform in England should consider developing and extending the model which gives local people the chance to become members of their NHS hospital foundation trust to primary care, so local people can have a greater voice in decisions about their local NHS. We should also advocate the greater use of personal budgets, not only as a means of giving patients greater control but also integrating NHS and social care funding streams.

Our Armed Forces retain a special place in the heart of the nation. Departure and homecoming parades should become the norm in every community where our troops are based. Attendance at Remembrance Sunday services could become a statutory part of the secondary school calendar. New lottery funding available for heritage projects could be used to clean up every cenotaph across the country.

By contrast, the European Union is an unpopular institution which is run by a remote bureaucratic and political elite. Labour must develop a reform agenda in consultation with the electorate. This starts from the basis that on economic, political and security grounds it is in Britain's national interest to remain in the EU and seek to play a leading role in influencing its future. However, pro-Europeans willing to make the case for the EU must show an equal determination to demand reform, much greater accountability and transparency. The public has a right to know and influence EU decisions which affect our way of life and sense of fairness, whether it be on issues such as budget priorities, value-for-money or prisoner votes.

### English identity
As I stated earlier, a resurgence in English identity raises profound questions for Labour. In the market towns, villages, council estates and suburbs there is a desire to express pride in

Englishness, partially born out of patriotism, partially as a cry of defiance from people who feel alienated from the mainstream political establishment. They write off politicians as being the same, are sceptical about progress and pessimistic about the future and feel their identity is being marginalised in their own country. Improving opportunities and raising aspirations as part of a new rights-and-responsibilities covenant would make a difference. But a major double-devolutionary shift of power and resources from Whitehall to English local government and on to local communities would also enable people to feel a greater sense of control and ownership over decisions which impact on their way of life. The Labour Party should consider the organisational, policy and campaigning implications of responding sensitively and seriously to the Englishness agenda. The argument for an English Parliament has not been won and there appears to be little public support for elected regional government as demonstrated by the north-east referendum result. But we should not and cannot close down the debate about the best way of ensuring English-specific issues are given a fair hearing.

**Controlled immigration**
Controlling immigration is both consistent with Labour values and a duty of all responsible governments.

We should maintain a points system and could consider establishing an independent body which would monitor immigration control, report regularly on the impact of all immigration, including from the EU, and consult the public. We know as a result of the immigration points system that we have skills shortages which can only be filled by non-EU migrant workers. Therefore, over the next decade we should set the education and skills system an explicit objective to eliminate this skills gap. This would not only reduce immigration but be a good test of our education system's progress.

Local authorities should receive tailored support to help

manage the impact on public services and community relations of new arrivals. Every effort should be made to match new migrants and asylum seekers with community networks to help with settling in and support integration.

The public does not understand why UK taxpayers should fund the cost of prison places for foreign nationals. We should explore how they can either be returned to their country of origin to serve their sentence, or for that country to be billed for all costs incurred. Similarly, there is a strong case for anyone granted UK citizenship who subsequently commits a serious crime to be stripped of their citizenship.

### Radicalisation and extremism

A new Prevent strategy should focus on both young Muslims at risk of radicalisation by extremists within their own community and young white people vulnerable to indoctrination by far-right groups. Inciting young people to commit acts of violence or hatred should carry aggravated prison sentences. Universities cannot be allowed to hide behind a free speech argument in failing to deal with conduct which oversteps the mark and becomes incitement or intimidation. In future, one option worthy of consideration would be to transfer the Prevent strategy and programme from government to an arm's-length charitable trust; a trust run by leaders and activists from the communities Prevent is seeking to influence. Like in any set of similar arrangements, the trust and its agents would have a duty to pass on information about any threats to national security to the relevant authorities.

A more explicit commitment to integration would also mean young people from different faiths and cultures should be supported to meet and learn about each other's lives and beliefs. As a strong supporter of faiths schools, I believe they would be strengthened, not weakened, by forming links with other faith and non-faith-based schools. This would also be relevant to schools serving very different socioeconomic and

ethnic populations. Under Ed Miliband's leadership, Labour
has begun a journey which provides us with a real opportunity to address these deep-rooted and challenging issues of
culture and identity. His focus on the 'squeezed middle', the
British promise, responsibility at every level of society, and a
wide-ranging policy review process provides a platform for us
to connect with the insecurities and aspirations of the mainstream majority. As we expose the poor choices being made by
this government we must reconnect our party with all sections
of the electorate and become the one nation party offering
hope and a better future to all. There should not be any 'no-go'
areas for Labour. Indeed, we will build organisational capacity
and arrange events not only in key parliamentary seats but in
parts of the country where Labour is less well established. As
well as working to rebuild trust among our core voters we can
be confident in taking our case to the village halls, golf clubs
and women's institutes of Middle England.

   This approach will be in stark contrast to the government
at Westminster and SNP in Edinburgh who are dividing our
country at a time when personal and collective insecurity is
crying out for a renewed sense of national unity and purpose.
New Labour, blue Labour, and anyone who wishes Labour
well will challenge conventional orthodoxies, promote new
ideas, sometimes disagreeing vehemently, but showing that the
British Labour Party can be the incubator that fuels the renaissance of social democratic parties across Europe. The party
which takes equal pride and inspiration from the anthems of
'Jerusalem' and the 'Red Flag' is well placed to address the new
complex cultural challenges our country faces. One Nation
Labour can once again ensure that hope triumphs over fear.

1. Richard English, *Is There an English Nationalism?* (London: ippr, 2011).
2. Nick Lowles and Anthony Painter, *The New Politics of Identity* (London:
Searchlight Educational Trust, 2011).

# Good government and thriving economies: rejuvenating England's cities

*Andrew Adonis*

Radical democratic devolution was the hallmark of the first two years of the Blair government. The Scottish Parliament, the Welsh Assembly, the mayor of London, the Northern Ireland Assembly – all were set up with significant powers following positive referenda. Each of them has been broadly successful, transforming democratic accountability and consent, and promoting better government.

But then it stopped. There was no devolution worth the name within England beyond London. Nor, apart from a few elected mayors for local authorities, has there been much local democratic innovation. In the decade after 2000, policy on decentralisation within England was largely a failure, bordering on fiasco in the case of the botched attempt to introduce regional government, defeated by four to one in the 2004 referendum in the north-east.

The consequences of this failure are serious. For all the Blair-Brown investment in public services, regional inequalities have not appreciably narrowed. Above all, this is a crisis of England's cities beyond London. Poverty, unemployment, poor skill levels – these bedevil virtually all of England's cities outside the south-east.

Visit these cities, and first impressions are generally favourable. City centres have undergone attractive regeneration.

University quarters, in particular, are thriving. But travel a short distance beyond and the view is very different. High unemployment, low skill levels, seriously underperforming schools, too few private sector businesses, social housing estates on-the-edge – for all the investment of recent years – and acute divisions between rich and poor districts: this is the general character of England's cities outside London. In income per head, public infrastructure and private sector business formation and location, they are virtually all poorer than a string of cities in Germany.

There are some partial success stories. Advanced manufacturing is alive and well in Sheffield and Bristol. Leeds has a concentration of legal and corporate services. Manchester boasts the greatest concentration of students west of Moscow, and the best tram system in Britain. But all these cities also have deep and wide concentrations of poverty.

Some major cities struggle to tell much of a positive story at all, in terms of their underlying economies. Liverpool has lost nearly half its population in the last fifty years; 40 per cent of its jobs are in the public sector. Newcastle and its conurbation are headquarters to only one FTSE 100 company – Sage – whose new chief executive has decided to locate to Paris. Four in ten of Bradford's population are in the bottom tenth of national income earners. Birmingham's population is still 100,000 lower than a generation ago; it has an unemployment rate twice the national average and among the lowest skill levels in the country. Type 'Made in Birmingham' into Google, and the first item listed is 'Birmingham's Industrial History Website'. According to economic projections prepared for the city council, Birmingham's employment is forecast to be 4 per cent lower in 2020 than in 2008. In the five years to 2008 the city gained 10,000 public sector jobs but lost 3,000 private sector jobs.

It is time for a fresh start. Labour needs a credible plan for devolution within England to promote local leadership, accountability and empowerment. This needs to start with a plan for radically improving the government of the major cities and city conurbations. Half of England's population lives in the major conurbations, yet outside London it lacks strong political institutions and voice; it is largely poor; and it is excessively dependent upon a public sector which is now being cut systematically.

I suggest three key policies for a renewed Labour policy on city empowerment:

- Elected mayoral authorities for the six major city-conurbations beyond London: Greater Manchester, Greater Birmingham, Greater Leeds, Greater Liverpool, Greater Newcastle and Greater Bristol (whatever the most popular names ultimately decided for them). Substantial powers should be handed down from Whitehall to the mayors of these city-conurbations, on a par with the mayor of London and the Greater London authority in respect of transport, policing, planning and economic regeneration;
- A requirement that city councils with weak leadership and a poor record of promoting jobs and growth should also adopt the mayoral model. Alongside mayors, there should also be pilots of 'city parishes' with their own councillors, budgets and responsibilities within city and large urban authorities;
- Far greater tax and fiscal incentives for local government at large to foster new businesses and – where there is demand – new housing, within a reformed council and business rates regime.

**City-conurbations**
The introduction of regional government into England foundered in 2004 not only on the absence of English regional identity, but also because the devolution plan itself was incoherent. It was extra bureaucracy to no clear purpose.

The key services and functions where the 'democratic deficit' needs redressing within England are policing, transport, infrastructure planning and economic development. These are handled, or best handled, not at a regional but at a subregional level. In respect of England's major cities, this means at the level of the city-conurbation because – with the partial exception of Birmingham, which with a population of one million is the largest single-tier local authority in Europe – no city council outside London is sufficiently dominant within its employment and travel-to-work conurbation to take responsibility alone for these major services and functions. The city of Manchester, for example, covers a population of less than 500,000 within the Greater Manchester conurbation of 2.6 million. In the north-east, Newcastle is not even clearly the largest city within the Tyne-and-Wear conurbation; Sunderland is about the same size.

Consider Manchester further. While the region of the 'north west' is purely a geographical expression, Greater Manchester is a recognised conurbation and the existing organisational basis for key services, including a police force and the Integrated Transport Authority responsible for local and regional public transport. But none of these services is directly accountable to the public. Who can name the chair of Greater Manchester's police authority or its ITA? Regional transport, in particular, needs dramatic improvement, while the imperative for more effective economic development and business promotion is obvious. Most of these points apply equally to England's five other city-conurbations outside London.

The coalition is seeking to introduce elected police commissioners to make the police more accountable. But policing is not the only conurbation-wide service which needs democratic leadership and accountability. Nor is it sensible to treat the police as a standalone elected service. The coherent policy is to create conurbation-wide elected authorities; and to do so by means of a mayor, promoting direct accountability and high-profile leadership rather than a new tier of political bureaucracy (which, for good or ill, the pre-1986 metropolitan authorities were seen to be.) Alongside these city-conurbation mayors there should be a small elected council to hold the mayor to account and agree the mayoral budget and major decisions.

This is precisely the model introduced by the Blair government with such success in Greater London. The mayor of London, elected alongside an assembly of twenty-five members, is responsible for policing, transport, economic development and has significant influence on skills policy through the London Skills and Employment Board. Much of this responsibility and power is in fact shared with others, including central government and the thirty-two elected London boroughs.

But by the nature of his profile and electoral mandate, the mayor has influence out of all proportion to the letter of statute. When I was transport secretary, hardly a week passed without Boris Johnson being in contact about some issue or other. The £16bn Crossrail project, which will transform east–west London rail connections, would not be happening without Ken Livingstone and Johnson – not only because of their successful lobbying of central government but, equally importantly, because of the impressive partnerships they built with the private sector, persuading central London's busi-nesses to pay a supplementary business rate which will finance a quarter of the cost. And London would probably not have won the Olympics without the mayor. It was only narrowly won and throughout the evaluation there were concerns at the state of London's transport and infrastructure, which Livingstone was able to assuage personally and categorically.

Greater Manchester, Greater Birmingham and the other city-conurbations need mayors to match London's. Establishing these city-conurbation mayors should be one of the first acts of the next Labour government.

## City mayors and city parishes

A starter for ten: name the leaders of Birmingham, Leeds and Manchester city councils, three of the largest cities outside London. Stumped? You are in good company. I have yet to meet anyone who can name all three, which sums up the weakness of democratic leadership and accountability bedevilling most of our cities. In some cases there is not only weakness but also chronic instability. Bristol has had seven changes of leader in eight years. Until last year, the leadership of Leeds alternated every six months between the Tories and the Liberal Democrats as part of an extraordinary coalition arrangement.

Compare Birmingham with San Jose in California and Cologne in Germany, cities of a similar size. Chuck Reed, mayor of San Jose, has a web presence thirty-three times as great as Mike Whitby, the leader of Birmingham City Council. Jürgen Roters in Cologne has a web presence nineteen times as great, and he has been in office only eighteen months. But you don't need to look abroad. A New Local Government Network poll conducted during the first term of elected mayors found that, just eighteen months after being elected, on average 57 per cent of people could identify their mayor, compared to only 25 per cent who could identify their leader in councils without a mayor.

Strong, accountable, high-profile political leadership is essential to transforming the cities. From national and international experience, directly elected mayors could play a positive role. Germany, for example, has now moved entirely to the elected mayor model for its cities, including in the northern German cities – within the post-war British zone – which previously had the leader-and-council model. None of these cities is proposing to change back.

The Blair–Brown governments should have moved decisively to introduce mayors into the major cities beyond London. They failed to do so not because of doubts about the policy – which both Prime Ministers supported – but because of vested local government interests which saw, and still see, mayors as a threat, when they ought to be welcomed as an opportunity for civic renewal. There are exceptions, notably Leicester, which in 2011 became the largest city outside London to elect a mayor. The first mayor of Leicester is Labour's Sir Peter Soulsby – who, tellingly, considered it more worthwhile to become mayor than continue as one of the city's MPs – winning the election with more than half the vote on a wave of enthusiasm for his candidacy and the office. But in most other cities, apart from Birmingham where Labour's Sir Albert Bore is in support, councillors of all parties are blocking this necessary reform.

Contrary to what many councillors allege, the experience of mayors has been largely positive. How many Londoners do you know who want to abolish the mayor? The London experience has been a spectacular success, which is highly relevant for the major cities and city-conurbations beyond London. Of smaller mayoral cities and towns, the mayors in Doncaster and Stoke-on-Trent have not been effective. In both cases, mayors were created to overcome chronic local authority dysfunctionality and it has not worked. But these are the exceptions, not the norm. In the other thirteen authorities with mayors, the record has been broadly positive. This, again, is particularly true in London. Hackney, Newham and Lewisham have all had successful mayors (Jules Pipe, Sir Robin Wales and Sir Steve Bullock respectively). All three are Labour, all three have a great track record, and all three were re-elected for third terms last year. And these are large authorities. Lewisham alone has a population almost as large as the city of Newcastle. Outside London, three of the four mayoral incumbents were re-elected this year, so, again, the public generally likes what it sees.

Nor is it the case that mayoralties breed maverick or irresponsible Independents. More Labour than Independent mayors have been elected so far. Of the Independents, most

– including Middlesbrough's Ray Mallon, Mansfield's Tony Egginton, and Hartlepool's Stuart Drummond (the so-called 'monkey') – are obviously competent, and have been re-elected and forged good working relationships with their councils.

In the case of cities with weak leadership and chronic problems, including Birmingham and Bristol, Labour should be supporting the introduction of elected city mayors in the referenda which the coalition is requiring to be held in May 2012. However, when Labour comes to decide its policy for government in respect of city mayors and new city-conurbation mayoral authorities, a requirement for referenda before implementation should not inevitably follow. Virtually all changes in local government organisation, including the creation of entirely new local authorities with substantial new powers, have not in the past involved referenda. A judgement needs to be made on the degree of political consensus supporting the creation of mayors and new metro-mayoral authorities. Labour should consult intensively on an outline reform plan before the election, shaping precise proposals, conurbation by conurbation, in response to this consultation. Provided these proposals generate a reasonable degree of consensus, they should, I suggest, be implemented on the back of clear manifesto commitments rather than referenda.

However, mayors alone will not reinvent city government, and they are only part of what needs to be done to build accountability and civil engagement. Even in cities with effective strategic leadership, such as Manchester, the councils themselves are too large either to hold the administration properly to account or to articulate local interests and concerns. Manchester has ninety-six councillors, Leeds ninety-nine, Liverpool ninety, Birmingham 120. Newcastle with seventy-six and Bristol with seventy seem positively small by comparison.

There is a case for reducing these numbers. This could take place alongside pilots in devolving power to 'city parishes'

– elected local ward communities – to foster greater local consultation and to extend local control and innovation in respect of local amenities, including libraries, parks, street-scapes and leisure facilities, which at present are too often neglected and undervalued as community resources. Such community councils might also attract more young people to take part in their local government. Until recently, Leeds council had more councillors over the age of eighty than under the age of thirty-five. There are few councillors in their twenties in any city council outside London.

## Incentives for growth

Every council leader worth their salt should have a plan for growth. But very few have. More effective strategic leader-ship – and the creation of mayors where appropriate – are part of the answer. Also important are stronger incentives for mayors and council leaders to promote planning, infrastruc-ture and development decisions which attract new and bigger businesses and foster substantial new housing – particularly brownfield development – where there is demand for it.

Local taxation is among the great minefields and grave-yards of British politics. The trauma of the poll tax is now past, but a new system of local taxation to enable councils to raise significantly more of their income locally – a desirable goal in itself – is still too risky a venture without stronger local leadership and consensus on key components (which would need to include fairer property valuations and/or a readiness to countenance an element of local income tax). However, within broadly the existing regime of council tax and busi-ness rating, significant new incentives should be provided for councils to promote growth.

To encourage extra housing where it is needed (as it is in much of the Midlands and the south in particular), there should be a significant council tax bonus for councils author-ising sustainable and affordable developments. The coalition has proposed a 'new homes bonus' matching extra council tax income from new housing developments for a six-year period. This is far too short to give a strong incentive for councils to agree to development and provide the associated infrastructure. The bonus should be for a fifteen- to twenty-year period, over which associated infrastructure and local amenities need to be provided and sustained.

To encourage new business activity, councils ought to be able to gain the business rate benefit accruing from new business developments to which they give planning consent, without losing the extra income to the national business rate pool and equalisation machinery. There are a number of options, including 'tax increment financing' (a method to use future gains in taxes to finance current infrastructure improvements) and a bonus to local tax revenue similar to that proposed in respect of housing. However, again, the bonus proposed is only for a period of six years; it needs to be for twenty or twenty-five years to maximise incentives and meet its purpose of enabling councils to plan and provide essential infrastructure.

An ambitious version of both of these policies is needed to provide strong incentives to council leaders to promote jobs and local investment. And the use of these incentives should then be at the heart of every city's plan for growth.

At the end of the nineteenth century, Joseph Chamberlain's Birmingham was commonly described as the best governed city in the world, and the city of a thousand trades. If Birmingham and England's other regional cities are to flourish anew, they need to compete hard for those two accolades in the twenty-first century, and Labour must provide them with the tools for the job. Good government and thriving economies go hand in hand.

# From centralism to localism: building cooperative communities

*Steve Reed and Paul Brant*

The welfare state has made Britain healthier, wealthier and better educated than ever before. But it has generated problems too. The tendency of the state to take over problems and create universalised solutions to meet them removes power from communities and can smother local innovation. In extreme cases we have created a culture of dependency instead of fostering self-reliance – a traditional working-class value that underpins aspiration and self-confidence.

People contrast unresponsive, top-down public services unfavourably with their experience elsewhere in life where, as consumers, their personal choices and preferences matter more. If we do not make public services more responsive we risk a loss of public confidence that will open up opportunity for more privatisation. That would create a more polarised and less fair society as the poorest, whose needs are less attractive to a profit-driven market, are left behind.

The progressive response should be a rejection of top-down services in favour of new ways of running services that draw on our party's rich mutual and cooperative traditions, with the aim of sharing power more equally between the citizen and the state.

Labour in power did not trust local government enough. By 2010 the Audit Commission recognised that local government was the most cost-effective part of all government.

Labour's inspection regime – the comprehensive performance assessment – helped drive this improvement by giving the public a way of measuring their council against others. But the CPA failed to reward success with autonomy, and the inspection regime eventually became overbearing, displacing local priorities with initiatives favoured by Westminster civil servants and generating a costly performance bureaucracy.

From time to time Labour talked about promoting localism, but double-devolution and the empowerment white paper were not followed through. Too often Labour sought to bypass rather than work with local government: arm's-length management organisations were an attempt to take housing out of local government control, academies were a first step in breaking up local education authorities. The problem with these reforms was that they did not hand more power to local communities, they centralised it in the hands of civil servants. This centralising tendency made Labour feel, and eventually become, more remote. We should have used local government, as the tier of government closest to communities, to enable communities to take control.

**Local government localisers**

Politicians now all talk the language of localism and empowerment, but they differ significantly in what they understand this to mean. The following chart shows how the differences cut across party lines. This explains why some Tories 'get' the 'big society' but others see it as a pointless distraction, and also why some Labour councils and ministers keenly pursue models of localism while others do not. The dominant model for public services in Britain is 'central-government centralisers' with a strong centre determining how services will be delivered locally. Some initiatives that appear localist – such as free schools – are not, because the funding and accountability are all dependent on national government and power remains in the hands of the people providing the service, not in the hands of the community using it. Other local authorities want to localise power as far as the council, but no further. This is local centralism – it does not empower communities, and it is how many local government officials think. This chapter argues that Labour needs to move our local government agenda towards a new form of double-devolution, where power is devolved to local government so that local government can devolve power to people and communities. We call this model of enabling local government 'cooperative councils'.

| Central government localisers | Local government localisers |
|---|---|
| Ministers that want communities to control services while bypassing local govt (e.g. free schools) | Councils that want to enable communities to control services (e.g. cooperative housing, community-led youth services) |
| Central government centralisers | Local government centralisers |
| Ministers that want to control centrally how services are delivered locally (e.g. benefits, tax, job centres) | Councils that want to control services delivered to communities (e.g. council housing, local education authorities) |

*(We thank John Anderson of KPMG for permission to reproduce the above chart.)*

## The case for cooperative services

Handing more power to communities and the people who use public services means a different role for local councils and councillors. Councils today are primarily top-down organisations that do things to communities. Services are channelled through silos, like housing, social care or youth activities, without much consideration of their cumulative impact on individual neighbourhoods. The community is relatively passive rather than closely involved, and is treated as a cohesive whole rather than a complex set of differing needs. Decisions about what a service looks like and how it works are taken by professionals who do not use the service and who generally do not live in the neighbourhood that is affected.

We must turn this traditional model upside-down to give the community more control. The council must become an enabling platform upon which community-led services are built. Council support would make community-led services sustainable by offering services such as IT, HR and people management, legal and regulatory compliance advice, and would intervene to resolve disputes or address serious failures in performance. The council would provide facilitators able to link communities with the resources available to help them analyse their needs and procure services to meet them. Making community-led services sustainable is critical to making the model work. Without this support, services moved into the community risk being gobbled up by the private sector if they are unable to match the economies of scale that would allow them to survive open tendering processes. This is cooperative commissioning, and it is one of a number of ways control over services can be devolved. Others include setting up trusts, social enterprises or mutuals led by the community.

Councils would be judged on their ability to help communities meet their own needs and solve their own problems. They would set an ethical and political framework to guide decisions over which needs to prioritise for investment. For the model to work to maximum effect, all local services, not just council services, should be included. This would break down the barriers between different services so communities can tie them up in ways that suit local needs. Building on the previous Labour government's Total Place pilots this would include current council services, local community health services, local police and other criminal justice services such as probation, employment and benefits services, as well as local schools and public housing. Communities would participate in allocating resources and challenging providers by having open access to performance and cost data to help scrutinise and shape services in a cooperative model of participatory budgeting.

Some communities have more capacity to participate than others, particularly those dominated by middle-class professionals. Councils would need to support more deprived communities so they can play a full part, including training and paying community facilitators and champions to engage excluded communities and individuals.

Of course, more variety in the kind of services on offer and how they work brings with it higher levels of risk. Some services will fail as new approaches are tried, but we need a different approach to risk if we want to create the space for communities to innovate, learn and do things differently. Robust contracting will allow councils to intervene if things go badly wrong or to guarantee access to everyone who should be entitled to use a particular service. This would prevent particular groups trying to exclude others.

The cooperative approach is about empowerment, it is not cuts-led. But at a time of austerity councils must deliver best value for money. By doing more of what communities want and less of what they do not want we stretch every pound of public spending. By opening up services to innovation we find new ways to help communities realise their ambitions, often at lower cost. Value, however, must be understood in its widest sense. It is because Labour understands the importance of social, economic and environmental value, as well as value for money, that we are proposing community-led delivery models rather than Tory-style competitive tendering based on price alone.

A common criticism is that community-led services are not accountable through the ballot box. We believe local control over services adds to the democratic mandate by making services more immediately accountable to the people who use them. Communities can use cooperative commissioning or their own representatives on trust boards to replace service providers or to reshape services as local circumstances change. Councillors will have a new role as community organisers, identifying local need and working with local community groups to link them in to resources that are available. Instead of being expected to provide all the answers, councillors will help communities find their own.

A major flaw in the Tories' 'big society' is the way it aims to replace skilled paid staff with untrained volunteers, deprofessionalising public services so they can be done on the cheap. Altruistic volunteering is immensely valuable and cooperative communities will need much more of it, but volunteering cannot be the heart of how public services work. The primary reason individuals will participate is reciprocity: you give to get. It is the principle that in previous centuries led miners in South Wales to set up friendly societies, or factory and dock workers to form trade unions. It recognises that 'we' is bigger than 'I'. Individuals will be able to influence the services that affect their lives the most and that is why they will get involved. But there is a place for more tangible incentives too. It should be possible to return the efficiencies of these new ways of working to the individual local communities themselves through discounted council tax, cut-price use of leisure facilities, community benefits, or access to job-skills training and apprenticeships

**The challenges facing local government over the next decade**
A combination of increased demand, decreased resources and the Tory reintroduction of a form of compulsory competitive tendering through the new 'right to challenge' means that councils will be hit from many sides in the coming years. Councils disproportionately provide services to the most vulnerable in society, particularly the young (education, child protection, youth services) and the old (care, sheltered housing,

transport). In some councils as much as 80 per cent of net spending goes on children's and adults' services. Demand in these areas is growing as high-cost new technology and medical procedures keep people with complex special needs alive much longer. Alongside a lower birth rate this has created an ageing society with a greater number of vulnerable people facing complex care needs.

Increasing demand for services runs up against radically reduced resources. We are already seeing the effects of this as councils restrict care services – home-helps, carers, residential homes – only to those in the most critical need. People with lower levels of need receive little or no help until their lack of support worsens their condition enough to make their needs critical. It is in lower-level categories of need that community-led services have an important role to play. By removing the assumption that the state will do everything, by delivering public services in ways that foster responsibility rather than dependency, we can promote the idea that it is alright to look in on elderly neighbours to make sure they are well, to offer to help with the weekly shopping, to use council funding in the form of personalised care budgets to pay neighbours or relatives to offer regular care and support where needs are not so great as to require more expensive professional help. Not only is this kind of neighbourliness good in itself, it is also preventative – it supports vulnerable individuals instead of letting them sink into a worse condition requiring more expensive interventions. Government funding cuts will force councils to move away from universal provision to more targeted and preventative services. Cooperative communities can help achieve this. Instead of just striving for 'more for less' we must learn to do things 'differently for less'.

A growing number of progressive Labour councils are working together to create a new cooperative model for local public services. The new Cooperative Councils Network, launched by Ed Miliband in July 2011, brings these councils together to learn from each other and produce a new local-ist agenda for Labour. The services that are emerging offer new ideas for the party nationally. It is shaping a radically different approach from old-style top-down public services. It offers the chance for the party to redefine itself to meet the demands of a modern, diverse and pluralist Britain while remaining true to our political heritage.

## A new settlement for local government

The UK suffers from the most centralised government in the world. Too much policy is driven by London-based policy groups, media and civil servants and Westminster politicians convinced that the political world revolves around them. Central government is too remote from local circumstances to act as the agent of empowerment for local communities. Only local government can play this role, but for that to happen we need to rebalance the power relationship between local and national government. The three necessary elements to achieving this are reform of the balance of taxation, local influence over national legislation, and the principle of subsidiarity.

Funding is the single biggest cause of local government's dependency on national government. The majority of local government funding is handed out by Westminster, allow-ing national government to dictate how it is spent. We have government capping of council tax, central control over fund-ing for housing, nationalisation of schools funding, central control over business rates, and – under Labour – hundreds of different ringfenced grants that limited local discretion. Local government currently exists on licence from national government in an unhealthy parent–child relationship that holds back local government's ability to develop.

If Labour wants to be really radical we need to tilt the balance of taxation so that it is more equally shared between national and local government. This is already common in other countries. Swedish municipalities levy income tax and charges and have significant discretion in deciding which services to offer. In the US, the federal government, the states and localities all raise taxes separately in a range of different ways but without sufficient redistribution to ensure that funding follows need. Any reform in the UK would need a redistribution mechanism, preferably controlled by local government as a whole rather than by Westminster. This is necessary to ensure that poorer areas are not left to decline as richer areas prosper. A land-use tax would help councils promote sustainable use of land and retain a property-based element to taxation, common in many countries.

Other countries include local government in their national legislatures. The German upper house, the Bundesrat, represents the regional Länder and has the power to veto legislation from the directly elected Bundestag. The US Senate has two representatives from each state regardless of size to counterbalance the House of Representatives, which is elected in proportion to the size of population. England is the constitutional poor cousin of the nations of the UK, with nearly all powers retained by a national government which can legislate ignorant of the pressures and needs at local level. A reformed House of Lords should have representation from the upper levels of local government, which can scrutinise legislation from this unique perspective. With the revising and scrutiny powers of the current upper house, the new chamber would ensure the interests of communities were not overlooked by the House of Commons. Local government representation on parliamentary select committees would ensure a localist perspective is involved in the scrutiny of all new relevant legislation.

The final piece in the jigsaw is subsidiarity – the rule that decisions should be taken at the lowest appropriate level of government as close as possible to the people. This principle is already enshrined in EU decision-making. Labour should apply the same requirement to national decision-making. Government should be required to justify why any legislation is taking place at national rather than local level. Enshrining this principle in law, creating a genuine devolution of power to councils and communities, would leave no need for a Department for Communities and Local Government. It could be abolished, with any residual functions transferred to the Cabinet Office, saving considerable sums of money.

Upper-tier local authorities, or groupings of them, should take over areas currently managed by quangos such as regional health authorities, national parks or planning authorities. Health, regional planning, regeneration and transport policy would all benefit from more local accountability. Where city-regions have directly elected mayors, it is appropriate for a forum of council leaders to hold them to account. In London a forum of this kind would replace the existing London Assembly, justifiable on the grounds that borough leaders have a clear and direct interest in decisions taken by the mayor of London and are therefore more likely to hold him or her robustly to account.

### Empowering people and their communities

Traditionally the left emphasises the rights of the collective while the right emphasises the rights of the individual. This led Margaret Thatcher to assert, 'There is no such thing as society', and the Labour Party's constitution to declare that 'By the strength of our common endeavour we achieve more together than we achieve alone'. In fact, both individual rights and the common good matter. They are mutually dependent on each other, so the point is to strike a balance between them and understand that you cannot empower individuals without empowering their communities, and vice versa.

We must also recognise that every locality is different, made up of different communities with different needs and ambitions. That is why localism is so important. A single top-down model of public services cannot meet all those different needs. The Beveridge-inspired model of public services this country created after the Second World War suited a country that was far more homogenous and was just emerging from the command-and-control wartime economy. That model no longer works so well in the more diverse Britain we know today. We need local flexibility and more local variation.

There is no single model we can apply to all public services. What matters is that individual service users and the communities they are part of have more control as a result of any change, are empowered to adapt the way those services are delivered to suit local circumstances, and as a result develop a stronger sense of self-reliance and the ability to work together in cooperation. The council, in this scenario, is the enabler – making available a set of resources that allows this to happen.

This is not about replacing skilled professionals with untrained volunteers. It is about placing the resources of the state at the disposal of the community who decide, with appropriate support and guidance, how best to use them. In each of these services the model is different but the approach is the same. The people who use the service have more control over it, and the outcome is better services that are more responsive and help build communities' control over their own destiny. It is an approach that Labour's cooperative councils are now seeking to extend across the full range of services they provide.

We can see how this might work by examining three different service areas.

*Community-led youth services*
Some urban estates and neighbourhoods suffer from high levels of youth offending, including violent youth gangs. Traditionally, young people getting involved in criminal behaviour are identified and targeted, with support. This usually

means professionals from outside the estate involving them in pre-existing projects and schemes designed to divert them away from offending. This way of working has only limited success because the services do not recognise the particular problems in a given neighbourhood, and it is often difficult to reach the most excluded and most vulnerable young people.

A community-led service would work differently. Turning Point, a leading national social enterprise, has developed a model of community control over services that works. It involves training members of the community to act as facilitators so they can engage with the people who live in an affected neighbourhood, including the most marginalised. Applied to youth services, the facilitators, supported by trained professionals, would help the whole community analyse the things that lead to offending, such as chaotic families, lack of positive activities for young people, low educational achievement or low aspiration caused by high levels of unemployment. The community would then decide what action is necessary to correct this, and choose organisations able to provide services to meet these needs. This is likely to create a very different set of services to that which is currently on offer, and there will be differences from neighbourhood to neighbourhood. This is a far more effective approach because it recognises that not all communities are the same and involves local people in a way that more remote models of service provision do not.

*Cooperative housing*
Cooperative housing makes up only 0.6 per cent of the total housing stock in England and Wales. In Sweden it is nearer 18 per cent, in Germany 10 per cent and Canada – where government funding has been available to start housing co-ops – around 10 per cent. Members of a Swedish housing cooperative elect their own board of directors annually from among the residents and manage their own block or estate. The board controls, within legal limits, who is allowed to join

the co-op as existing members move out. Tenants in privately owned housing developments are allowed to form their own cooperative and make an offer to the owner to buy it. If the owner decides to sell, the cooperative has the first right of purchase as a shared equity scheme where every member owns shares which may be purchased through bank loans like a mortgage.

While they are relatively few in number, there are many different forms of housing cooperatives in the UK. Watford Community Housing Trust is a 'gateway' model that allows residents in the formerly council-owned housing estates to opt into becoming shareholders in the trust by purchasing shares. The resident-owned trust manages the estates and all housing services. Other cooperative schemes allow people on low or fixed incomes to become property owners without running the risk of taking on unaffordable mortgages because they can choose the amount of equity they purchase. If a buyer's income suddenly collapses, instead of losing their home they simply reduce their monthly equity purchase but retain what they have already built up. This is a socially responsible form of the right-to-buy that offers a progressive response to Margaret Thatcher's flagship policy from the 1980s without the risks associated with subprime lending or a reduction in the amount of affordable housing. It creates mixed-income housing neighbourhoods rather than ghettoisation of the poor. It also offers a route for first-time buyers to get a foot on the housing ladder – important when you consider that today buying your first home is so difficult that the average age of a first-time buyer is thirty-seven. Councils can use their land assets, planning powers, housing policies or make investment available to promote more cooperative housing as part of the UK's housing mix.

*Mutualised care services*
For many frail, elderly or disabled people the experience of

coping with disability is deeply distressing if, after a lifetime of self-reliance and independence, their lives are suddenly taken over by professionals. They are told which daycare centre they will attend, when and where respite care is available, when their home will be cleaned, and even what meals they will eat or when they will go to the toilet. Instead of this, many councils now offer personalised budgets where care users receive a budget worth the value of the care services they would have been allocated. Instead of being assessed and told what services they will get, an adviser helps them choose what they want to do with their lives and what services they need to achieve that. They often choose radically different things to what the state gave them, and they end up more satisfied.

Councils can push this model further by supporting the development of micromutuals of personalised budget-holders. This brings together groups of people who share a similar type of disability, care objective, faith or ethnic background, or who live in the same area. By pooling their care budgets they can use their strengthened purchasing power to force faster change in the care services that are available to them. For instance, if older Somali women want care provided in the daytime by other women, they can band together and purchase care in this form. The point is that the people who use the services are in control, not the professionals.

### Trusting communities

The time has come for Labour to trust local people more. A new form of enabling local government can reinvigorate communities and give them back the power that top-down public services have taken away. Labour must never cede the political territory of communities, participation and mutualism to the Tories. It is part of our political DNA.

The 'big society' started life as a longer phrase: 'big society, not big government'. The Tories fail to understand that the state stepped in to support vulnerable groups because the Victorian mechanism for helping the 'deserving poor' was more full of holes than a Swiss cheese. They aim to marketise public services, extend the profit motive, break up state provision, and treat people only as consumers or providers of services in a market. They fail to realise that communities and the people who make them up are about more than commercial transactions.

Where the Tories want to roll back the state, Labour must change the role of the state. Labour must argue for the socialisation of public services – putting them under the control of reinvigorated communities whose energy, insight and creativity will deliver better outcomes. It is only when we acknowledge the human relationships that make communities work that we can build public services that support cooperative communities.

# Letting the people decide: redistributing power and renewing democracy

*Stephen Twigg*

In the aftermath of the failed referendum on the Alternative Vote, and with tricky waters ahead for House of Lords reform, it might look like the end of the road for democratic reformers. Pigeonholed as the concerns of out-of-touch, metropolitan elites, there is a danger that the notion of redistributing power through democratic methods will be quietly forgotten. It simply is not a priority for many Labour people, given the financial crash and the Tory assault on public services. After all, they say, when the house is falling down all around you, there is no point in tinkering with the foundations. But for me, democratic reform is about addressing the public's lack of faith in politics. Clearly the British public was not persuaded that AV would make any positive difference. So, where do we go next?

Democratic power, put in the right hands, can be powerful indeed. From the Suffragettes to the Chartists to the civil rights movement, democratic power can help to shift huge power blocks in society down to individuals. When there is no obvious pressing need for democratic change, however, little steps in the right direction can seem too much trouble for too little gain, particularly when progressives are already in positions of power or hoping to achieve it. If we know how to get our hands on powerful levers, the argument goes, why can't we simply gain control of the establishment and use the levers of power to promote progress?

Progressives need to turn this thinking on its head. Is it up to politicians to determine how power is wielded? Even when parties like Labour get into government, does it necessarily follow that, as rational actors, politicians want to give the people more power when it is easier to do things for them? Have not politicians themselves become part of the powerful and lost touch with the public? Often too many of us in politics assume that we know what the public wants, taking away their capacity to effect change themselves. In the Arab world people are risking their lives for democracy. Yet, here in the UK, it is widely believed that politics is all about power, patronage, privilege and pecuniary advantage. Of course, this is anything but true. Elected representatives do sometimes give away power, for example, as Labour did through devolution or by establishing elected mayors. Most work hard for our constituents. Yet there is a powerful lack of trust in UK politics and politicians.

Given the intractable problems with achieving solutions for national politics, perhaps democratic reformers should focus on the local. After all, this is where people themselves feel they can make more of a difference. In this year's Hansard Society audit of political engagement, 51 per cent of respondents agreed with the statement: 'When people like me get involved in their local community they really can change the way their area is run.' This compares with only 30 per cent who agreed that they can change the way the UK is run by getting involved in politics at a national level.[1] If people feel that they can have an effect on the way things are run at a street level, they could be persuaded that they can also have an impact on national policy.

In politics, everyone says they would like increased citizen involvement, but often forget why. As Stella Creasy wrote in her pamphlet *Participation Nation*: 'Engagement and empowerment activities can unleash ... "civic energy" within society by helping the public to learn the skills and confidence they need to be able to participate in either civil or civic action.'[2] By involving the public in civic activities, they are more likely to continue to support a policy or government activism because they feel ownership of the process. Rather than feeling something has been done to them, it has been done with them. But by its very nature, public engagement can be messy, fractious and counterproductive if it is conducted in the wrong way, or if politicians over-promise.

This chapter investigates the avenues which democratic reformers should explore by weighing up which mechanisms would redistribute power the most. As we saw with the electoral reform referendum, saying that a change is for the people does not mean that the people will necessarily be in favour. Therefore, finding the reforms which genuinely redistribute power and then making the case for them must form the focus of any next steps by progressives. Banging the same old drums and hoping that someone will listen is not an option.

### Who wants to become a Labour MP?

The phrase 'you're all the same' has become a truism on the doorstep for politicians of all hues. It is generally taken to mean that all governments make the same mistakes, and all politicians are greedy and corrupt. Many of us spend our time trying to disprove that claim. But there is one way in which politicians are becoming the same as each other, and rather different from the population. House of Commons research shows that 90 per cent of the 2010 intake of MPs are university-educated, compared with 20 per cent of the adult population. More than one-third of MPs attended fee-paying schools, while just 7 per cent of the population did. Despite the increases in female and BAME representation, 62 per cent of the House of Commons is still white, male and over forty.

One of the reasons for this may lie with how people get involved with political parties and the way our candidates are selected. In 2005 only 1.3 per cent of the electorate was a member of a political party, a fall from 4 per cent in 1983 and much lower than the average membership of European political parties.[3] Labour has seen an encouraging rise in membership since the general election, but at around 200,000 this is still a large drop from the 400,000 members it had in 1997. Most analysis of the fall in the membership of political parties agrees that it is due to a number of factors including changes in the socioeconomic make-up of the UK, the explosion of single-issue groups, and the pressure on people's time.

The fall in membership has resulted in fewer people being involved in selecting Labour's MPs. The average constituency Labour Party has around 300 members. This equates to a very small percentage of the local population. When candidates were selected by large memberships fifty years ago, it was easier to see how they reflected the wishes of the local population.

How, then, could Labour seek to increase the influence of ordinary people over the decision of who represents them? One way would be to introduce closed primaries. I do not advocate open primaries where supporters of other parties could vote in Labour selections. Voting in a closed primary would be restricted to Labour supporters. To guarantee the sanctity of party membership, members should still have the important responsibility of selecting the shortlist which would then be opened up to a vote by registered supporters of the Labour Party. Not only would this help to involve a wider group of local people in the selection of their Labour candidate, it could, contrary to popular assumption, also help to increase Labour membership.

By showing that Labour members have the opportunity of selecting the shortlist of local candidates, Labour could market membership to registered supporters on the basis that they get to have a wider choice in the primary if they join. Research by Will Straw conducted for Progress has shown that the introduction of primaries has historically been 'grounded in two principles: an optimism about the power of activist-based politics to change society for the better, and a belief that citizens should be able to hold their politicians to account'. As such, they are a good candidate for redistributing power.

Primaries by themselves will not, of course, automatically increase working-class or other representation. All-women shortlists and other mechanisms to increase representation, such as mentoring, will need to continue. But, crucially, primaries could show the electorate that our doors are open to our supporters.

In the US, Barack Obama reached out to unregistered voters, ethnic minority voters, young people and trade union members to register them as supporters for his primary campaign. The fact that he had to build a base of support before he went into the presidential campaign meant that far more people were engaged than might otherwise have been. The French socialists are now holding an open primary to choose their presidential candidate as a way of reinvigorating the party. The party itself runs the primary, setting up 10,000 polling booths and allowing anyone to vote for one euro, including fifteen- to eighteen-year-old members of the party's youth organisation.

In 2004 the Greek socialist party PASOK organised primaries in which 900,000 Greek citizens were said to have voted out of a population of eleven million, particularly engaging working-class supporters.

There is a key opportunity for Labour to seize the moment as the government has performed a somewhat unnoticed U-turn on its agreement in the coalition programme to fund 200 primaries.[4] Once again, it looks like the Conservatives were only interested in primaries as a way of decontaminating the Tory brand. Instead, Labour should seize the primaries, mantle and campaign for the money to conduct primaries to be made available as promised. This would also help to show the public that Labour is prepared to try out different ways of engaging them in the high end of politics.

As Ed Miliband has said, consideration should also be given to auto-registering trade union levy payers whose union is affiliated to Labour as full Labour supporters. In leadership contests, this would mean that Labour's union members would be canvassed in their own right. Instead of the paltry 9 per cent turnout in last year's leadership contest, the fact that candidates could canvass all parts of the membership, would mean that political levy payers would be engaged with. Imagine if Labour's leader could say he or she had the support of a million members rather than 200,000. It is also important that the oddity of multiple voting in leadership elections be abandoned. In many cases, individuals have a number of votes to cast because they are a member of different affiliated organisations. Affiliated organisations could still engage in the voting process, but if people are members of the Labour Party they should not be allowed to vote more than once.

Opening up access to the Labour Party and how it operates should be an important organisational goal. Following the Refounding Labour consultation, the party must focus its efforts on building local parties' capacity to organise in the community. Labour needs to be seen to be the trailblazer on the local issues which matter to people's everyday lives. This is not simply good politics, it will help to ensure Labour activists are talking about the changes people wish to see and campaigning on practical measures that make a difference in the here-and-now. It will mean that more members are indeed the change they wish to see in the world, to quote Mahatma Gandhi. The concurrent effect will be that the party's eyes and ears will be as close to local people as possible. Being active in the community will also help Labour to identify future leaders, both for their communities and to stand as representatives of the party.

## Let the people decide

As part of the coalition deal, the Liberal Democrats negotiated another attempt to reform the House of Lords. Labour champions a fully-elected chamber. The arguments for democracy in the upper House have been rehearsed ad infinitum. It goes without saying that people who set the laws that govern the people should have a mandate from the people to do so. No matter how talented, independent or hard-working peers might be, it does not change the fact that they are accountable to no one and yet can have a strong impact on our legislation – just look at their refusal to back the equal age of consent, the ban on hunting or the introduction of proportional representation in European elections.

Labour should support the use of the Parliament Act if the Lords, inevitably, put up a fight for their lives. But what if Lords reform does not go through this time? Labour's thirteen years of government was littered with long-grass moments and most constitutional observers expect the new legislation to run into trouble. Perhaps the answer is to return to the option of a citizens' convention, a deliberative body of at least 100 people selected from the electoral roll and charged with putting a series of proposals to Parliament to improve British politics. This mechanism would be the best way of avoiding the inevitable compromises and vested interests within and between political parties, and would allow the public to take charge of creating the change Britain's democracy so sorely needs.

Taking constitutional decisions out of the hands of politicians and giving it to the people would be a hugely symbolic redistribution of power. It would show that not all political discussions need take place in the confines of Parliament and would deliberately give the public a reason to be interested in democracy issues. While the final decision to change would, of course, be taken by elected politicians, the process of deliberation by a random jury of the public could help to stimulate what is often a dry and technical discussion. It would ensure that the case for change was made by the consumers, not the producers, of politics, and that any systems that were put forward were chosen not on the basis of partisan interest, but for the benefit of the public.

It is clear that if the public is to feel closer to the decisions that are taken in its name, Labour must embrace the importance of local government. Progressives should campaign for local authorities to have more power to scrutinise local providers both within the public and private sector. Councillors should have the legal power to insist bodies and companies give information to scrutiny committees and attend scrutiny meetings. The public does not always have the time or inclination to follow the detail of public sector finance, commissioning or contracting-out arrangements, but councillors should, in its name.

More and more local services are now being delivered in partnership with the local council, but current powers limit the way in which council scrutiny committees can hold them to account. The Centre for Public Scrutiny, in its recent commentary on the Localism Bill, recommended 'that scrutiny's powers over partners should be brought broadly into line with those over the authority itself – the power to require attendance at meetings, to require the provision of information, and certain rights to make recommendations which go beyond what is provided at present'. It is particularly important that scrutiny committees are given the powers to refer decisions to the secretary of state. Not all local issues can be resolved at a local level because of national government decisions, and such referral powers help to put pressure on central government to reconsider.

As the coalition pursues its ideological break-up of local service delivery, the role of local scrutiny will become more important. As more academies and free schools fall outside of local statutory control, and GP commissioning starts to undo the NHS monopoly of service provision, it will be up to local councillors to ensure that services are providing value for money, ensuring that they meet their contractual obligations, and highlight practices which are damaging to the wider community, for example, 'cream-skimming' where contractors pick the easiest users to provide services to.

What about decisions which cannot be taken at a local level, but should be at a regional or city-region level? The Conservatives are proposing referendums next May on the creation of directly elected mayors in England's twelve largest cities outside London. I know there are different views in the Labour Party about this proposal in different cities and I anticipate that some will say 'yes' and others 'no'.

There are important lessons to learn from the Greater London experience. Following Margaret Thatcher's abolition of the Greater London Council in 1986 the capital city was run by a series of quangos and joint boards until the restoration of democratic city government in 2000 with a mayor and London Assembly. Even sceptics in London accept that the Greater London authority has been a success.

The main functions of the GLA are city-regional in character – policing, fire and rescue, economic development, transport and strategic planning. If strong city-regions are part of how we deliver growth outside of London, might these regions learn from the governance model which works in the capital?

Merseyside has five local authorities, none of which has opted for an elected mayor. Under Conservative plans, the city of Liverpool will vote on having a mayor next year. Would it not make more sense, as Andrew Adonis argues in his chapter, for the Merseyside city-region to have a directly elected mayor with responsibility for the key strategic functions that are already exercised on a joint-council basis, like police, fire and transport, but with the crucial addition of responsibility for economic development? As an aside I think this model would provide the democratic leadership that the government claims for elected police commissioners without the many disadvantages that this Tory reform entails. And, on the central issue of economic renewal, this would give Merseyside (and the other English city-regions) a stronger voice.

City-regions can make a real difference. It might be that this can be achieved without creating directly elected mayors, but I do think (whatever people's views of Boris Johnson or Ken Livingstone) that the GLA's success is in part a product of having a mayor directly accountable to the voters.

Beyond city-regions, there is a broader argument here about the distribution of power between Whitehall and local government. There is a very legitimate centre-left case that fears that the Tories' localism will result in a further redistribution of resources from the poorest to the more affluent parts of the country. The challenge for Labour's decentralisers is to develop a model that retains the redistribution of resources while fostering greater local independence, including greater scope for local fiscal flexibility. Our ultimate goal is an economy where the gap between rich and poor localities is narrowed so that there is less need for such redistribution. That laudable goal is a long way off and until then it is vital that we defend the principle of a fair redistribution of resources – otherwise our proper desire for a more equal distribution of power could work disastrously against our goal of a more equal distribution of life chances.

## Redistributing political power to the powerless
One group of people who have no political power are sixteen- and seventeen-year-olds. Despite paying tax and engaging in a whole range of adult activities, this section of the population cannot vote. Labour was committed to introducing votes

at sixteen in its manifesto and should continue to support the extension of the franchise. Young people are bearing the brunt of the Tories' policies, which have hiked up university fees, abolished the Future Jobs Fund and slashed the education maintenance allowance. It is crucial that they are recognised as full citizens and given the power to determine the decisions which are made in their name.

Voting inequality is rife in the UK. If you are old, white and rich your voting power is three times that if you are young, black and poor. According to research by ippr, the gap between the rate at which the youngest and older age groups, vote has grown consistently since the 1970s. While in 1970 there was an eighteen-point difference between the 18–24 age group turnout rate and the 65–74 age group rate, by 2005 the gap was forty points.[5] Non-voting has become entrenched in many poor communities, leading to a concurrent loss of voice in the political process. Combined with our electoral system, which forces political parties to focus on marginal seats, the fact that young people, poorer people and some ethnic minority communities do not vote skews politicians' incentives to concentrate on high-turnout areas.

Introducing compulsory turnout in the UK could help to combat this. Such a reform would require cross-party support so Labour would have to tread carefully. If the trends continue, the only voters will be those who already hold a good deal of power because of their wealth and status. If everyone has to turn up to the polling station, political parties might be forced to win over undecided voters, rather than concentrating all their efforts on turning out those voters they know already support them. In the absence of electoral reform, this could help to change the way we conduct politics. Since turnout is lowest in local government elections, perhaps a pilot on compulsory turnout could be run in receptive local authorities to see if the public takes to it? Of course, voters would remain free to spoil their ballot paper or vote for none of the candidates.

The future for democratic reform lies in the local, the personal and the practical. As fewer people feel like politics has anything to offer them, new ways of allowing citizens to participate in political activity with as few barriers as possible is the only way of trying to halt the downward trend. A healthy democracy is predicated on societal involvement – leaving things up to politicians creates a disconnection between what the state does in the name of the people and how they receive it. While Whitehall might be good for pulling levers, it is not so good at bringing about long-term change in communities. As Tessa Jowell argues, if public services need to become more relational, so does politics. Understanding that political parties need to change to accommodate new ways of reaching out to supporters and electors will be key to Labour's renewal in opposition. So too will finding new ways, such as a citizens' convention, to ensure that the redistribution of power goes straight into citizens' hands, rather than solely to another layer of government. If Labour can redirect its reforming efforts from the top to the bottom, it has a chance of re-engaging with the public in a way which could finally help to change the political consensus for good.

---

1   *Audit of Political Engagement 8: The 2011 Report* (London: Hansard Society, 2011).

2   Stella Creasy (ed.) *Participation Nation: Reconnecting Citizens to the Public Realm* (London: Involve, 2007).

3   John Marshall, 'Membership of UK Political Parties', House of Commons Library Note, 17 August 2009.

4   'An end to open primaries?', BBC, 3 May 2011.

5   Emily Keaney and Ben Rogers, *A Citizen's Duty: Voter Inequality and the Case for Compulsory Turnout* (London: ippr, 2006).

# Conclusion: a progressive future for Labour

*Robert Philpot*

New Labour's achievements in government are detailed throughout this book. Just three of them illustrate the historic nature of what the party achieved during its time in power. Alan Milburn and Liam Byrne identify Labour's efforts to tackle poverty and raise the glass ceiling on aspiration. 'Our record fighting poverty,' argues Byrne, 'was, quite literally, one of the best in the world.' Jenny Chapman and Jacqui Smith suggest that, for all the liberal-left's criticism of Labour home secretaries' alleged populism, 'Labour left government with crime lowered. There were fewer victims and the chance of being a victim was at a historic low.' No other post-war government can make such a claim. And Andrew Adonis believes that 'radical democratic devolution was the hallmark of the first two years of the Blair government'. The Scottish Parliament, Welsh Assembly, the mayor of London, and Northern Ireland Assembly were, he notes, successful in 'transforming democratic accountability and consent, and promoting better government'.

But, as our authors also detail, where New Labour fell short it did so because of a failure to develop a wider understanding of the strengths and weaknesses of the state and markets.

New Labour's embrace of the market economy in the mid-1990s both reflected political realities – as Douglas

Alexander notes, 'In retrospect it is hard to overestimate the scale of intellectual defeat felt by the centre-left in the wake of the 1992 general election defeat' – and brought with it huge benefits. As Tristram Hunt reminds us, New Labour used the 'proceeds of the growth over which it presided to rebuild the public realm'. Nor should we fall for the myth that New Labour did not challenge the unequal distribution of power in the market economy: the significance of measures such as the minimum wage, tougher competition laws and a host of new rights in the workplace – including the right to join a trade union – should not be underestimated. Moreover, as Peter Mandelson notes, with his arrival at the Business Department in 2008, New Labour embraced an industrial activism strategy that challenged 'the belief that markets alone must deliver sustainable and balanced growth'.

However, New Labour's approach to the market now needs to be rethought not just because of the failures of regulation and overreliance on the financial services industry, that the banking crisis exposed and which, in the words of Alexander, 'left Labour looking as if we had confused good times with a good system'. Just as crucially, even before the onset of the financial crisis and recession, New Labour's original promise to promote economic efficiency and social justice was being undermined by the fact that, as Liz Kendall outlines, 'while productivity has continued to grow, the gains have not fed into pay packets, particularly of low-to-middle income earners'. Byrne points to the startling fact that in 2009, workers' share of national earnings was around £768bn. Yet if workers' share of the national economic pie had matched the post-war averages, an extra £23.4bn would have ended up in people's pay packets.

And this is not simply the result of the financial crisis and recession. Both the Resolution Foundation's first report for the Commission on Living Standards and earlier work for the TUC outline the manner in which, outside London, disposable income was falling for those in the 'squeezed middle' in the five years prior to the onset of the recession.[1] Its impact, in turn, suggests that it will not be until 2015 that living standards return to their 2001 levels.

New Labour revised, but did not fundamentally alter, the revisionist critique of the market developed by Tony Crosland in *The Future of Socialism*. Put simply, this rested on the notion that economic growth – and through it stronger public services and resource-based redistribution – would allow the state to correct and compensate for the weaknesses of the market.

Whatever its past strengths, the limitations of this essentially statist approach are now apparent. As Hunt argues, 'sober assessment of the long-term economic trends would suggest that, even were such statism still desirable (and it is not), we are unlikely to enjoy the conditions favourable to its enacting that we enjoyed pre-2008, if and when we return to power'. Moreover, not only did New Labour most definitely not put an end to 'boom and bust', but ensuring resilience to future fluctuations will require a tighter fiscal policy and a 'less cavalier attitude towards borrowing'. The stubborn persistence of long-term unemployment and poverty underline that resources are nothing without the power to use them. However important, tax credits and unemployment benefits alone cannot transform the lives of those living at the sharpest end of the market's failures.

Three interrelated responses are required. First, a greater recognition, through the kind of industrial activism that Labour began to embark upon before it left office, of the need to promote the kind of private sector growth which is sustainable and which, as Mandelson argues, is 'based on new sectors and growing businesses ... that successfully combine our manufacturing prowess with the expanding demand for services'. Second, what Hunt, drawing on the writings of the political economist Jacob S. Hacker, terms a shift from redistribution to 'pre-distribution', that is 'the way in which the market distributes its rewards in the first place'. This will require market reforms that promote a fairer distribution of economic power but the political prize is one that will 'avoid the perennial ... pitfall that excessive reliance on redistribution generates: the ease with which the Tories deploy their populist, well-rehearsed "tax and spend" arguments'.

Finally, as John Woodcock argues, Labour must not lose sight of the fundamentally empowering nature of markets: 'Markets have provided the majority of working people in Britain with standards of living that previous generations could not have dreamed of through ensuring lower costs and greater availability for food, consumer goods and travel. In recent decades, the market was the essential basis of the information technology revolution, which has served not only to support wealth creation, but has facilitated a shift of power towards individual consumers and has been both a trigger and tool for movements demanding greater democracy.'

But if Labour was at times too hands-off with the market it was also, as James Purnell and Graeme Cooke argued in *We Mean Power*, 'too hands-on with the state'.[3] Mandelson suggests that 'Labour's approach to public service delivery meant change was rapid in some areas but also too top-down and driven too much from the centre in other cases. With the collapse of our ideas for regional government we did little, outside Scotland and Wales, to reverse Britain's historic trends towards centralisation.' At the same time, as Alexander argues, Labour's comfort with the notion of market failure was not matched by a similar scepticism of the state: 'By focusing on how the state could do good, at times we lacked a language for state failure. And that left us fighting a referendum on the virtues of the public sector – the big state versus small state argument – rather than on a choice between action and inaction.'

Nowhere, perhaps, was New Labour's statism more apparent than in its attitude towards local government. As Steve Reed and Paul Brant write, 'Labour in power did not trust local government enough… From time to time, Labour talked about promoting localism, but double-devolution and the empowerment white paper were not followed through. Too often Labour sought to bypass rather than work with local government.'

Indeed, as Paul Richards argues, Donald Dewar's description of devolution as 'a process, not an event' was turned on its head as it became 'a series of events, not a process'. Regional government for England, the creation of a democratically elected House of Lords, the much-promised referendum on electoral reform, elected mayors – each of these remained 'unfinished business' by the time of Labour's departure from office.

What Patrick Diamond terms 'New Labour's heavy-handed and centralist approach' was also apparent in its public service reform agenda. Thus, while the Blair government was, as Richards suggests, correct to recognise that monolithic state institutions were incapable of meeting modern demands, its greatest missed opportunity was the failure to introduce local ownership and democratic control over public services. 'They remained services done to people, not co-authored or co-owned,' he rightly argues.

There was one exception to this: the creation of foundation trust hospitals, which – with their local memberships, governors and boards – offer a possible template for Labour's future public service reform agenda. Indeed, this major expansion of the mutual principle into public services saw nearly two million people become members of their local foundation trusts – more than the membership of Britain's three political parties combined.

And, indeed, what could have turned into another powerful example of the merits of locally run and controlled public services was missed when Sure Start centres' original cooperative and self-governing ethos was snuffed out after 2005, as Whitehall effectively turned them into just another centrally run government programme.

The fate of Sure Start under the coalition government illustrates the fatal political error of Labour's failure to truly devolve power in our public services. Had the assets and control of these hugely popular centres been located locally, rather than in the hands of the Department for Education, the coalition would have found it far less easy to begin the destruction by stealth upon which it is now engaged.

While acknowledging that local ownership and control of public services does not come without risks, Diamond makes the wider case for such an approach: 'If communities feel a stronger sense of ownership, new coalitions of support will be forged that help to sustain public investment. The pace of improvement might be slower, but change is more likely to embed and endure.' However, as Milburn argues, the statist approach actually ends up promoting public cynicism and undermining public confidence in the ability of government to affect progressive change. 'People are left confused and disempowered,' he writes. 'Governments end up nationalising responsibility when things go wrong without necessarily having the levers to put them right.'

Nor should we forget the waning capacity of statism to deliver even on its own terms: its inability to deliver greater equity or social mobility in an age where global economic competition demands a more responsive, agile and strategic state and where an increasingly diverse society means that needs and aspirations – and therefore the responses to them – differ greatly between localities.

The promise to create a future 'fair for all' was at the heart of Labour's bid for a fourth term. Unfortunately for the party's attempts to attain it, Labour's conception of fairness and that of large numbers of the public were increasingly at odds. As Alexander writes, the party was 'challenged for too little action at the top of the income scale and, simultaneously, for too much action at the bottom of the income scale'. Government appeared to lack a response to voters' anger at runaway pay at the top of the public and private sectors, while some of the policies it employed to make society fairer – like housing benefit – became a source of resentment. 'Too often they reinforced a sense that when we talked of fairness we were talking about someone else,' suggests Alexander.

In his chapter, Frank Field underlines this problem with his attack on New Labour's use of means-testing in its welfare policy: 'In place of Labour's traditional, contributions-based contract [Gordon Brown and Tony Blair] put means-testing at the heart of New Labour's strategy, entirely disregarding the fact that the values it instils, and its impact on behaviour, are totally the opposite to what had gone before. By simply concentrating on the levels of poverty (as defined by income) New Labour stripped out the wider providential role welfare plays in working-class budgets. Fairness ceased to be based on contributions and reciprocity and was supplanted by a single mechanical calculation of supposed need. This fundamental change in direction amounted to a war of attrition against working people's moral economy.'

The lesson here is clear: a party that believes in the utility of government activism can never be, as Labour appeared, indifferent to the values that that activism appears to promote.

### Restoring Labour's economic credibility

Labour left power with its reputation for economic credibility dented but not shredded. But despite the anaemic recovery over which the coalition has presided, a relentless assault on its record has left most voters more confident in the current government's ability to manage the economy than in Labour's. Restoring faith in Labour's economic credibility is the cornerstone on which the party's political and electoral viability – and thus all of the aspirations contained in *The Purple Book* – rests. This imperative features in many of our authors' contributions.

Labour's response to the banking crisis and recession was

the correct one, and the Darling Plan's careful emphasis on a
balance of tax rises, spending cuts and growth measures to cut
the deficit was the right judgement. However, as Mandelson
also notes, 'our mistake was not to spell out in more detail the
implications of the spending cuts so that people could see
we were serious. By refusing to be clear that our deficit plans
were sufficient, we were unable to persuade the public that
the Tories' plans were excessive.'

This is a crucial lesson for Labour as it attempts to regain
the public's confidence. As Kendall argues, 'Ed Miliband and
Ed Balls have made it clear that Labour will not oppose every
cut. This is crucial, particularly as we approach the next election, as it would risk raising expectations that every cut will be
reversed if Labour regains power, which is neither convincing
to the electorate nor realistic for a party that is determined to
demonstrate that we are a government-in-waiting.'

Hunt, too, is correct in his analysis that, while the coalition has turned the 'means' of deficit reduction into an 'end
in itself', Labour needs to be clear that it is a vital means
because 'there is nothing progressive about running a large
budget deficit or wasting money on interest repayments that
could be invested in schools, hospitals or Sure Start centres'.

There is another strong progressive argument for controlling spending: the need, highlighted by Diamond, 'to take
more citizens out of the tax system, progressively reducing the
tax burden through fundamental reform of the tax system'.
Indeed, given the continuing pressure on real incomes, any
Labour strategy to tackle the plight of the 'squeezed middle'
that does not go beyond critical work–life balance issues to
the fundamental question of how we reduce the taxes of those
on low and middle incomes will be necessarily incomplete.

Tax reform is clearly part of the equation here, but so, too,
will be Labour's commitment to being, in the words of the
1997 manifesto, 'wise spenders, not big spenders'. This, in turn,
will require more clarity from Labour over time on the 'how' of

its own deficit reduction plans and thus its own future priorities. To make a reality of social mobility, Milburn argues for 'a commitment to invest more of our national wealth ... in schools and early years'. This, he says, should be 'top of New Labour's policy and political priority list'. Similarly, Kendall suggests there are 'compelling reasons why Labour should now place a greater emphasis on championing childcare and care for the elderly'. The former because it is critical to promoting higher employment levels among women, thus supporting the long-term sustainability of the welfare state, tackling child poverty and promoting social mobility; the latter because it will not only improve the quality of life of older people, but also deliver significant savings in NHS spending.

Picking priorities requires, of course, difficult and tough choices. Kendall calls, for instance, for Labour to 'consider how to strike a better balance between funding for tax credits and benefits, and funding for services like childcare and care for the elderly'. The implications of such a debate will not be easy but a progressive case can be made for them. Prioritising funding for childcare and primary education over and above universities, for instance, can be argued for on the basis that they are crucial to whether young people from disadvantaged backgrounds get into higher education in the first place. Similarly, redirecting expenditure from wealthier pensioners – like winter fuel payments, for instance – to help fund universal social care will help meet the challenge of an ageing population and again relieve pressure on the NHS.

Other authors point to further elements of the agenda that Labour will need to pursue to restore its economic credibility. Diamond, for instance, emphasises the need for far greater tax transparency to ensure citizens can 'make informed decisions about how their taxes are spent, and to what effect'. Similarly, the measures outlined later in the 'Reforming the state' section to deliver 'high-octane reforms to an excessively centralised and bureaucratic state' will demonstrate Labour's commitment to ensuring that maximum value is wrung from every pound of taxpayers' money.

By making the case that Labour needs to finally abandon its embrace of statism, *The Purple Book* seeks to make another, related, contribution to the issue of Labour's restoration of its economic credibility – demonstrating that the party will not respond to every problem with a new central government programme, and thus higher taxation and spending. Equally, though, our desire to develop an alternative to statism differs fundamentally from that of the Conservatives in that we are seeking to put genuine power in the hands of citizens – through new rights to redress in failing public services and guaranteed national minimum standards, for instance – to enable them to hold services to account and thus ensure those services become better than ever.

## Power and responsibility

The redistribution of power is, of course, not a new objective for Labour. The new Clause IV calls for 'power, wealth and opportunity' to be placed in the hands of the many, not the few. Neither is the redistribution of power a replacement for Labour's historic commitment to promoting equality and freedom. Hunt captures the links between the three thus:

'The exercise of power is the most basic, fundamental political act for any member of a free and fair society; in its absence, citizens lack the capabilities to lead a full life of their choosing. The type of freedom brought about by the distribution of power is positive freedom, the freedom to carry out a given act, physically. This contrasts with negative freedom, freedom from interference, which is the only freedom that animates the right. In choosing positive freedom, we reject the false dichotomy of choosing between freedom and equality, as greater equality is instrumental in creating the kind of society required by the pursuit of positive freedom.'

Similarly, Diamond – in keeping with a number of our

other writers – draws on the writings of Amartya Sen and his conception of 'capabilities' to define our conception of power, suggesting that it amounts to 'a strategy of equalisation through empowerment: enabling individuals and communities to take greater responsibility for their own lives'.

Responsibility is, of course, the counterpart to power, and any agenda to redistribute power must ensure that it is part of what Byrne terms a 'something-for-something deal'. There is a moral and a political case for this argument. Morally, the pursuit of equality is, for instance, farcical if some people are being held to different standards, or to account for their behaviour in different ways, than others. This goes as much for those in receipt of housing or out-of-work benefits as bankers or those seeking to exploit tax loopholes. Politically, as Byrne suggests, quoting the work of Samuel Bowles and Herbert Gintis, support for the welfare state cannot rest on notions of 'unconditional altruism'. Instead, it must reflect 'deeply held notions of fairness, encompassing both reciprocity and generosity'.

So what might this all mean in terms of a governing agenda? *The Purple Book* authors share a belief in the need for reform of the state, market and our political system in order to redistribute power. The specific policies contained within the book, however, are advocated by each author alone – although similar approaches and proposals can be seen in different authors' proposals. However, what follows is a summary of the principal proposals contained within the book.

**Reforming the state**

First, we need a major devolution of power from Whitehall and Westminster to local government and local communities:

- The principle of subsidiarity – the rule that decisions should be taken at the lowest appropriate level of government as close as possible to the people – is enshrined in EU decision-making. It should now be applied to national decision-making, with government required to justify why legislation is taking place at a national rather than local level;

- Half of England's population is in the major conurbations, yet outside London strong, responsive political institutions are lacking. Elected mayoral authorities should, therefore, be established for the six major city conurbations beyond London: Greater Manchester, Greater Birmingham, Greater Leeds, Greater Liverpool, Greater Newcastle, and Greater Bristol. As in London, powers over policing, transport, planning and economic regeneration should be transferred to the mayors. City councils with weak leadership and a poor record of promoting jobs and growth should also adopt the mayoral model, and 'city parishes' with their own councillors, budgets and responsibilities within the city should be piloted. Outside of urban areas, upper-tier local authorities, or groupings of them, should take over areas currently managed by quangos, like regional health authorities, national parks or planning authorities;

- In order for it to exercise real power, the balance of taxation between local and national government needs to be tilted. A redistribution mechanism – preferably controlled by local government – should be retained, but greater tax and fiscal incentives to foster new businesses and encourage the building of more homes should be granted to local government. A reformed council and business rates regime should be examined, as should proposals for a land-use tax to promote the sustainable use of land and enable the retention of a property-based element to taxation, and the granting of local authorities in England the power to vary the basic and higher rates of income tax by 3p in the pound, subject to a popular mandate through a local referendum;

- Local authorities should have more power to scrutinise local providers both within the public and private sectors, including the right to insist information is provided to scrutiny committees and representatives attend scrutiny meetings;
- The devolution of power to local government needs to be accompanied by a devolution of power to local communities, building on the principles of the 'cooperative councils' model. Community-led commissioning should be promoted, with communities using cooperative commissioning or their own representatives on trust boards to replace service providers or reshape services as local circumstances change. Locally generated efficiencies should be returned to individual local communities, while credit-based time-banking, to allow residents to give their time in return for financial and other benefits, should be examined. We should consider how to give local communities a right to request participatory budgeting and more rights to community ownership – for instance, of leisure facilities, public amenities, or children's centres – with the value of any public assets turned over 'locked in' to ensure long-term community benefit and prevent any future privatisation.

Second, we need to reinvent central government, deliver high-octane reform and build a decentralised state:

- The structure of central government departments should be reviewed and major reform of the civil service undertaken. As a first step, the Department for Communities and Local Government should be abolished with residual functions moving to the Cabinet Office, while the Wales, Scotland and Northern Ireland offices could be merged into a single Department of the Nations;

- All central government programmes and agencies should be subject to a 'public value' test: decentralising and removing functions altogether, focusing resources on the frontline, local neighbourhoods and communities.

Third, the tax burden should be kept as low as possible, with far greater transparency employed to ensure taxation is meeting citizens' priorities:

- Given the squeeze on real incomes, a future Labour government should seek to take more citizens out of the tax system, progressively reducing the tax burden and fundamentally reforming the tax system;
- A hypothecated NHS and social care insurance fund, merging income tax with National Insurance, should be considered;
- The use of time-limited levies for special capital expenditures and the earmarking of environmental taxes for specific tasks should be encouraged;
- All citizens should receive an annual statement explaining how the tax system works and public spending is allocated, with an expert audit by an independent fiscal authority, accountable to Parliament, also provided.

### Reforming public services

First, we need to ensure more power is transferred to public service users and local communities:

- Citizens should have new rights where services are failing. For instance, if schools fail to meet minimum attainment standards for more than three successive years a competition should be triggered to bring in alternative providers. Parents should also have the right to trigger competitions for new schools where standards fail to improve;

- To encourage greater social mobility, we need to take radical steps to empower parents in schools that are officially assessed as consistently poor. They would have the right to choose an alternative state school, and be granted an education credit worth 150 per cent of the cost of educating their child in their current school;
- We should widen the use of personalised budgets, including for adult skills and the long-term unemployed. Local authorities should support the development of micromutuals of personalised budget holders, allowing them to pool their care budgets and use their strengthened purchasing power to force faster change in care services;
- We should provide legally enforceable rights for the victims of crime, with a sentencing framework that puts victims' experience first and gives them a greater say in determining the nature of community sentences, while exploring the possibility for them to make recommendations on the length and type of sentence, within clearly defined ranges. 'Justice mapping', where communities can see what happens when a crime is reported, could allow communities to work together to reduce crime. Such communities should be rewarded with money from confiscated assets to reinvest in priorities they have chosen to prevent crime;
- We should examine how we give social housing tenants the right – and the ability – to actively shape where they live. This should include looking at how those who wish to move towards a community-led mutual model of housing might be able to do so. We should also look at how we empower people to hold their landlords to account and drive up standards in the private rented sector. By introducing a landlords' register, for instance, government could ensure that housing benefit was only paid in respect of properties that met the Decent

Homes standard. This could empower people renting privately, and drive up standards without requiring an overly burdensome regulatory system;

- We should examine turning the BBC into a mutual organisation, so that all who pay the licence fee become its members and owners with, for instance, rights to elect the trustees who oversee its operations and direction;

- We should consider transferring the Prevent strategy and programme – which combats extremism and radicalisation – from government to an arm's-length charitable trust, run by leaders and activists from the communities the programme is seeking to influence.

Second, we should free public services from centralised control, while ensuring proper local accountability:

- We should create more self-governing institutions, built on the model of foundation hospitals, with local democratic control and ownership. We should consider, for instance, applying this model to primary care;

- We should guarantee all schools the chance to become autonomous, with a variety of models – from academies to trusts, parent-owned or community-controlled – all provided as options.

Third, we should ensure our public services respect the values of the public: providing opportunity for all, demanding responsibility from all, and helping to strengthen communities:

- We should renew the welfare state so that it more clearly combines an attack on poverty with the rejuvenation of the social insurance principles upon which it was originally based. We should consider moving towards a salary-based insurance system where higher salaries require higher contributions, but also provide higher benefits to those who lose their jobs. This would help people to protect their incomes in the first period when they are out of work, as they do successfully in Denmark. We could also consider the costs of long-term care as a part of the new insurance-based system. National Insurance would be converted from a state-run scheme into one which is mutually owned by its members;

- We should consider other ways in which public services can reward those who contribute in the widest sense. As innovative Labour local authorities like Newham and Manchester are doing, we should consider, for example, how social housing could be allocated on the basis of rewarding good tenants and good neighbours. Conversely, we should consider 'Hasbo' eviction orders against antisocial neighbours: a simple mechanism for the police to employ where a household is reported repeatedly for antisocial or violent behaviour. This would be a power for residents to petition the police, to submit complaints confidentially, leading to a magistrate's order banning people from living within five miles of the area.

Fourth, government should encourage the development of 'asset-based empowerment', building the framework in which individuals can make their own decisions and choose to live the life they want:

- We must ensure the 'auto-enrolment' principle behind the pensions reforms introduced by the previous Labour government is a success and revisit the position of those – mostly women – whom the coalition's changes have sought to exclude;
- We should examine how the principles behind the child trust fund can be renewed, while also improving

any new scheme so it reaches those our previous policy did not. Utilising credit union networks – and allowing them to expand via the Post Office network – could be one option;

- We should reform pensions tax relief by removing the 50 per cent rate of tax relief and exploring replacing tax relief with matched contributions or a system that is even more progressive, offering higher relief to those on lower incomes than those on higher incomes;
- We understand that giving people a stake in the property market also allows them to build up an asset base. To assist those struggling to get onto the housing ladder, we should be looking to new and underdeveloped models of home ownership. We should consider the power of equity release, on fair terms, to transfer assets from one generation to the next. We also need to examine how we can get greater private sector involvement, from both developers and lenders, in shared ownership schemes and how we can encourage the development of mutual home ownership. To encourage the latter, councils should use their land assets, planning powers, housing policies, or make investment available.

Finally, we should prioritise tackling the 'care crunch':

- Labour should consider placing a greater emphasis in terms of investment on early years services and care for the elderly, which are crucial for improving working opportunities, reducing poverty and increasing living standards for those on low-to-middle incomes;
- We should have as our goal the transformation of childcare and elderly care into universal public services. The Teach First model – which brings the brightest graduates into some of Britain's poorest schools and

communities – would be applied to childcare with the piloting of Teach Early Years First;

- Labour should consult with business about how family-friendly working can be strengthened in the future. This could include offering the right to request flexible working to all employees, including agency workers, from their first day of employment. It should also examine the case for redistributing maternity leave time more fairly between mothers and fathers, with a separate and increased entitlement for fathers.

## Reforming the market

First, we should encourage new models of ownership in the economy to empower employees in their workplaces, thereby ensuring a fairer distribution of rewards:

- We should actively encourage the formation of mutuals and cooperatives and other inherently democratic models of the firm through tax breaks, incentives and reducing the regulatory burden for new mutual start-ups or spin-outs;
- To further employee share-ownership, we should consider reintroducing the tax break on creating employee benefit trusts abolished in 2003, but hard-wire in progressive principles by ensuring the tax break only applies where a significant threshold of shares have been distributed to all members of staff;
- We should consider improving on whatever investment the Conservatives provide for the Big Society Bank, to ensure new mutuals have adequate access to capital.

Second, to help create a more balanced, stable and secure financial system, we should encourage a new generation of financial cooperatives and mutuals:

- We should provide incentives for other banks to capitalise fledgling mutuals, provide community investment tax relief for people who use them, and expand the Share Incentive Plan so that it benefits all members of the firm and is not merely a way of enhancing executive salaries;
- We should commit to the remutualisation of Northern Rock;
- We should consider ensuring that the 600 branches that the interim report of Sir John Vickers' Independent Commission on banking ordered Lloyds TSB to sell off are sold to new or existing mutual organisations.

Third, we should look to develop strong, well-funded regional investment funds to encourage regional, inclusive growth.

### Reforming the political system
We should increase the power of citizens over who represents them:

- We should introduce 'closed' primaries for the selection of Labour parliamentary candidates;
- We should support the creation of a fully elected second chamber, while considering the manner in which – as is the case in the upper chambers of many other national legislatures – it might also include representation from the upper layers of local government;
- If Lords reform stalls during this parliament, we should consider the option of a citizens' convention. Taking constitutional decisions out of the hands of politicians and giving it to the people would be a hugely symbolic redistribution of power. It would show that not all political discussions need take place in the confines of Parliament;
- To ensure politicians do not simply focus on high turnout areas, we should consider the introduction of

compulsory turnout, with pilots run in receptive local authorities.

*The Purple Book* represents simply the first chapter in what we hope will be the new story of Labour revisionism and revival. Our focus has been on the domestic agenda – and important elements of that, like environmentalism are, we are aware, largely absent from these pages. Similarly, the challenge of assembling an agenda for how Labour might in government contribute to the redistribution of power internationally – from promoting democracy and human rights overseas to trade justice and widening the circle of winners from globalisation – was, unfortunately, beyond the scope of this project. But it is one that progressives within the party must return to.

For all the many achievements that Labour governments have to their name – and now, more than ever, these are important not to forget – there is a pattern to what has limited their ambitions and weakened their political and electoral viability: the common thread running through the 'stern centralism' of the 1945 government; Labour's inability in the 1970s – exemplified by its attitude to the 'right-to-buy' and the Bullock report – to understand new desires by the public to own, participate and control; and New Labour's own missed opportunities and unfinished business, is the party's overreliance on Whitehall-driven 'mechanical reform' at the expense of the creation of new centres of governance, power and wealth creation. Despite differences of approach and emphasis, our authors are united by a belief in the importance of Labour rediscovering its decentralising tradition and thus discovering new ways to redistribute power in the second decade of the twenty-first century.

But this book and project has been guided by another strongly held belief: that with boldness, radicalism and a willingness to think anew about how it can make real its progressive aspirations, Labour can, to paraphrase R. H. Tawney, once again become the author of its own fortunes.

1. Stewart Lansley, *Life in the Middle: The Untold Story of Britain's Average Earners* (London: TUC, 2009).
2. James Purnell and Graeme Cooke (eds), *We Mean Power: Ideas for the Future of the Left* (London: Demos, 2010).

# Author biographies

**Andrew Adonis** is a member of the House of Lords and was Secretary of State for Transport, minister for schools and head of the No. 10 Policy Unit in the last Labour government. He is currently director of the Institute for Government. His book, *Academies: The Reinvention of English Education*, is published in the autumn.

**Douglas Alexander MP** is shadow Foreign Secretary and the Member of Parliament for Paisley and Renfrewshire South. Between May 2001 and May 2010 he served in a wide range of ministerial positions, including Secretary of State for International Development and Secretary of State for Transport. He is a qualified lawyer.

**Paul Brant** is deputy leader of Liverpool City Council, where he has served as a councillor since 1995. He stood as Labour's parliamentary candidate for Southport in 2001 and 2005. He is also a Co-operative Party member. Professionally he practises as a barrister and has previously been selected as *The Times* lawyer of the week.

**Liam Byrne MP** is shadow Secretary of State for Work and Pensions, coordinator of Labour's policy review and the Member of Parliament for Birmingham Hodge Hill. As immigration minister, he created the UK Border Agency and led the biggest overhaul of Britain's border controls since the Second World War. He joined the Cabinet under Gordon Brown and in 2009 was promoted to Chief Secretary to the Treasury, where he negotiated Labour's deficit reduction plan across Whitehall.

**Jenny Chapman MP** is the Member of Parliament for Darlington. Her interest in the criminal justice system grew from working in the prison service in her early twenties. She went on to work for the former Health Secretary to Alan Milburn and has served as a councillor in her local community.

**Patrick Diamond** is Gwilym Gibbon Fellow at Nuffield College, Oxford, and a visiting fellow in the department of politics at the University of Oxford. Now a member of Southwark Council, he was the former head of policy planning in 10 Downing Street and senior policy adviser to the Prime Minister. He spent ten years as a special adviser in various roles at the heart of British government, including 10 Downing Street and the Cabinet Office.

**Frank Field MP** is the Member of Parliament for Birkenhead. He was director of the Child Poverty Action Group between 1969 and 1979. He was chair of the social security select committee in the run-up to the 1997 election and minister for welfare reform in the early years of Tony Blair's government. More recently he was asked to report to the Prime Minister on poverty and life chances. His latest publications include *Attlee's Great Contemporaries: The Politics of Character* and *Saints and Heroes: Inspiring Politics*.

**Caroline Flint MP** is shadow Secretary of State for Communities and Local Government, and the Member of Parliament for Don Valley. She currently chairs Labour's housing policy review. She held a number of ministerial posts in the last Labour government, including minister for Europe. As housing minister her achievements included a £1bn housing package, new shared ownership and shared equity schemes to help first-time buyers, and a mortgage rescue scheme.

**Tristram Hunt MP** is the Member of Parliament for Stoke-on-Trent Central, elected in May 2010, and is a vice chair of Progress. Prior to entering Parliament, he was senior lecturer in history at Queen Mary, University of London. As a historian and broadcaster, he was the author of numerous books, TV and radio series, and served as a trustee of the Heritage Lottery Fund.

**Tessa Jowell MP** is shadow minister for the Cabinet Office and the Olympics, and the Member of Parliament for Dulwich & West Norwood. She served as a minister throughout the last Labour government, spending eight of its thirteen years in the Cabinet. As Secretary of State at the Department for Culture, Media and Sport between 2001 to 2007 she pioneered London's successful bid for the Olympic Games in 2012 and remains on the Olympic Board.

**Liz Kendall MP** is the Member of Parliament for Leicester West, elected in May 2010, and is a vice chair of Progress. In October 2010 she was appointed to Labour's frontbench team as a shadow health minister. Her previous roles include director of the Maternity Alliance and of the Ambulance Service Network. She was an associate director at the Institute for Public Policy Research, where she led work on health, social care and children's early years. After the 1997 general election, she was special adviser to Harriet Harman MP and then Patricia Hewitt MP.

**Ivan Lewis MP** is shadow Secretary of State for Culture, Media and Sport and the Member of Parliament for Bury South. Prior to becoming an MP he was chief executive of two voluntary organisations, Contact Community Care Group and the Manchester Jewish Federation, and served as a Bury councillor for eight years. During Labour's period in government he served in five government departments, including the Department for International Development.

**Peter Mandelson** is a member of the House of Lords. He was elected to Parliament in 1992 and entered British government in 1997, serving as Secretary of State for Trade and Industry and Secretary of State for Northern Ireland. In 2004, he became EU commissioner for trade until 2008, when he re-entered the British government as Secretary of State for Business, Innovation and Skills, and First Secretary of State until 2010. He published his autobiography, *The Third Man*, in 2010. He is currently chairman of Global Counsel and senior adviser to Lazard.

**Alan Milburn** was Member of Parliament for Darlington between 1992 and 2010. He served in the Cabinet as Chief Secretary to the Treasury, Secretary of State for Health and Chancellor of the Duchy of Lancaster. He has chaired the Panel on Fair Access to the Professions, and is currently the independent reviewer on social mobility for the government, reporting on child poverty and social mobility.

**Ed Miliband MP** is the leader of the Labour Party and the Member of Parliament for Doncaster North. He served in the Labour government between 2007 and 2008 as minister for the Cabinet Office and as Secretary of State for Climate Change between 2008 and 2010. As climate change secretary he led the British delegation to the Copenhagen summit and worked to ensure that a global agreement was established.

**Robert Philpot** is director of Progress and editor of its monthly magazine. He is a former special adviser to Peter Hain MP and to Tessa Jowell MP. Before joining Progress, he was a graduate teaching assistant at Brunel University, teaching American politics and history. He has written for publications including *The Guardian*, *New Statesman*, *Tribune* and *Renewal*.

**Steve Reed** has been leader of Lambeth Council since 2006. He is pioneering new cooperative models of running local services and aims to make Lambeth Britain's first cooperative council. He is also deputy leader of Local Government Labour and London Councils board member for children's services and employment. He was this year named by the *Local Government Chronicle* as one of the three most influential council leaders in the country.

**Rachel Reeves MP** is the Member of Parliament for Leeds West, elected in May 2010, and is a vice chair of Progress. In October 2010 she was appointed to Labour's frontbench team as shadow minister for pensions. As a member of the Business, Innovation and Skills Select Committee, she challenged the government's decision to cancel a loan to Sheffield Forgemasters. Previously, she was an economist at the Bank of England, British Embassy in Washington and at Halifax Bank of Scotland.

**Paul Richards** is a Labour activist, columnist and author. He joined Labour in the mid-1980s and has served as a branch chair, party press officer, parliamentary researcher, parliamentary candidate in 1997 and 2001, and special adviser to two Cabinet ministers. He was chair of the National Organisation of Labour Students, and chair of the Fabian Society. His books and pamphlets include *The Case for Socialism*, *Labour's Revival*, *Tony Blair In His Own Words*, and *How to Win an Election*. He was one of the founders of Progress in 1996, and has written for *Progress* magazine regularly ever since.

**Jacqui Smith** became Britain's first female Home Secretary in 2007. Following a successful teaching career, she was elected to Parliament in 1997, became a member of the Treasury Select Committee in 1998 and was appointed a minister in the Department for Education in 1999. In a ten-year ministerial career, she held many roles, including minister for equality, when she was responsible for the Civil Partnerships Act. She left Parliament in 2010 and now works as a consultant and broadcaster.

**Stephen Twigg MP** is the Member of Parliament for Liverpool West Derby, elected in May 2010, and is chair of Progress. In October 2010, he was appointed to Labour's frontbench team as shadow minister for Africa and the Middle East. He has been an active member of the Labour Party for twenty-nine years, holding many roles including MP for Enfield Southgate, deputy leader of the House of Commons and general secretary of the Fabian Society. He is a member of Usdaw, the shopworkers' union.

**John Woodcock MP** is the Member of Parliament for Barrow and Furness, elected in May 2010, and is a vice chair of Progress. In October 2010, he was appointed to Labour's frontbench team as shadow transport minister. Before entering Parliament he served as political spokesman for Gordon Brown and was special adviser to former Cabinet minister John Hutton MP. He became chair of Labour Friends of Israel after the death of David Cairns MP.

**Progress** is an organisation of Labour Party members, aiming to promote a radical and progressive politics for the twenty-first century. It seeks to discuss, develop and advance the means to create a more free, equal and democratic Britain, which plays an active role in Europe and the wider world. Diverse and inclusive, it works to improve the level and quality of debate both within the Labour Party, and between the party and the wider progressive community.